ANNA
KOMNENE

To the memory of my fathers:

George D. Kolovos; astronomer, wise in all things that matter

Fr John Maitland -Moir; holy, good and kind

καὶ ἐν τούτοις ὁ αὐτοκράτωρ τὴν ἱερὰν ψ [υχὴν] ἀφῆκε Θεῷ,
καὶ ὁ ἐμὸς ἥλιος ἔδυ.
and then the emperor surrendered his sacred soul to God, and
my own sun set.

Alexiad 15.20.11, line 10

To the memory of Ruth J. Macrides

Καὶ δακρύσονταί σε καὶ ἐπαινέσουσιν …
And they will shed tears for you and they will praise you …

George Tornikes, Funeral Oration for
Anna Komnene

ANNA KOMNENE

AND THE ALEXIAD

THE BYZANTINE PRINCESS
AND THE FIRST CRUSADE

IOULIA KOLOVOU BA (HONS), MSC, PHD

PEN & SWORD
HISTORY

AN IMPRINT OF PEN & SWORD BOOKS LTD
YORKSHIRE – PHILADELPHIA

First published in Great Britain in 2020 by
PEN AND SWORD HISTORY
An imprint of
Pen & Sword Books Ltd
Yorkshire – Philadelphia

ISBN 978 1 52673 301 6

A CIP catalogue record for this book is available from the British Library.

Typeset in Times New Roman 11.5/14 by
Aura Technology and Software Services, India.
Printed and bound in the UK by TJ International.

Pen & Sword Books Limited incorporates the imprints of Atlas, Archaeology,
Aviation, Discovery, Family History, Fiction, History, Maritime, Military, Military
Classics, Politics, Select, Transport, True Crime, Air World, Frontline Publishing,
Leo Cooper, Remember When, Seaforth Publishing, The Praetorian Press,
Wharncliffe Local History, Wharncliffe Transport, Wharncliffe True Crime and
White Owl.

For a complete list of Pen & Sword titles please contact
PEN & SWORD BOOKS LIMITED
47 Church Street, Barnsley, South Yorkshire, S70 2AS, England
E-mail: enquiries@pen-and-sword.co.uk
Website: www.pen-and-sword.co.uk

Or

PEN AND SWORD BOOKS
1950 Lawrence Rd, Havertown, PA 19083, USA
E-mail: Uspen-and-sword@casematepublishers.com
Website: www.penandswordbooks.com

Contents

Abbreviations

BMGJ: *Byzantine and Modern Greek Journal*
CEEOL: *Central and Eastern European Online Library*
DOP: *Dumbarton Oaks Papers*
EHR: *English Historical Review*
JGH: *Journal of Garden HistoryJHF: Journal of Historical Fictions*
JMH: *Journal of Medieval History*
REB: *Revue des études byzantines*
TLG: *Thesaurus Linguae Graecae*

Foreword

Anna Komnene is one of the most intriguing figures in the history of an intriguing empire. The Eastern Roman Empire, as it was properly called, or Byzantine, as it is mostly known, took over from Rome in 330 AD and flourished for over a thousand year until it fell to the Ottoman Turks in 1453. Anna was an imperial princess, daughter of Emperor Alexios I Komnenos (r. 1081–1118) and his wife, Empress Eirene Doukaina. A woman of extraordinary education and intellect, Anna Komnene is the only Byzantine female historian and one of the first and foremost historians in medieval Europe.

Yet not many people know her outside the rather narrow world of Byzantine Studies. And those who do know her have generally received a biased, skewered impression of the intellectual princess and powerful author, mediated through centuries of misreading and misogyny. They see her as an angry, bitter old woman who was forced to live the cloistered life of a nun for over thirty years as punishment for her murderous intentions. She had wanted the throne, the story goes, and coldheartedly conspired to overthrow and kill her brother, the lawful Emperor John II Komnenos. She was the ultimate 'nasty woman', the unnatural shrew whose arrogance, ambition, and fury at having been thwarted led her to write an account of her father's reign undoubtedly vivid and fascinating yet false, hypocritical, and vengeful. Right?

Wrong.

Recent scholarship, new editions of old texts, modern readings help to establish the facts of Anna's life in a very different light. Anna Komnene was an intellectual of an unprecedented calibre, author of an epic history of her father's reign, the *Alexiad*, styled on the classical tradition in which Anna was raised and educated. She did write that history in her later years, after her husband, an aristocratic statesman and soldier, and a historian too, died and left her a widow, and she did write it in a convent which her mother built and endowed and of which Anna was the governor. But she was not exiled, and she was not a nun, at least not until the very last hours of her life. Her history could be said to be biased, but no more biased, and probably much more rigorous, than many of the historical accounts of her own time. And most importantly, she was not a conspirator, in spite of the historical tradition, formed on conjectures many decades after her death and prevailing for centuries due to the facility with which strong, self-asserting, authoritative women are condemned and maligned even in our own, more enlightened times.

This book aims to present Anna Komnene, the fascinating woman, pioneer intellectual, and charismatic author to the general public. Drawing on original medieval Greek texts as well as on the latest academic research to reconstruct Anna's life, personality, and work, it moves away from the myth of Anna the conspirator and 'power-hungry woman' which has been unfairly built around her over centuries of misrepresentation. At the same time, it places Anna Komnene in the context of her own time, the medieval Eastern Roman Empire, known as Byzantium for its capital city, the ancient Greek colony and later magnificent city of Constantinople. A world renowned capital city of dazzling wealth, beauty, spirituality, and mystery (at least in Western eyes), Byzantium or Constantinople is the setting of an epic clash between East and West, of power games among the big aristocratic houses for the crown and the purple mantle and scarlet buskins – the Byzantine insignia of imperial power. The book sets Anna in the context of her own powerful family, whose strong women maintained the gilded throne for the dynasty for over a century; and all this within the epic power struggles of the great aristocratic houses against each other and against the rising powers of Western crusaders and Seljuk Turks.

My main source for the Greek primary texts was the amazing digitalised corpus of ancient Greek texts at the University of Calinforina, Irvine, the *Thesaurus Linguae Graecae: A Digital Library of Greek Literature*. The TLG has all the latest editions of Greek texts, and sometimes links to English translations in the public domain: http://stephanus.tlg.uci.edu/Iris/demo/browsers.jsp. Some of the texts cited below are freely accessible, others require registration and an account. All the original Greek texts cited were retrieved from the TLG in the editions as cited in Primary Sources. The translations throughout the book are mine unless otherwise stated.

Foreword

I wrote this book in an effort to give the general public an idea of
Anna Komnene and her world. I hope it will motivate readers to seek
Anna's book and know her through her own writing. In her inimitable
Alexiad, Anna Komnene's voice comes clear and convincing, the voice
of a strong, intelligent, opinionated, exciting woman, as relevant, and
perhaps more today as in her own time.

Glasgow, June 2019

Cast of Characters

Anna Komnene – princess *Porphyrogenita*, author, historian, intellectual.
Alexios Komnenos and Eirene Doukaina – her parents, emperor and empress of Byzantium.
Maria, John, Isaac, Evdokia, Andronikos, Theodora, Manuel, Zoe – her siblings.
Nikephoros Bryennios (the Younger) – her husband.
Alexios Komnenos Bryennios, John Doukas Bryennios, Eirene Doukaina, [Maria] Komnene Bryennaina – her children.

Paternal family

Anna Dalassene and John Komnenos – paternal grandparents.
Manuel Komnenos, Isaac Komnenos, Adrian Komnenos, Nikephoros Komnenos – her uncles.
Evdokia, wife of Melissenos; Theodora, wife of Constantine Diogenes – her aunts.
John Komnenos, Isaac Komnenos' son; Maria Komnene, Isaac Komnenos' daughter – her cousins.
Manuel I Komnenos – her brother John's son, her nephew and emperor.

Maternal family

Maria of Bulgaria and Andronikos Doukas – maternal grandparents.
Anna Doukaina – her aunt, wife of George Palaiologos (Anna's favourite uncle).
Kaisar John Doukas – her great-grandfather, aristocrat, kingmaker, and '*éminence grise*' of the Byzantine Empire in the 1060s, 1070s and early 1080s.

Emperor Michael VII Doukas – his brother.

Constantine Doukas, prince Porphyrogenitos, Emperor Michael's son – her fiancé.

In-laws

Empress Maria of Alania – Constantine Doukas Porphyrogenitos' mother, wife of Emperor Michael VIII Doukas and after his abdication wife of Emperor Nikephoros III Botaneiates daughter of King Baghrat of Georgia.

Nikephoros Bryennios the Elder – grandfather of Anna's husband.

Friends

George Tornikes – scholar and metropolitan bishop of Ephesus; belonged to Anna's circle of friends and wrote her obituary in the mid-1150s, within a year or two of her death.

Nikephoros Diogenes – son of former Emperor Romanos IV Diogenes, conspirator.

Enemies

Bohemund of Taranto, later of Antioch – crusader.

Prologue

Time, which flies irresistibly and perpetually, sweeps up
and carries away with it everything that has seen the light
of day and plunges it into utter darkness, whether deeds
of no significance or those that are mighty and worthy of
commemoration … Nevertheless, the science of History is a
great bulwark against this stream of Time; in a way it checks
this irresistible flood, it holds in a tight grasp whatever it
can seize floating on the surface and will not allow it to slip
away into the depths of oblivion.

> (Anna Komnene, The *Alexiad*, tr. E.R.A.
> Sewter revised by Peter Frankopan)

The past is a place / And it is lost / In the gloaming
> (Martin Cathcart Froden, 'Fickle Fortune')

Constantinople, Year of the World 6657 (AD 1147)

For the duration of that autumn, Constantinople, ancient Byzantium,
Queen of Cities, the World's Desire, had resembled an ocean hit by
tempest. With approximately a quarter of a million permanent inhabitants
plus thousands of visiting merchants, mercenaries, foreign envoys,
scholars, pilgrims, and curious travellers of all colours and tongues, the
city had always attracted the attention of the world. Often this attention
has been unwanted and frightening, like recently when foreign armies
stopped in the city, whether as friends or enemies it was not clear. These
armies were on their way to liberate the Holy Land, ironically looting and
burning and killing fellow Christians in their passage. Emperor Manuel
Komnenos had received the leaders of those armies. King Conrad of
Germany, his own kinsman, brother of his wife, Bertha of Sulzbach, and

King Louis of France with his beauteous queen, Eleanor of Aquitaine stayed in his splendidly refurbished Palace of Blachernai, while their uncouth, undisciplined soldiers vandalised the suburbs of the great city itself, terrorising the populace. Such acts stirred the memories of another such passage, fifty years earlier, rekindling old fears.

For this was not the first time that Western armies had descended upon the city on their way to the Holy Land. Emperor Manuel would not remember; this was long before his time. His grandfather Emperor Alexios Komnenos had been sitting on the gilded throne then and his father, Emperor John Komnenos of blessed memory, had only been a child of 10. But there was one member in the family old enough to remember: his aunt Anna, the eldest sister of his late father, estranged from palace and court for as long as Manuel could remember. He was not interested in old aunts, especially when they were as terrifyingly clever and sharp-tongued as his Aunt Anna, an unusual woman whose intelligence and erudition frankly made everyone uneasy. His own mother of blessed memory, Eirene Piroska of Hungary, and his wife Eirene-Bertha, both silent, unobtrusive ladies of foreign royal blood, quietly preoccupied with their children and charitable works, were the proper models of what an imperial woman should be like. What business did a woman have being a scholar and a philosopher?

***

Not far from the Palace of Blachernai, in the western part of the city, in the neighbourhood called Defteron, the night is drawing in over the convent of Theotokos Kecharitomene (Mother of God Full of Grace). The air is ringing with the insistent metallic rapping of the *semantron*, calling the small congregation of twenty-five nuns to Vespers and Compline, its call reciprocated from the adjacent male monastery of Christ Philanthropos. Intricate patterns of sound waft towards a palatial building situated within the high convent walls, but set well apart from the nuns' quarters, separated from them with extensive, leafy grounds and a low wall with a door locked on both sides. In a high, airy, comfortable room, filled with books and papers, infused with light from the large windows in daytime, but now obscured with the long shadows of the evening, well-trained servants enter and begin to light the lamps, filling the room with pools of soft yellow light.

An aged lady is sitting at the scriptorium by the window, still working on a manuscript in the gloaming. She is dressed in austere black robes and maphorion, a black veil covering her head and shoulders; her garments, of the very best quality money can buy, are not those of a nun but of a widow. Her face is still beautiful, largely unlined, somewhat retaining the bloom of youth; it is an arresting face, with brilliant, penetrating eyes under arched eyebrows and an aquiline nose. The servants glide around her silently, respectfully. She puts down her pen and rubs her tired eyes and aching temples and fingers. She has been working all day; beyond the physical exertion of writing, it is the efforts of the mind that have exhausted her the most. She has been recalling events that took place a good many years ago, more than the lifespan of many of her servants and of the nuns who are now filing into church for the last service of the day, blissfully unaware of such toils as hers. They pray; she writes. Hers is a long and arduous task, for she is building up a rampart against time, against forgetfulness which like an immense river threatens to drown heroic deeds of men long gone. Her rampart is made of memory and its name is History. She, Anna Komnene, princess Porphyrogenita Kaisarissa, is writing about her father, Emperor Lord Alexios I Komnenos of blessed memory, dead for over thirty years, but now slowly coming back to life, resurrected in the writing of his daughter.

***

Anna Komnene's historical work in fifteen volumes, entitled *The Alexiad* – an homage to Homer's *Iliad*, the model for many authors writing in the classical tradition – is one of the most important medieval Greek works of history and the only one in the whole corpus written by a woman. The *Alexiad*, as the name itself betrays, focusses on Alexios as the main hero of the story. In a brilliant and colourful narrative, Anna describes Alexios' rise to power and his ceaseless, untiring efforts to limit the damage done to the empire by half a century of feckless predecessors and almost two decades of disastrous civil wars. A vast array of other characters, major players in the events of the late eleventh century, march through Anna's pages, vividly and shrewdly described. Many of them were personally known to Anna or were even members of her own family, since she was related by blood or marriage to many of the most important families in the empire. Much of her information comes straight from the sources, from the personal reminisces of historical events which she heard straight from the protagonists – a privileged position for a historian. Additionally, she spoke to many other eyewitnesses or to those who had collected information from those witnesses, 'men who are now mostly in monasteries and who have written down their accounts of those events in plain language' and she had access to many of the state archives and documents. What is more, she had the best models for writing history, the great classical historians of Antiquity Herodotus, Thucydides, Polybius, and the best guides for literary style, among whom Homer was most prominent.

Anna's history reconstructs a time when her world came into large-scale contact, initially with wary friendliness, later with open hostility and violence, with Western Europeans, at the time of the Crusades. Anna witnessed the First Crusade (1095–1099) and was the only Greek historian to write about it. According to some modern historians, it was Anna's father, Emperor Alexios Komnenos, who triggered or incited the First Crusade by his call for help to Pope Urban II in 1095, as the empire was threatened in its eastern borders. Whether Alexios' desperate plea at a time when his empire was besieged by the Seljuk Turks was the definitive reason for the Crusades or not, it is certain that the history of the Eastern Roman Empire would from now on be inextricably linked with the West, for better or for worse. Anna Komnene, writing her historical work on the First Crusade possibly at the time of the Second (1047–1049), seems to have been the first and possibly only historian of her time to grasp the significance of those events for the future of the empire, which was ruled by her own family.

Anna Komnene's formidable intellect and acute historical perception were admired by Edward Gibbon, if we consider real admiration to reside in acts rather than words: Gibbon used Anna's history extensively as source in his magisterial *History of the Decline and Fall of the Roman Empire* (1775–1881) and essentially agreed with her judgments, nevertheless disparaging her as a 'vain female author' in the misogynistic context of his era. The fact that Anna was a woman played an important part in how she was perceived not only as an author but as a historical character as well. The denial of authority to women, pervasive in the pre-modern and early modern eras, meant that a woman with the intellectual authority of a historian was viewed suspiciously as a trespasser into fields of masculine authority, and therefore as an unnatural, 'manly' woman.

In Anna case, things became a little more complicated by the fact that she was the first-born daughter of an emperor, married to a powerful aristocrat, Nikephoros Bryennios the Younger (*c.* 1078–1138), whose grandfather Nikephoros Bryennios the Elder had been a contestant for the throne in the civil wars of 1070s. The younger Bryennios had great power and influence at court and was a great favourite with his mother-in-law, Anna's mother, Empress Eirene Doukaina. As other historians of the time noted, on the day Alexios Komnenos died, the behaviour of his son and heir John Komnenos (1088–1143), who abandoned his dying father to rush to the Great Palace and by tricking the Varangian Guard to enter and establish himself as emperor, was rather strange, giving rise to gossip about imminent moves of other members of the family to grab power; some of the gossip implicated Anna indirectly or, later, directly. Byzantine historian Niketas Choniates (*c.* 1150–1127), writing about ninety years after these events, presents it as a fact that Anna herself had conspired against her brother for the throne, although no contemporary source confirms this view.

But consequent historians by repeating Choniates' story with interpretative comments of their own, consolidated Anna's reputation as a 'power-hungry' woman, a conspirator, and a traitor who ended up writing her history in bitterness and regret for the lost throne she had allegedly coveted. But recently this view has been undergoing some revision, as the historical evidence is re-examined and Anna's place in history reconsidered. Literature saw in Anna the 'power-hungry', masculine woman, but also the first model of a modern intellectual woman striving to balance family and writing. At the same time, her *Alexiad* is still in print (in the English language it is available in the Penguin Classics series in an excellent and flowing translation, doing justice to Anna's vibrant storytelling). Her vivid and powerful writing makes its own case for Anna's value as a historian and writer, regardless of whether she was a conspirator and usurper manqué.

Much of what we know and can surmise about daily life in general and Anna Komnene's life in particular also comes from texts. The following portrait of the family is reconstructed on the basis of contemporary sources, beginning with Anna herself, who left us descriptions of her parents and some of her siblings in the *Alexiad*. Her historian husband, Nikephoros Bryennios, wrote in detail about the generation of their parents and grandparents. Anna's contemporary and friend George Tornikes, Bishop of Ephesus, wrote a long obituary full of details about her personal life and character. Although we must be aware that much of what he says may be an idealised rather than a factual account of

Anna's character and features, we still manage to get a glimpse of her life and get as near Anna as possible beyond her own writings. Another contemporary, historian and judge John Zonaras, presents some of the dysfunctional aspects of the Komnenos – Doukas family dynamics in his critique of Alexios Komnenos and his regime; and Niketas Choniates, a historian and courtier who wrote many decades later, paints an even darker picture of Anna and her family.

There are snippets of information to be gleaned in court poetry written mostly by Theodore Prodromos or other court poets at the occasion of important family events, such as weddings and funerals, some of them involving Anna's children. The foundation charter written by Eirene Doukaina, Anna's mother, for the convent she established in Constantinople in the 1110s, gives us clues about Anna's final years. Finally, we have the intriguing prologue to Anna's own last will and testament, but sadly not the body of the will itself. But we must make do with what we have, which is enough to allow a glimpse of Anna's life at home, making allowances for the unavoidable rhetorical exaggeration and decorum of the sources.

***

As Anna Komnene puts her pen down after a day of hard work at the scriptorium, she has a strong sense of the importance of her book and of history books in general: history, she tells us in the prologue of her book, is a dam erected by the historian to stop the river of time from letting important events sink and perish into the sea of forgetfulness. As a historian, it is her duty not to allow the deeds of Emperor Alexios Komnenos to sink into obscurity. The act of writing history is also an act of personal commemoration: these are the deeds not only of important historical characters but also of members of her family, people she has known and loved and now are long gone. The act of history is also an act of mourning, inevitable when recalling the past and all that was lost. As the sun sets over the land, Porphyrogenita Kaisarissa Lady Anna Komnene Doukaina Bryennaina, daughter, sister, great-niece and aunt of emperors, the most educated woman of her times, recalls the dead as their dear faces rise in the gloaming. Putting away her pen, she prepares to turn in for the night. Tomorrow she will continue building her bulwark of memory against oblivion.

Chapter 1

Power Games

Unto Darius and Parysatis two sons were born

(Xenophon, *Anabasis*, 1.1)

He hath put down the mighty from their seats and exalted them of low degree

(Luke 1:52)

In this way and no other did Komnenos summon power, that is by the right of blood, as he was by birth one of the Komnenoi, and kinship, as he was by marriage a close relative of the Doukai

(Nikephoros Bryennios, *Materials for History*, P.9.lines 9-12)

The Komnenoi: Early Years

It all began with two brothers, Isaac and John Komnenos, orphaned at a young age. Their father, Manuel Erotikos Komnenos, high-ranking army officer and aristocrat from the Thracian town of Komne, whence his surname, with considerable estates in Paphlagonia by the Pontic Sea, died in 1020. His wife had been long dead. Emperor Basil II, known as the Bulgar-Slayer (r. 976–1025), the archetypal warrior-king who would become the model for the Komnenos emperors, took the orphan boys under his wing. He placed them as his wards in the monastery of Stoudion, one of the largest and wealthiest establishments of its time in the west end of Constantinople, with easy access to hunting grounds and training fields outside the Golden Gate. The emperor personally supervised the Komnenos boys' education, making sure they would be especially trained in the military arts, offensive and defensive: riding, archery, spear-throwing, and most importantly for their future career, as army generals,

1

tactics and the art of war. The boys must have been close to the emperor and sincerely loved and admired him; many years later, Isaac Komnenos as emperor would reminisce and tell stories to his entourage about Basil.

Their education completed, the Komnenos brothers entered the imperial service as members of the hetaireia, the imperial guard consisting of aristocratic sons. Suitable brides were found for them. Isaac married Katherine, granddaughter of King Samuel of Bulgaria. John's bride was the daughter of Alexios Charon, governor of Italy. Whether Charon was his real name or a cognomen gained by his uncanny aptitude for killing every single one of his enemies (Charon is the Greek name for the Grim Reaper), he did not bequeath it to his children: his daughter Anna Dalassene, John's 15-year-old bride, was known by the surname of her mother's more illustrious family, the Dalassenoi, one of whom would come very near to marrying Empress Zoe, the niece of Basil II. By their marriage, John and Anna had eight children: Manuel, Maria, Isaac, Evdokia, Alexios, Theodora, Adrian, and Nikephoros. [Tables 1 and 3]

Basil died and the members of his family, brother Constantine VIII, niece Zoe with her three successive husbands Romanos III Argyros, Michael VI Kalafates and Constantine IX Monomachos, and finally niece Theodora, succeeded him to the throne one after the other between 1025 and 1056. Basil II, as thrifty as he was warlike, had left the coffers of the treasury filled to the brim at his death in 1025; it only took one generation to spend the lot on expensive vanity projects, on frivolous gifts to favourites, and on the luxurious and indulgent lifestyle of the imperial families and their courtiers. Sadly, no money was spent where it was mostly needed for the survival of the empire: the army. With the death in 1056 of Empress Theodora who, like a famous English queen a few centuries later, did not want to marry and share her throne with anyone, ended the line of the Macedonian dynasty, considered by many historians as the apex of the Byzantine Empire for its territorial expansion and economic stability. The court and senate chose as emperor an elderly man whose cognomen Stratiōtikos (military) was as misleading as his appointment was misguided. What the empire needed most at a time when new fierce enemies overrode its borders – Seljuks in the East, Normans in the West, Cumans and Patzinaks in the North – was a warrior-emperor; what it got was an administrator in the civil service who had no actual battlefield experience whatsoever and cared not at all about the security of the empire. The military coup that ousted him was only a matter of time.

Meanwhile Isaac and John had brilliant careers, although John was much less ambitious than his hardy brother. Isaac became domestic of the schools (Domestikos tōn Scholōn), or commander-in-chief, of the battalions of the East, gaining the love and loyalty of the army. In return, the army acclaimed him emperor in the summer of 1057, raising him on a shield in the old Roman fashion. Isaac Komnenos was just the kind of emperor needed at that critical time for the empire. But Isaac did not last long on the throne. He had the temperament of a soldier and did not possess the skills for subtlety and negotiation to deal with the conflicting interests and powers at court. He primarily thought of himself as a warrior-emperor: he had coins minted that showed him holding a naked sword; he was reported to have said, 'This, and only this, is what procured me the empire.' In his urgency to reform the army he sought funds from the Church, but his heavy-handed approach made some very powerful enemies for him there, no less than the patriarch himself, Michael Keroularios, the obstinate protagonist of the schism between Eastern and Western church in 1054. Isaac's abdication, nominally attributed to health problems, was more prompt than his coronation. One source narrates that Empress Katherine tried to stop him, begging him to consider how dangerous it would be to abandon her and their daughter Maria to the mercy of their enemies, but her efforts fell on deaf ears; soon Isaac, Katherine, and Maria withdrew into respective monasteries. The imperial crown was then offered to Doux Constantine Doukas, of the illustrious House of Doukas. However, another source states that the conjugal quarrel was not between Isaac and Katherine, but Isaac's brother John Komnenos and his wife, Anna Dalassene. In this version, John Komnenos was offered the crown by his brother but refused to take it out of modesty, or because he saw it for the poisoned chalice that it was. Similarly, Anna's passionate pleading failed to convince her husband, and she had to swallow the bitter pill of losing the throne to Constantine Doukas.

Which of the two versions is true, or rather which set of protagonists is the right one? Probably neither. Classical historians tended to add such anecdotes to the narrative to strike a point home. The point here was that the Komnenoi men were unworldly and virtuous in their scorn of imperial power in favour of morally higher things, whereas their women were power-hungry and overly ambitious; for any instance of power-crazed act on their part, the reader would know whom to blame

This appears to be a thread running through historical narratives related to Komnenian women. Anna Komnene would also be painted in similar negative overtones.

Emperor Constantine Doukas' reign began in 1059 and ended with his death in 1067. His relative longevity on the throne was largely due to the support of his brother, the powerful Kaisar John Doukas, a shrewd and ruthless man. In the years to come, John Doukas' support for Alexios Komnenos would prove indispensable to the latter's cause, but for the time being the two houses were set against each other as rivals and even as spiteful enemies. From his marriage to Empress Evdokia Makrembolitissa, niece of the intransigent Patriarch Michael Keroularios, Emperor Constantine had six children. [Table 2] The eldest, Michael (the future Emperor Michael VII), was still a minor when his father died; normally, the young prince should be acclaimed emperor, with his mother and her uncle the patriarch as regents until he came of age. But this is not what happened.

The empire was still, and perhaps more than ever, in trouble. Severe losses of Byzantine territories in southern Italy and Sicily to the Normans, and the increasing raids of Seljuk Turks in the east who quickly turned from mere marauders to settlers meant disruption of normal economic activity and consequent loss of income from taxation for the royal purse, not to mention the waves of refugees from the provinces to the capital. Difficult times required urgent measures: a warrior-emperor to deal with the external dangers and a spirit of unity to deal with the serious problems besetting the empire. The first of these two requirements was met in the person of Romanos Diogenes, an aristocratic soldier whose manly beauty and military training stole the heart of Evdokia Makrembolitissa, the widow of Constantine X. Ignoring the advice and wishes of the living and the dead – her late husband had made her sign a pledge at his deathbed that she would never marry again, and the Doukai, particularly her brother-in-law Kaisar John Doukas, wanted to make sure she kept it – Evdokia rushed into marriage with Romanos. The ceremony took place on 1 January 1068, only seven months after Constantine's death on 22 May 1067. Never did the proverbial 'marry in haste, repent at leisure' prove as apt as in the case of Evdokia's marriage. Although the premise of the marriage was not unsound, for a strong military emperor would be better able to restore the fortunes of the flailing empire and hopefully defend the rights of his stepson to the throne, this particular marriage proved an unmitigated disaster. Romanos began to treat Evdokia shabbily within days after the wedding, concentrating all powers into his own hands rather than sharing it with her as she had imagined and keeping her isolated in the women's quarters. They soon had children together, two sons – Constantine and Nikephoros, whom we shall meet again later. More heirs to complicate the succession! The Doukas successor were set aside and naturally the Doukai who resented this worked ceaselessly to bring Diogenes down; but their family loyalties and political plans did not bode well for the second urgent requirement in those hard times, unity in the face of the common danger. Under such circumstances, Romanos Diogenes began to prepare for war against the Seljuk Turks.

Much as it was a blow for the House of Doukas, the rise of Diogenes to the throne was a blessing for the House of Komnenos. Their fortunes, which had deteriorated after the Doukas succession, now faced an up-turn. The head of the family for some time had been Anna Dalassene, who was arguably the best thing that ever happened to the House of Komnenos. On 12 August 1068 John Komnenos died, leaving Anna a widow. She was only 40 years old, but she had 'an old head in young shoulders' as her namesake and granddaughter would write admiringly some eighty years later. Anna Dalassene managed the family fortunes, both financial and political, with unerring instinct and an iron hand. Blessed with a large family of children, Anna made everyone work towards the ultimate goal, the throne of Byzantium; she pushed for her sons' promotions in the army and court and she arranged marriages for all her children with suitable members of practically every single important family in the realm. With Romanos IV Diogenes on the throne, who was her kin by marriage as well as by blood, the Komnenoi stood very close to it once again. Anna's eldest son, Manuel, was married to a Diogenes bride, whose name sadly is not recorded for posterity, and he was made great domestic (chief commander) of the East by the emperor. Manuel's premature death at the age of 25 or 26 by a sudden illness – an ear infection that went wrong – almost broke Anna's heart and for a short time stalled the Komnenos fortunes; but she had a plan B and a plan C, her sons Isaac and Alexios, who were now teenagers and getting ready to enter the world of politics and power in their own right.

Alexios especially appears to have been something of a favourite, a precocious lad with as much ambition as his mother would have wished of him. He was too young to participate in Romanos IV's campaign against the Seljuks, no more than 14 or 15, 'soft down only starting to grow on his face', and yet he begged the emperor to allow him to go. Diogenes was moved and impressed but told the lad that he could not do this to his dear mother Anna Dalassene (who had begged him earlier not to allow Alexios to fight), so recently bereaved of one son. Thus Alexios was spared for future greatness and did not participate in that fateful battle in which his future father-in-law, Andronikos Doukas, and his future adversaries Nikephoros Bryennios the Elder (future in-law), Basilakes, Roussel of Balliol, and Nikephoros Botaneiates were all field commanders.

Sadly, and unpatriotically, the Doukai were willing to pursue their self-interest at a high cost for the empire at its worst hour of need. In the battle of Mantzikert, on 26 August 1071, where Romanos IV faced the Seljuks in what he had hoped would put an end to Turkish incursions in Asia Minor, the Doukai let the emperor and the empire down, according to many narratives. The Byzantine attack fell apart, partly owing to the unexplained, or downright treasonous, moves of Andronikos Doukas, commander of the rear-guard of the army who abandoned the battle and called an early retreat. Although General Nikephoros Bryennios, the commander of the left wing, tried to keep some order, the attack fell apart and in the subsequent chaos many Byzantine troops were captured by the Seljuks. Among them was the emperor himself. The Doukai had managed to get rid of him in the most dramatic way possible.

Mantzikert was the beginning of the end for Diogenes – a tragic end. Captured alive by the Turks, he was allegedly treated well and even honoured by Alp Arslan, the Seljuk leader, who eventually released him. But his enemies in Constantinople made haste to depose him and put his stepson, the Porphyrogenitos Michael Doukas, on the throne. Diogenes, with the help of the Turks, tried to get his throne back, but it was a hopeless case. Captured by his nemesis Andronikos Doukas, he was imprisoned and blinded. It was a horrible affair. According to a near-contemporary source, they so seriously botched the job of cutting his eyes out and not taking proper care of the wounds that his head festered and stank and his eye sockets crawled with worms. In this pitiful condition he was carried to Proti, one of the Princes Islands. Soon after that he died, mercifully, and Empress Evdokia gave him a splendid funeral service and burial on the island.

This version of events emphasises prejudiced views of the Byzantines as treacherous, untrustworthy, disloyal villains, drawing a sharp contrast with the allegedly chivalric behaviour of the Turk Alp Arslan – in the pattern of Sir Walter Scott's novel *The Talisman* (1826), where the wicked Italian Conrad of Monferrat is the polar opposite of the noble 'Arab' Saladin. Here Diogenes is the noble hero, betrayed by his own people and honoured by the enemy. However, the facts can be interpreted in a different way: when Diogenes was deposed after his capture and defeat, he struck a deal with Alp Arslan who saw an opportunity for the Seljuks to gain territories and wealth by helping Romanos to gain back his throne. Seen this way, Diogenes is as much a traitor as the Doukai, if not worse, for promising the Turks what belonged to the Romans. Losing the battle of Mantzikert was also largely his fault, first for refusing to negotiate with Alp Arslan when he clearly had the upper hand, and then for falling into the trap of the retreating Turks, following them into their own territory – one of the most common tactics used by the Turks. At least this was the version that the Doukai put about to explain their behaviour after the defeat: in only a week's time after the battle, with the news of Diogenes' capture hardly having reached Constantinople, his stepson Michael Doukas, son of Evdokia and Constantine X Doukas, was proclaimed emperor through the ceaseless activity of his uncle John. The fortunes of the Komnenoi were once again at stake, as full-blown civil war broke upon the empire like a fierce forest-fire, wreaking more havoc than the Seljuks themselves had ever done.

The downfall of Diogenes almost took the Komnenoi down as well. Michael VII Doukas was crowned in October 1071, after John Doukas half-convinced, half-coerced the Empress Evdokia with the 'help', or rather the threat of the Varangian Guard, to withdraw to a monastery. In the political purges that followed in the winter 1071–1072, Anna Dalassene was charged with treason; she had allegedly conspired to bring Michael VII down in letters that were caught and brought to the court. She denied all accusations as made up, in the words of historian and future grandson-in-law Nikephoros Bryennios, by a 'malevolent, envious, viper-tongued individual' who remained nameless.

Anna withstood the accusations with a temper of steel, which she was too clever to show to her accusers. Instead, she stood in the courtroom playing the long-suffering poor widow and mother of a large family of orphaned children. At a crucial moment during the trial, seemingly unable to support all the lies that were hurled against her, she rose fiercely from her seat and drawing an icon of the Christ from under her cloak, she showed it to the judges and cried, 'Behold my Judge and yours today; look at him as you cast your vote, which must not be unworthy of that Judge who knows all that is hidden.'

Anna was an astute judge of human nature and had a reputation of being righteous and godly. Her stunt did not result in full acquittal but convinced the court that she was not guilty of treason; yet she was deemed dangerous enough to be punished with exile as a preventive measure. Together with her family she was sent to the beautiful Princes' Island in the Bosporus. It cannot have been such a terrible exile, but for Anna Dalassene to be kept away from the centre of power and, above all, to be defeated by her old enemies the Doukai must have rankled. At any rate, this exile did not last long. Within the next few months, Diogenes was dead and Michael VII Doukas fell out with his uncle the kaisar. Anna Dalassene and her brood were soon recalled from exile and restored to their fortune and their palatial mansion in the capital city. The Komnenoi were now serving the ruling emperor; their mother continued managing the family fortune and building up her networks of support, casting her net as far and high as the imperial family.

Maria's Two Emperors: Doukas and Botaneiates

Michael VII Doukas' reign was another example of the cognitive dissonance which seemed to have struck the imperial court at the time and led it to act as if completely oblivious to the multiple troubles of the empire. Michael was as scholarly and out of touch with reality as his father Constantine X had been. The assailants were too many and hard to defeat even with military experience, as the tragic case of Romanos IV Diogenes had shown. Michael's marriage to the beautiful Georgian princess Maria (more on her later), a foreign bride with no connections or family to offer the support of a network, did not help him win any loyalties either. Interestingly, it is precisely for her isolated status that Michael had chosen Maria – in addition to her fabulous beauty – as he 'did not want to be burdened with a demanding family to whom he would be obliged to render favours.'

Maria of Alania was originally Martha or Mar'ta. She was the daughter of King Bagrat of the mountainous kingdom of Georgia and his second wife, Borena of Alania (modern-day North Ossetia). Georgia, which also comprised Abasgia, was called Iberia by the Byzantines. Maria's brother was the future King Giorgi II of Georgia. Interestingly, Maria was called the Alan, or of Alania, and not Georgian or Iberian; whether this was a Byzantine nickname or Maria's own choice, we do not know. In Georgian sources Maria is only even mentioned as Mar'ta (and later as Mariam), but never 'of Alania'. She received a new name when she married the emperor, as was the custom with foreign brides.

Maria must have arrived at the court of Constantinople as a hostage first in 1056, at the age of 3 possibly (Her father King Bagrat IV and her grandmother, Queen Mariam, had also been hostages there in the late 1040s–early 1050s for a short time), then returned to her own country until her second and final return possibly ten years later, this time as a bride-to-be. Apparently, a holy man from Mount Athos, from the monastery named Iviron (i.e. of the Georgians – still thriving today), had predicted that little Mar'ta would one day be Queen of Byzantium. The story goes that little Mar'ta entered the empire (or the city of Constantinople, the text is not very clear) on the very day that Empress Theodora of Byzantium died in August 1056. Then the holy man, Giorgi of the Holy Mountain, prophecied: 'Let everyone know that today the Queen has departed and the Queen has arrived.' A few years later, when Mar'ta (now renamed Maria) married Emperor Michael VII, her grandmother Queen Mariam informed the holy man that his prophecy had come true.

To be fair to Michael, he did try to do something about the trouble from the West, where the Normans had been steadily hacking at pieces of the Italian and Sicilian territories. He forged an alliance with the fearsome Norman warlord Robert Hauteville 'Guiscard' (i.e. the Weasel) by engaging his only son, the Porphyrogenitos Prince Constantine Doukas, to Robert's daughter Olympias, who was renamed Helena according to the Byzantine custom of renaming foreign brides. But the East was beset by the Seljuks; they overwhelmed Anatolia and the territories by the Black Sea and practically reached the gates of Constantinople, installing their own rule in the ancient walled city of Nicaea in Bithynia, under the very nose of the emperor. The temporary lull in hostilities within the empire itself after Diogenes' defeat did not last very long. Michael VII, who must have resented and possibly feared the influence of his formidable uncle Kaisar John Doukas, fell out with him and became the dupe of a very astute and capable eunuch, Nikephoritzes; his name, a diminutive of Nikephoros, may refer to his short stature or his ambivalent status as a castrated man. Byzantines were as keen on nicknames as their Greek and Roman predecessors, and as merciless. John Doukas withdrew to his large estates in Asia Minor and occupied himself in activities common to aristocrats of his stature, hunting and managing the affairs of his house; he was also beset by personal tragedies, such as the death of his wife and even more devastatingly, his son Constantine, brother of Andronikos Doukas, Anna Komnene's maternal uncle. [Table 2]

Michael was unpopular for his fiscal tightening of the purse strings in his effort to generate some income for the empire. His reformations earned him the nickname Parapinakes – 'minus-a-quarter' – when the gold coin lost a quarter of its value due to inflation. He also neglected the army and let the Turks invade Asia Minor; the loss of land caused famine, and the famine caused plague and death. Michael, however, did not seem to be aware of any of these evils, preferring to spend his time composing poems and discussing literary texts with his tutor and mentor Michael Psellos. Again it was a matter of time before various aristocratic generals or foreign mercenaries – for this was also a new reality in an empire that did not focus enough on defence – began to see an opportunity. Michael could not deal with them himself. Instead, he used the services of two young but ambitious and highly promising generals – the brothers Isaac and Alexios Komnenos. Anna Dalassene had done really well: her eldest living son, Isaac, married right into the imperial family and allied himself to the emperor by taking as his bride Eirene, first cousin of the Empress Maria of Alania. Michael Doukas had realised that he needed the support of other powerful families, after all, and the two Komnenos brothers were loyal and capable; now that his uncle the kaisar had turned against him (or he against his uncle), their mother's feud with him did not bother Michael at all.

When in 1078 the army decided that they had had enough of Michael's incompetence, he was forced to abdicate in favour of Nikephoros Botaneiates, another Mantzikert veteran. Michael was forcibly removed and tonsured in the Monastery of Stoudion. Ever-vigilant of the rights of the Doukai, Kaisar John Doukas, who had by now returned from his self-imposed exile, and his son Andronikos convinced Empress Maria of Alania to marry Botaneiates. The idea was that the new emperor would protect the right of his little Doukas stepson, the Porphyrogenitos Prince Constantine, Michael VII and Maria's son. But both Maria and Nikephoros Botaneiates had living spouses, and Botaneiates had already been married twice; a third marriage was not then allowed in the Orthodox Church. Additionally, the former Empress Evdokia Makrembolitissa – a very handsome and intelligent woman now in her late fifties, nearer Botaneiates' age than Maria – had written to Botaneiates from the monastery of her exile to offer her hand to the new emperor, and Botaneiates, a lifelong admirer of Evdokia's, was keen. However, the kaisar prevailed, persuading him to marry Maria instead. He whisked Botaneiates and Empress Maria to the palace chapel, but the officiating priest refused to conduct the service of a marriage so blatantly against canon law and stayed inside the sanctum. Time was pressing; the marriage ceremony had to be completed before the patriarch got wind of what was happening and stopped it.

The kaisar, in a sequence that echoes a mafia modus operandi, made a sign with his eyes to his grandson Michael Doukas. The young man got up and left; within minutes, he returned with another priest, loyal to the Doukai (aristocratic families had their own church people as part of their retinue and staff), whom he bade to stay aside and wait; he then went up to the altar and called the first priest. When the priest came out to see what was happening, Michael Doukas grabbed him firmly by the vestments and led him quietly outside. The Doukas priest then stepped in and officiated the wedding.

Sometime in the latter years of Emperor Michael's reign, Alexios Komnenos had been engaged to be married to a girl from the House of Argyros, but his fiancée had died, and a new suitable bride was sought. Anna Dalassene was considering Zoe, the youngest daughter of Empress Evdokia Makrembolitissa. But another candidate was proposed from a totally unexpected quarter, given the history of the two families: Eirene Doukaina, daughter of Andronikos Doukas, son of Kaisar John Doukas. The daring plan was the idea of Maria of Bulgaria, Andronikos' beautiful and clever wife, who convinced her husband to propose it to Alexios. Maria was a scion of the royal family of Bulgaria on her father's side – she was a granddaughter of Czar Samuel – and of the old and wealthy Byzantine families of Kontostephanos, Avallantes and Phocas on her mother's side. Her older daughter Anna was married to George Palaiologos, another son of a great house (who was to become

Anna's favourite uncle – the House of Palaiologos would eventually give Byzantium its last dynasty of emperors many centuries later); her younger, Eirene, was only a child. As her future grandson-in-law Nikephoros Bryennios would write in his history later, everyone in the household of the kaisar went berserk with this preposterous idea. Maria had to work very hard to convince her father-in-law the kaisar and Anna Dalassene, who hated one another. And yet somehow she did, and somehow Alexios and Eirene found themselves engaged to one another. But it was not love that brought them together, and the road to the matrimonial happiness that their daughter would describe many years later was long and strewn with obstacles.

The Komnenian Coup

In the evening of Saturday 18 February 1081, eve of Cheese-Fare Sunday, last day of the three-week unruly carnival festival of Triodion before Lent, the mansion of the Komnenoi in the aristocratic south side, not far from the Great Church, was all in a bustle. This had been a busy week of comings and goings, of secret negotiations and plans and tonight, these plans were coming to fruition. The Komnenos brothers Isaac and Alexios were about to flee the city, only to return ahead of an army and claim the throne of Byzantium.

At the start of Emperor Nikephoros III Botaneiates' reign, the Komnenoi had done very well. Both Isaac and Alexios attained high offices: Isaac became doux of Antioch and Alexios great domestic of the West. The emperor, an old soldier, took much pleasure in the company of the young military-minded men; he liked to have them in the palace and often invited them to his own table. Both of them were also very close to the empress, Isaac because of their kinship by marriage – he was married to her cousin Eirene – and Alexios because he was a charmer and Maria liked him a lot and considered him her friend and ally (and according to some, her lover) so much so, that she formalised their relationship by officially adopting him. Anna Dalassene, always quick to form strategic alliances, had connected the families of Komnenos and Botaneiates by betrothing one of her granddaughters to Botaneiates' grandson. [Table 3] The boy lived in her household with his tutor. With Isaac's marriage connection to Empress Maria and the prospective marriage of the grandchildren, the Komnenoi were practically within the inner circle of the imperial family.

But recently their situation at the palace had become untenable. The quick rise of the brothers in the favour of the imperial couple had created many enemies. The 'Scythian barbarians' Borilos and Germanos, eunuchs, servants and close confidants of the elderly emperor were particularly incensed by the success of the Komnenos brothers. 'Those slaves', Anna Komnene says, 'hated their master, like all slaves do, but because they could not strike directly at him, they struck at others who served him.' Borilos and Germanos, fearing Isaac and Alexios' influence especially with Empress Maria and desiring the throne for themselves, decided to act quickly and brutally. Their plan was to seize the brothers and blind them. Apart from the terrible injury that might result in death as in the case of Diogenes, blindness would also forever disqualify them from the throne, since the emperor ought not to have any visible disability. The only way that the Komnenoi could get out of this alive and undamaged was to hatch a counterplot of their own.

The imperial court, teeming with factions and rivalries, was a dangerous place where power and wealth were brokered in a game of very high stakes. The Komnenos brothers were expert players, trained by the best of them all, their mother and head of the family. But their rivals were strong and cunning. Now they realised that their mother had been right all along, like that other Caesar, Julius of the old Roman Empire, who had said that the only safe place in Rome was at the very top.

The rift between the Komnenoi and Botaneiates was deepening. Maria's support for Alexios, whether as a lover or as a promising young general who would help her son to the throne, was indisputable. The emperor was becoming suspicious of the Komnenoi brother's constant presence at court. He too would have heard the gossip about his wife and the charismatic Alexios; perhaps it is true that someone in his entourage of relatives from Cappadocia, Turk mercenaries, and old military men who now frequented his table, alerted the emperor to the dangers involved in a young man constantly in and out of the empress' private rooms, adopted son or not.

Maria was the only ally of the brothers in the palace now, together with a network of palace people who were loyal to her. In her palace apartments, which were a veritable 'centre of intrigue and clearing-house for seditious information', Maria received Alexios and Isaac freely owing to their family ties, exchanging information, offering advice, and receiving reports from her own network of spies, whose duty was to inform Alexios and Isaac of all that was going on in the palace, especially as it related to their own standing there. The Komnenoi knew that to be forewarned was to be forearmed; they wanted the latest news and developments as soon as – and sometimes even before – they reached the emperor's ears. It was thanks to this network of spies that the brothers found out about the dark designs of the eunuchs, Borilos and Germanos, to seize and blind them.

During a dinner party which must have been particularly fraught and tense, a servant – one of Maria's men – communicated to the brothers that some distressing news had just arrived. As the emperor and his people were sitting at the table too, the man ('a cook' according to Anna), had to be discreet: he made signs and as Alexios followed him outside he informed him that the Turks had invaded the city of Kyzikos, across the city on the opposite shore of the Sea of Marmara. This was disastrous news for the realm and for the Komenoi; they would surely be blamed for that calamity, since they were the commanders-in-chief of the army, East and West. It would look as if they had not done all in their power to stop the Turks, whose hold of Asia Minor was now becoming all the firmer, their boldness growing after their success over a decade earlier in Mantzikert, as the event of Kyzikos proved. But one of the things that distinguished Alexios Komenos from other men was his ability to turn a difficult situation into an opportunity for himself. At once he ordered a massive movement of the armies he commanded from East and West to the environs of Constantinople, purportedly in order to organise a campaign to regain Kyzikos. But Botaneiates and the enemies of the Komnenoi saw this as a definitive proof of Alexios' intention to lead a rebellion against the emperor. Having quashed at least three such rebellions before, Alexios was in a better position than anybody to have learnt from his enemies' mistakes and to make sure he would not repeat them.

Whether rebellion was really the intention of Alexios initially, it is not clear. Perhaps he was really pushed to it by the hardening of Botaneiates towards him and by fear for his own and his brother's safety. It would not be the first time in the history of the world that an event one fears comes to pass precisely because one gives way to fear. On the other hand, one must keep in mind that the ambition to sit on the throne was never far away from the mind of the Komnenoi, who had been raised and trained for this purpose from a young age by their formidable mother. The way their flight was orchestrated, as well as the course of action taken by the women of the family that very night, suggest that the Komnenoi had been preparing for this night and that it was all done not at the spur of the moment but as part of a well-laid out plan.

As they made their escape from the city to meet their supporters and gather their armies, the Lady Anna Dalassene was silently hustling the women and children of the family out of the house. Careful not to wake up the Botanieiates grandson and his tutor, who were sleeping in their separate apartment, they headed for the Great Church. They were disguised as provincial women from Anatolia, draped in long veils which hid their faces, carrying baskets of food and bedding, as if they had been travelling from afar and needed their provisions for the road, Anna Dalassene leading them like a brood of hens. When they reached the adjacent chapel of St Nicholas 'The Refuge', they knocked and asked to be let in. To the sleepy monk who guarded the chapel they said they were pilgrims from the East who wanted to worship at the sanctuary before setting out for home. They spent the night there. On the following day, the emperor send two envoys to bring them back, but Anna Dalassene (in a scene evoking the future Queen Elizabeth Woodville in a similar situation but in a very different place and time) held on tight to the sanctuary door and refused to let go, informing them that they were welcome to cut off her hands if they so chose, as this would be the only way to prise her from the door of the sanctuary. One of the envoys, appalled at the thought, took out his crucifix and offered it to her as a token that he meant no harm. Anna would have none of it and demanded a bigger cross, visible to everyone there, on which he would swear that she and her family would be safe. In the end, the impasse was resolved when the emperor sent reassurances that he did not hold her personally responsible for her sons' defection and would only keep her and her family of women under house arrest in the convent of Petrion. The women were allowed to have their own provisions and food stores and to bring in anything that might add to their comfort. By the orders of the emperor, Maria of Bulgaria, Eirene's mother, joined them in their imprisonment (by that time Alexios and Eirene had been married, but it is doubtful that they lived as husband and wife yet).

As well as being the most beautiful woman of her generation, Maria was also very astute: by bribing the guards with food and other gifts, she kept a steady stream of news coming into the convent and not a single detail of the rebels' progress was lost to the ladies. What is more, she persuaded her son-in-law George Palaiologos to participate in the Komnenian coup, a move that would greatly contribute to its success.

Pillage and Murder on the Way to the Throne

The six weeks of the Great Lent passed quickly. Alexios and Isaac, with all the charisma of the one and the intelligent analysis of the other, supported by other great families, among them the Doukai and the Palaiologoi, marched towards the walls of the city. Alexios had been acclaimed emperor, chosen over Isaac with the support of the Doukai. The match with Eirene was now paying off. A great part of the army was on his side, and apparently, the Almighty as well: one night when the brothers were returning home from the palace, before their insurrection, an old white-haired, long-bearded man who looked like a priest or like St John the Theologian had appeared out of nowhere and hailed Alexios calling him emperor, then vanished. Although Alexios dismissed the story as claptrap, Isaac took it to heart and surrendered the throne willingly to his brother.

Now all they needed was to take the city. For Alexios the formidable ramparts were not a problem; he knew that the walls of a city are as good as the men who guard them. It did not take very long to persuade the German guards near the Char(i)sian gate to open it; money talks, and money in the hands of the Komnenoi was particularly eloquent. The Komnenian army rushed into the city on Maundy Thursday; it was April in the fourth indiction of the Year of the World 6589 (AD 1081). The soldiers, disrespectful of the day and hungry for loot, were unleashed upon the inhabitants of the capital with the fury of wild fire. They pillaged, raped, and killed the natives of the city acting exactly like the barbarians with no compunction. The terrible events of that day would make Anna cringe as she wrote about them over half a century later. The sons of Anna Dalassene, schooled in piety by their strictly religious mother, must have been horrified to behold the monster which they had let loose upon the populace. It was victory, but a victory bought with blood and dishonour.

16

By the time Alexios entered the Great Palace a crowned emperor, it was Easter; normally the sombre ascetic regime of the Holy Week would be followed by merriment and feasting in celebration of the greatest festival of the year for the Orthodox Christians. But there would be no celebrations in the imperial palace. The whole family of the Komnenoi had to make penance for the atrocities committed. For forty days, the emperor and all his household would be sleeping on the floor, dressed in sackcloth, their hair covered in ashes, eating only stale bread and drinking only water. This was probably Anna Dalassene's idea; she was a woman practised in the ascetic life, which she seemed to prefer by temperament and habit. Steely personalities like hers tend to thrive on that kind of regime. There would be plenty of time for celebration later; expiation in the eyes of God and the people of Constantinople came first.

There was still the matter of the crowing of the empress. Things had become strangely fraught there; Eirene Doukaina, although nominally under the care of her mother-in-law, had been sent to the Lower Palace, together with her sisters, her mother, and her grandfather the kaisar, while Alexios, his mother, and his brothers went to the Palace of Boukoleon. Empress Maria was in that palace too, with the Komnenoi. Malicious tongues wagged, claiming it was Anna Dalassene's doing, that she was seeking a quick divorce for her son, so he could abandon the Doukaina and marry Empress Maria instead; it was common secret, they said, that she and Alexios had been lovers.

The army of the Komnenoi had taken over the city, and now the fleet led by George Palaiologos was coming to port at the Palace of Boukoleon. As the troops were acclaiming Alexios and Eirene, some men from the palace leaned over the ramparts and asked them to stop linking Alexios and Eirene's names together like that. George Palaiologos was furious and did not mince his words: 'Either we acclaim Eirene together with Alexios, or we withdraw our support from you. We are in this for Eirene, not for Alexios.' The message was clear and hit the mark in one. The Komnenian party shut up. Anna Dalassene would not have her way. Immediately the name of Eirene was ringing over the water and across the city walls together with that of Alexios.

But Anna Dalassene would not give up that easily. She resisted to the bitter end, trying at least to avert the coronation of Eirene as empress. But she found resistance where she was not used to expect it: Patriarch Cosmas was adamant that Eirene had every right to be crowned as the lawful wife of Alexios. Anna threatened to depose him; she meant to replace him with a favourite of hers, the eunuch Eustratios Garidas, an insignificant monk who had pleased her with prophecies about the greatness of her family. Cosmas did not care; he would happily vacate the patriarchal throne for any successor the mother of the emperor pleased to appoint, but his last act as patriarch would be to crown Eirene Doukaina empress of the Romans. This was promptly done. Urged, convinced or coerced by the Kaisar John Doukas, Maria moved out of the Great Palace and into her own luxurious apartments in the Palace of Mangana, together with her young son and her large retinue. The Doukai and the Komnenoi were both satisfied; their united houses now possessed the throne of the greatest Christian realm in the world. Their mutual support and cooperation would be the necessary guarantee for the stability of their rule. All they needed now was an heir to fix the union.

Chapter 2

The Chamber of the Porphyra

At dawn (it was Saturday) a female child was born unto
them, looking like her father, as they said, in everything.
That child was I.

(Anna Komnene, *Alexiad* 6.8.1)

How great was their desire for her when she was born! For
not a short time had passed after they became emperor and
empress and the fear of childlessness distressed them, which
even to private citizens is such a great cause for despondency,
but even worse to kings, and to women more than to men; for
children become an unbreakable bond between husbands and
wives and kindle their affection even more.

(George Tornikes, *Discourse on the Death of the
Porphyrogenita Lady Anna the Kaisarissa*,
14.247. 7-11)

Among the many splendid palaces, churches, and public monuments
gracing the shoreline of the Bosporus in the south side of the imperial city
of Constantinople, beneath the lighthouse, the small Palace of Porphyra
stood sedately apart, secluded but not isolated. From its narrow, arched
windows it offered a view of the elegant Palace of Boukoleon: orderly
rows of double-arched windows poised above the private harbour where
the imperial dromon was usually moored, the marble statues of the ox
and the lion giving it its name entwined in deathly struggle over the
water. But now, in the dark hours before dawn on a cold winter's night,
the harbour was empty and a constellation of flaring lamps, torches and
beacons was reflected on the dark waters along the shore.

Despite the late hour, lamps were burning in a small square room high
up on a tower of the Porphyra. Under a pyramid-shaped roof, the walls lined
with dark-red porphyry stone, the hangings of purple silk, warm and dark

and opulent, created an effect not unlike the inside of a womb. A fitting atmosphere for the purpose: this was a confinement room, a birthing chamber. On the bed a young woman of 19 was half-sitting, half-standing, contorted with the pains of labour; she was flanked on either side by two midwives, their strong, bare arms under her armpits offering support as she writhed and strained. This was her first birth; fear and inexperience added to her agony and the three women glistened with sweat. The young mother-to-be was the empress of the Romans, Eirene of the great House of Doukas, wife of Emperor Alexios Komnenos, first of his name but not of his House to become emperor of the Romans barely two years earlier.

A very handsome older lady, the insignia of her court title of protovestiaria clearly marked on her luxurious robes, stood next to the young parturient, whispering softly into her ear: 'Give birth, woman, like Mariam gave birth to Christ, like Elizabeth gave birth to John; come forth, child, Christ is calling you and the earth is awaiting you.' The young woman barely listened as she alternately whimpered and screamed, begging the Mother of God to release her from the unbearable pain. The older woman, Lady Maria of the royal House of Bulgaria, whose similarity of facial features showed her to be the young empress' mother, smiled to herself as she remembered that only two days ago in this very room her daughter had made the sign of the cross over her bulging belly and said to her unborn baby: 'Wait, my little one, and do not come forth until your father is home.' The emperor was away in the West, fighting a long war against the Norman Robert Guiscard, and no one knew when he would return. Lady Maria had told her daughter off for speaking such nonsense: 'Suppose the emperor is not back for another month,' she had said, 'how will you bear the pangs of childbirth *for a whole month*, pray?' But now she refrained from making any comments; her first-born daughter was suffering enough as it was, finally giving birth to a long-awaited first child.

Eirene had been married for four years already and tongues had been wagging. Childlessness was one of the worst misfortunes that could befell an ordinary couple, but for a royal union it could be fatal. The marriage between Alexios and Eirene had been fraught with difficulties from the start. Anna Dalassene, the emperor's formidable mother and matriarch of the House of Komnenos, disliked her daughter-in-law and loathed her family, the Doukai. She particularly hated Lady Maria's father-in-law and Eirene's grandfather, Kaisar John Doukas, with a bitterness that went many decades back. Anna Dalassene had only reluctantly agreed to the match between the families which resembled more a business merger than a matrimonial affair based on love and affection. The Komnenoi had needed the Doukai in their precipitous ascent to the throne of Byzantium. But it was a common secret that Eirene and Alexios were not happy together. In the hotbed of gossip that was Constantinople, it would not go unnoticed that no heir arrived within the first three years of marriage; Alexios had a reputation as a womaniser despite his mother's draconian watch over him, and there were nods and whispers whenever the name of Empress Maria of Alania, a famous beauty from Georgia who promoted Alexios' case when he was still a promising general, was mentioned. Putting two and two together, the wagging tongues of city and palace lived in anticipation of Alexios and Eirene's divorce and Alexios' instant remarriage to Maria. And yet, here was Eirene, about to give birth to a child that would grace both the great Houses of Komnenos and Doukas and forever silence the nasty rumours.

What were Eirene's thoughts as she laboured in the Porphyra? Childbirth was a particularly dangerous time for women, generating a great number of superstitions. The fear of the female daemon Gello or Gillou, who killed new mothers and snatched babies from the cradle, created the need for ecclesiastically approved protection, granted to the mother-to-be via prayers, icons, holy relics and blessed water. But for good measure, pre-Christian and traditional magical remedies were also adopted: incantations, special amulets, and magical practices of a great variety. Other pregnant women were not allowed in the birthing chamber; all knotted laces or threads were loosened so as not to prevent quick resolution to the mother's suffering – a superstition that survived from classical Greece, where goddess Eileithyia, she who loosens and releases, was the protectress of parturient women, before this role was handed over to the Holy Mother of God and St Domna, the patron saints of childbirth. There was also the very real fear of death: Eirene may have heard horror stories including the terrible fate a few centuries earlier of another empress whose stillborn baby the doctors had to cut up and extract piece by piece from her womb, resulting in the horrible death of the mother (most probably from toxaemia). This terrible fate would not befall Eirene; young, strong, healthy, surrounded by wealth and privilege and all the additional resources of her imperial status, she would live on to bear another eight children and she would die an old woman, surrounded by her children, grandchildren, and great-grandchildren. But at the time she could not know the future as she laboured in agonising pain.

The women bustled about in the room, wiping the empress' brow and refreshing her with rose water, massaging her lower back and belly, bringing basins of warm water and stacks of clean linen, when a servant girl who had been stationed at the window overlooking the harbour let out a cry: 'The imperial dromon is coming! The emperor is here!' 'Glory be to God!' Lady Maria said, as her daughter let out a rending cry. The midwives announced that the baby was now about to emerge. Lady Maria grabbed a boy eunuch who was hovering at the door, his golden locks and long legs making him look like a young Hermes ready to fly, and ordered him to run to the Sacred Palace and inform the Lady Anna Dalassene, regent of the emperor in his absence, that the baby was now unmistakeably arriving at the same time as the emperor himself. Torches flickered and horse-hooves thundered, while the clattering and ringing and loud voices a little further down the shore signalled the docking of the imperial vessel. From the Great Palace the black-clad Lady Anna Dalassene with her retinue of monks – a true conspiracy of ravens – descended hastily upon the Porphyra in time for the arrival of her son and his heir, her first imperial grandchild. In the midst of all the hustle and bustle of guards, messengers, servants, and family members, the puny whimpers of the new-born were hardly heard.

And yet there she was, little Anna Komnene, tiny and radiant and destined for eternity, arrived just as dawn was breaking. As the first child of the House Komnenos to be born a Porphyrogenita, she was marked out as heir to her father, who was there to pick her up in his arms and rejoice.

Anna's narrative of her own birth and in particular the little vignette of her mother's bidding her to wait and the miraculous coincidence with her father's arrival is the sort of anecdote that classical historians would add to make a point about the character of a historical person. Anna uses this as an instance of what she presents as her main feature: her love for her parents and submission to their will. Her obedience to her mother, manifested before she was even out of the womb, and her birth in sync with her father's arrival, mark her relationship with them throughout her life.

Born on Saturday, 2 December, in the Year of the World 6592 (AD 1083), Anna Komnene is the most famous baby girl to be born in the Palace of the Porphyra. Many decades later, writing a description of the room and of her birth, she would be keenly aware of her special status as Porphyrogenita born in that chamber. For this was not merely a luxurious room lined with a stone so rare and ancient that no money in the world could acquire it, even in the richest city of Christendom, where fabulously wealthy people and magnificent rooms and palaces abounded. The place of royal confinements and birthing possessed a quality of timelessness and uniqueness that could not be reproduced by the *nouveau riche*. When the capital of the empire moved from the Old Rome to the New Rome, i.e. Constantinople, the room was transported from the old palace to the new one exactly as it was, a symbol of continuity and stability and uninterrupted glory. A place in the Porphyra could only be inherited, not bought. Emperor Alexios himself was not a Porphyrogenitos; although his uncle Isaac had been the first Komnenos to sit on the throne a quarter of a century prior to Anna's birth, Alexios was a usurper whose blood-stained coup only two years earlier had left a black stain on his reputation that was never to be completely removed, even after almost four decades of rule which only ended with his natural death. He needed legitimacy in every way he could get it. His first child's birth in the Porphyra was a step towards the right direction, sealing the ascendancy of House Komnenos.

Anna's birth consolidated the marriage of Alexios and Eirene which had united the two great imperial Houses of Doukas and Komnenos. It was an uncontested proof that the marriage was fertile and therefore blessed. In that Christian empire, in which Greco-Roman and biblical traditions mingled, a fruitless marriage was considered failed and even cursed, and one of the greatest anxieties of the Byzantines was the begetting of children. But the healthy baby girl who emerged from the body of Empress Eirene was indisputable proof that Alexios and Eirene were blessed by God; and if their first-born was not a boy, it hardly mattered. They were young and fertile, and from fertile families, and they would hopefully have more children. In Byzantium, as everywhere else in the medieval world where the line was secured via the male descendants, a son was much preferable to a daughter; however, a daughter was not to be dismissed either. Judging by narratives in the ever-popular Lives of Saints, a widespread form of entertainment at the time which has been compared to the TV dramas of our days, the birth of a female child to a previously infertile couple was a great miracle – the Holy Mother of God herself was such a case – and was much more preferable than no child at all. Heiresses were not uncommon; the relatively recent examples of Empress Zoe (d. 1050) and Empress Theodora (d. 1056) indicated that female descendants could inherit the throne, albeit as a last resort. By their marriage they would install an emperor: a royal husband in the Byzantine Empire would not be a consort but a ruler in his own right. It can be safely assumed that the minute the little princess saw the light of day, plans and speculations were made about her future marriage in several quarters in Constantinople.

Anna's birth brought joy to a great many people beside her parents, starting with their respective families. By that time both her paternal grandfather John Komnenos and maternal grandfather Andronikos Doukas had been dead – the former for a very long time – but her grandmothers were very much alive and present in her life one way or another. Even if she disliked her daughter-in-law, Anna Dalassene would be happy for her son and no doubt would already think of political alliances and ways to consolidate power for her family through a suitable marriage for the girl. As the paternal grandmother, she would expect as a matter of course that the new granddaughter would be named after herself; it was the custom (and still is in Greece) to honour one's parents by naming one's children after them, starting from the father's family. As the first-born daughter, the little princess would be called Anna. When a second daughter arrived two years later, she would be called Maria, after Eirene's mother. When the long-desired boy finally came, the future emperor John II Komnenos, he took his long-deceased paternal grandfather's name, John Komnenos; the next boy was named Andronikos after their maternal grandfather. Once the grandparents' names were all given and thus the couple's two sets of parents were honoured, then other family members' or saints' names would be chosen. Tradition and continuity, as well as honour to the ancestors, were thus the most important considerations in the naming of a child in Byzantium. In the Komnenian dynasty, unfortunately this means that many family members had the exact same names. No less confusing than the Henrys and Edwards and Marys and Elizabeths and Janes of the English great families, they are a veritable headache for the historian who encounters in the sources no less than twenty-five members of House Komnenos named Alexios, seventeen Johns, fourteen Isaacs, eleven Manuels, fifteen Marias, thirteen Annas, ten Theodoras, and eight Eirenes.

Anna's maternal side of her family, the Doukai, were particularly happy with Anna's birth. For Maria of Bulgaria it must have been an important moment to see the first grandchild from her daughter the empress, particularly after all the worry and trouble she had been through concerning Eirene's marriage. Anna was very fond of her maternal grandmother whom she describes as kind, sweet-natured, and so beautiful that all men felt compelled to help her. She probably spent time with her as a child and had the opportunity to hear her and her mother reminisce about her own birth several times, especially the episode of her mother's and grandmother's altercation regarding her arrival in time with her father's. Anna mentions that the closest relatives of her mother the empress were ecstatic with joy when she was born; as far as they were concerned, this was not just a Komnenos but a Doukas heir as well. Anna did not seem to have a very affectionate relationship with her other grandmother, the awe-inspiring matriarch, although she expresses great admiration for Anna Dalassene's unprecedented political and administrative powers and the relationship of trust she had with her son, as well as for her strength of character, strict morals and deep piety.

But we can easily imagine that for Maria of Bulgaria, as for the whole House Doukas, Anna was something more than a power asset. Anna appears to have felt a strong connection with her mother's family all her life; her own favourite daughter was named Eirene Doukaina, taking both her maternal grandmother's – Anna's mother's – name and surname. For the Doukai, Eirene's safe delivery and the birth of a healthy baby daughter must have been a great source of happiness, in the knowledge that now Alexios and Eirene's marriage would be much harder to dissolve. It is not surprising then that the empress' family, as Anna herself says, danced with joy at the good news of Eirene's safe delivery and birth of a healthy daughter.

There was a particular member of House Doukas by marriage who must have responded to the news of a baby girl with a sigh of relief: none other than Maria of Alania, twice empress by her marriage to Michael VII Doukas, Empress Eirene's uncle, and to Nikephoros Botaneiates, and for a while adopted mother of Alexios I Komnenos. The woman who might have been the cause for a rift between Alexios and Eirene, if the rumours and whispers in the gossip-loving court were true, had her own reasons for being happy on the day of Anna's birth. Maria had given birth in that same chamber herself only seven years before. Her young son, Constantine Doukas Porphyrogenitos, was according to many the true heir to the royal throne, as we shall see in the next chapter. The birth of a little girl and not a boy to the Komnenos-Doukas union meant that the perfect solution to the problem of succession and legitimacy was now available. Little Anna would make a very suitable bride for the young Porphyrogenitos prince and, in Maria's anxious point of view, she would guarantee his succession to the throne of which he had been wrongfully kept away, not only by his young age but also by two successive coups and usurpation, first by Nikephoros Botaneiates (his mother's second husband, who eventually dashed Maria's hopes of safeguarding her son's rights by appointing his own kinsman Synadenos as his heir), then by Alexios Komnenos.

The fact that the baby girl and Maria's darling boy were related by blood and marriage was a problem, of course. The Church was very strict about consanguinity, and canon law forbade marriage between relatives not only by blood or marriage, but also by baptism or adoption. Constantine was first cousin to Anna's grandfather Andronikos Doukas, and her father Alexios was the adopted son of Maria, making the prohibition to the marriage all the more powerful. But the Komnenoi, in spite of their professed piety, did not care very much for canon law: the patriarch's power was in their gift and depended on their pleasure. One patriarch, Kosmas, had already been replaced by Anna Dalassene's own favourite, the eunuch Eustratios Garidas; Kosmas' mistake was to unequivocally support Eirene when Dalassene had wanted to get rid of her, right after the success of Alexios' coup. The secular power of the great families could be greater than the Church. The Doukai themselves had broken canon law when they made sure that Emperor Nikephoros III Botaneiates married Maria of Alania (who had a living husband shut in a monastery against his will), breaking every religious and moral law. Consanguinity may have been a problem for lesser folk but not so much for the imperial families of Byzantium.

Finally, the birth of a royal child was a great source of joy for the people of Constantinople, high and low alike. Anna mentions that the celebrations at her birth lasted for days, with public banquets set not only for dignitaries in the court and in the city, where many of the old Roman institutions were still alive, but for everyone. The patriarch would be summoned to the palace to be told the joyful news and bless the new-born and the mother; gifts of money, food, and drink would be distributed to the men of the imperial guard, the army and the navy; the court officers and senators with their wives would visit the emperor to formally offer their best wishes and the emperor in his turn would grant them gifts and promotions, a ceremony normally reserved for specific feast days. Food and money would be distributed to the people, churches would be holding celebratory services, and the Hippodrome would ring with acclamations.

In his famous *Book of Ceremonies*, which records in detail the complex and elaborate ceremonies of the Byzantine court, the ninth-century emperor and author Constantine VII Porphyrogenitos, himself another baby of the Porphyra, describes in detail the joyful atmosphere in the city when a prince or princess was born in the Porphyry Chamber. The demes, the organised factions or associations of supporters of the city's teams in the Hippodrome would gather at the fountain near the Sigma, a public space just outside the Great Palace complex (marked 22 in Illustrations 3 and 4). Their heralds would then lead on the supporters to a series of call-and-response chants: 'A good day for victories!' 'Lord, send good days to our rulers and the Porphyrogenita! 'Happy birthday to the Porphyorgenita born unto us!' 'May they always win!' 'May they live long and reign!' The crowds would erupt in joy and alms would be tossed out in small coins. In the Forum of Constantine in the area of the Augoustaion – the large open public space between the Great Palace and Hagia Sophia – and in the main forums and thoroughfares of the city tables laden with food and drink would be set for the populace. The lochozema, a broth or gruel made with roasted semolina or flour and honey, would be offered in the palace and in the streets so that everyone could toast the happy occasion.

A few days later, more celebrations would follow with the ceremony of the baptism, performed with solemnity and grandeur in the baptistery of the Church of God's Holy Wisdom, known as Hagia Sophia (Aya Sofia, today a museum in Istanbul and a top destination for tourists, but at that time the world's greatest Christian cathedral). Baptism usually took place a short time after the birth, traditionally on the eighth day, or after the forty days of 'lying-in' and subsequent 'churching' of the woman. This very long and almost universal tradition of postpartum confinement was strictly followed in Byzantium. For the six weeks after birth, the mother would keep to her room and rest in bed with her baby. As she was considered 'unclean', she would not have been able to attend the baptism, or to breastfeed and even to touch her baptised infant afterwards, if the baptism took place before the 'churching', a ceremony in which she would present her baby to church and a blessing would be read over them both.

Baptism was the official integration of the child into the Church of Christ. In the Orthodox Christian tradition, holy baptism is followed immediately by the holy sacrament of Chrismation or Anointment (known in the Western world as Confirmation). As the infant is unable to recite the catechism, it is the duty of the godfather or godmother to do this on the child's behalf, reciting the creed and renouncing the Devil. The infant is then fully immersed in the water of the font and subsequently chrismated or anointed. Another ceremony integrated with the baptism, kourosyna or the cutting of the hair, signifies the dedication of the child to Christ. During the ceremony, the child's godparents – in Anna's case, very important men and women from among the aristocracy, some of them likely her uncles and aunts – would be standing in a line around the font holding handkerchiefs of gold cloth sewn together. The priest would cut two small clumps of hair crosswise and hand them over to the first of the godparents who would wrap them in the gold cloth. Because Anointment is so closely linked to kingship, and because of the liturgical connections between coronation and chrismation (those who remember the elaborate liturgical service of Queen Elizabeths II's coronation service might not be surprised to know that much of that ceremonial was taken or inspired by the Byzantine service), it is likely that the day of the baptism was also the day when a royal child was confirmed as his or her father's heir.

It is not unlikely that Anna's betrothal to Constantine Doukas was also celebrated at the same time. Little Anna was crowned with tiny purple imperial robes and shoes and a diadem, and acclaimed, together with her fiancé: Constantine and Anna, Anna and Constantine, Porphyrogenita Princess and Porphyrogenitos Prince. The whole of Constantinople rang with those two names for a long time afterwards, as her Doukas relations would often tell Anna later. After the horrible atrocities connected to Alexios' ascent to the throne only two years earlier, this joyous event and the non-stop street party celebrating it, which must have lasted for at least a week – there were traditionally eight days between a birth and christening in the Orthodox Church – was surely just the thing that was needed to heal the trauma and lay the past to rest.

This was the nearest that Anna Komnene would get to the throne of the Byzantine Empire; an occasion she would not have remembered herself and only known about by stories told to her later. At the time, she did not care at all about the fuss made around her. Cosy and warm in her swaddling of gold and purple, ensconced in the care of her doting mother, father, grandmothers, aunts, uncles, family friends, and hosts of servants, eunuchs, and slaves, she was completely unaware of the celebrations all over the great city of Byzantium for an event that promised some long-desired peace and stability after many turbulent years.

Chapter 3

A Girl Grows Up in Byzantium

Then a second child was born unto the emperor and empress, a female, goodly fruit from such goodly trees, but as in birth also in graces in second place. Then a third one was born, a male, a star of great brightness, and he was pronounced the heir to the empire.

(George Tornikes, *Discourse on the Death of the Porphyrogenita Lady Anna the Kaisarissa*, 14.251.3-6)

He gave to his own relatives and to some of his servants wagonloads of money and apportioned to them hefty yearly stipends, so that they were surrounded by great wealth and by retinues more fit for kings than for private citizens; and they possessed mansions that resembled entire cities in size, their luxury not dissimilar to that of palaces in every aspect.

(John Zonaras, *Synopsis of Histories*, 767.2-8)

The Imperial Family at Home

As Anna grew up in the 1080s, change was in the air, transforming the empire and the world. Every generation aims to do things differently and better in our progress-obsessed modern world, but not in pre-modern Byzantium, where emulation of the past and upkeeping of traditions were paramount. Yet the era of Alexios Komnenos was undoubtedly an era of change. The empire was porous, open to new influences, as the world around it seemed to press even harder on its boundaries. Enemies had always threatened the empire, but this time it was different: the Seljuks in the east and the Normans in the west were here to stay. At the time when Alexios Komnnos came to power, most of Anatolia had been lost to the Seljuks, and southern Italy and Sicily had a new master, Alexios' arch-enemy Robert Hauteville, known by the nickname Guiscard (Fox or Weasel).

Change was also happening within. The golden era of military triumphs and economic stability of the Macedonian dynasty which had reached its summit during the reign of Basil II was undone by successive waves of spendthrift emperors and civils wars. The financial crisis that had cost Michael VII his throne was not an exception but the norm. The powerful military aristocracy of which the Komnenoi and the Doukai were the cream of the crop, was gradually replacing the palace bureaucracy as main power brokers. As the empire shrank there was a notable downsizing, a shift from the public and monumental to the private and more intimate. A telling example is church architecture. The large basilicas of the early years of the empire, with their soaring domes and many windows that allow dazzling light to flood the vast space within, gradually gave way to much smaller, cruciform churches, their interior fragmented into small separate spaces lit by narrower windows and by the more mellow, muted, flickering light of candles.

The family and the house (in Greek, the word *oikos* signifies both the building and the extended family) became the epicentre of imperial power and imperial life, public and private. As public wealth decreased, less money meant less pomp and circumstance; the long, intricate and expensive ceremonies of the palace appear to have fallen out of fashion. Anna hardly ever mentions any official ceremonies, as opposed to her fellow Porphyrogenitos Constantine VII, whose most famous work is dedicated to them. Life was elsewhere: the palace-like seats of the great aristocratic families, like separate cities within the city protected by their own private armies, became centres of power, wealth, and influence in their own right, fostering art and literature. From such a mansion the Komnenoi had set out to conquer the city and the throne. When they succeeded, they did not want to live in the Great or Sacred Palace, the vast, sprawling complex of public and private buildings in the south side of Constantinople that had been the pinnacle of imperial splendour for so many centuries. Instead, they moved to the Palace of Blachernai, at the opposite end of the city, adjacent to the very end of the land walls, overlooking the Golden Horn and the shores of Asia across the water.

The Komnenoi preferred Blachernai to the Great Palace for many reasons. Its proximity to the lush woods and parks of Philopation with their abundance of game was important to the sport-loving Komnenoi men, who had a particular fondness for hunting. Anna's great-uncle Emperor Isaac I Komnenos was the first of the family to renovate and inhabit that ancient, suburban palace so he could be near the hunting grounds. The courtier and intellectual Michael Psellos mentions with a somewhat condescending amusement how the emperor loved shooting arrows at flying cranes, rejoicing like a small child every time he hit one and watched its magnificent tumble from the skies. There may have been another subliminal reason for the choice of Blachernai as the family residence: a need to make a clean start on moral terms, abandoning the decadence and corruption linked to the older and much grander palace. Anna Dalassene, according to her granddaughter and to the customs of the age which made her the de facto ruler of her son's household, imposed an almost monastic discipline at the palace with strict meal times and compulsory attendance of frequent church services for both the family and their servants. As a young wife and mother in the 1040s, Dalassene would have been horrified to see Emperor Constantine IX bring his mistress Maria Skleraina to live in the palace in a menage-a-trois with his wife Empress Zoe; the scandal did not end there, for after Skleraira's death a young Georgian princess took over as imperial mistress, scandalising the matrons of Constantinople once again. Moving away from the palace must have felt like a clean break from that morally polluted past, a fresh start.

Blachernai was Anna's first childhood home; the first seven or eight years of her life were spent there. She refers to it several times in the *Alexiad*, offering us scenes of private family life which are quite endearing and much nearer our own experiences of daily life: her father and her uncle playing chess together before dinner, her mother reading difficult theological-philosophical texts at table and explaining her taste for them to a sceptical teenage daughter, Anna and her sister Maria hovering nervously outside the private chapel where their parents were at prayers, making desperate signs to their mother that she is urgently needed. But let not these fond memories of a private life fool us: Anna's life would be as private as a huge army of servants and eunuchs, courtiers, state officials, foreign envoys, relatives, friends, hangers-on, and petitioners constantly moving around the imperial family would permit. Even if the large bulk of government business was conducted elsewhere, the emperor was always the epicentre of endless buzzing activity. Even if Anna does not mention any official ceremonies taking place in Blachernai – except perhaps the taking of oaths of the crusader princes – we know from other sources that at least one great church synod took place there in Alexios' reign. Anna offers a vivid image of business being conducted in the palace, with which anyone who has ever participated in a large conference, assembly, or summit meeting will be quite familiar: sessions going well into the night, the emperor presiding over the proceedings and patiently listening to the endless interventions and long-winded speeches of self-important Franks, while fed-up, exhausted secretaries and attendants abandoned all decorum to lean against walls, some even sitting on the floor, nodding with sleep as the night went on and little progress was made in the negotiations.

Anna, first-born and dearly loved, spent the first years of her life in the Palace of Blachernai with her parents and siblings, whose number grew almost yearly. What was her life like then? We catch glimpses of Byzantine childhood in the material culture of the age, in icons, murals and frescoes, and in manuscript illuminations. In these, babies are bathed and swathed and cradled, children pore over books, pray, attend ceremonies, assist their working parents in the fields and markets, watch as soldiers are trained, serve wine to their masters and fan their mistresses, play games in the street or with their pets, swim, run, pull wheeled toys, beg for bread, and steal fruit. The Lives of Saints present a much more tame and rather idealised image of children; the male or female saint is generally presented as a model child. We do not hear the voices of the children themselves, understandably; but there are passages in the *Alexiad* which may reveal something of the feelings of a child, a clever and precocious child observing her parents like a portrait-painter. Many years later she would depict them in her work with a vitality which brings them to life for the modern reader, albeit with a generous dose of rhetorical idealisation.

Descriptions of Alexios and Eirene

The emperor and father, Alexios Komnenos, was not a handsome man, but must have possessed considerable charisma. He was dark, black-bearded, with bright grey eyes under strong arched eyebrows, which made his face look both kind and awe-inspiring. His impressively broad shoulders and chest, muscular arms, and straight bearing suggested a seasoned soldier. Standing up among other men, he did not make much impression, for he was a rather short man; but on horseback or sitting on his throne he looked formidable. Obviously, the Komnenos charm lay not in looks but in personality. With a mind as quick and inventive as that other Greek king of old, Odysseus of Ithaka, Alexios made many friends who helped him on his way to the gilded throne. He was also kind-hearted, another Komnenian trait: philanthropy was honest in his case and not just for show. He endowed the Orphanage, a charitable institution 'as big as a city' that was much more than just an asylum for orphaned children. It covered a wide range of social services, providing residential care to the poor, to immigrants (many foreign languages were heard in there, Anna tells us), to the sick and disabled as well as to orphaned children, who were also schooled in the institution, not least in Greek, for long the official language of the Byzanine Empire. Judging by the place it takes in her narrative, Anna appears to consider the Orphanage Alexios' greatest legacy.

One may accuse Anna of bias on behalf of her father. But here is what another contemporary historian wrote about Alexios:

> The man was not contemptuous nor arrogant nor irate, nor did he care very much about money to the degree that he would bury and keep hidden treasures, but neither was very much left in the coffers after his death; he was inclined to mercy, not too keen on punishment, moderate in character, approachable, not a glutton and not a drinker; he heeded and honoured those who led a virtuous life; he was lenient even with those who did not treat him with due respect and talked and joked with them almost as if they were equals; which encouraged them to behave brazenly, as long as the empress wasn't there; but they drew back when she was present.

The author of this appraisal, John Zonaras, a senior palace official and judge who withdrew to a monastery and critiqued Alexios severely, did not have any reason to praise Anna's father; on the contrary, he had a few bones to pick with him and he makes this very clear.

As a private man, he says, Alexios was good and worthy of praise; his kindness, moderate behaviour, mercy, and good temper were notable. But as a king, now that was a different matter. Alexios treated the state as his private property, as if it were his own house rather than the common property of the politeia (republic); he did not honour the senate and he favoured his own kinsmen and family members to a degree that was unacceptable. But on the whole he was not a bad emperor as emperors go, for not one of the Roman emperors would be found perfect if judged on every aspect of his rule. This is where Anna the daughter and Zonaras, the disaffected civil servant who belonged to that class of senators that Alexios overlooked, beg to differ.

Next to the easy-going, talkative Alexios, his empress the Augusta Eirene Doukaina was serene and silent. Tall and slender like a young cypress tree, blue-eyed and pale like the moon, she looked like a statue of the Greek goddess Athene (Minerva in Roman mythology). She was as different from Alexios in appearance as in temperament and character. She was grave and distant while he was affable and fond of a good joke. Her presence checked him; when she walked into the room, it was the end of all the familiarity and rowdiness with his men, to which he was accustomed from his life as a soldier. She disliked small talk and displays of wit, while he was eloquent and fond of a good argument. Being in the room with her and her entourage was like being in church, so rigid and silent they all sat there, eyes fixed straight ahead, still as statues.

In the early years of their marriage, Alexios and Eirene were not close. He was rumoured to have passionate sexual liaisons with other women – Empress Maria was only one of them. Their marriage had begun as a business arrangement, not an affair of the heart. But there would come a time when Alexios would come to depend on Eirene, and they would be inseparable in the last years of his life.

In the description of Anna's childhood, her obituarist George Tornikes has drawn an intriguing picture of the Komnenos family at dinner, and Anna herself has let slip a few details. It is almost certain that the grand ceremonial etiquette surrounding the emperor's daily activities were abandoned in favour of a less formal atmosphere. Alexios and Eirene were close to their large families and various Komnenoi, Doukai, Palaeologoi and other member of the great aristocratic families would be frequent guests. Anna mentions listening to stories about war campaigns from her father and her uncles at table. The imperial couple were hospitable and charitable, and many poorer relations or unrelated needy people were their guests. Despite their long-held wealth as scions of old aristocratic families, they had simple tastes and abhorred luxurious excess. Even if their table was filled with rich dishes, as it befitted a royal table, they did not partake much themselves, but instead urged their guests to eat and made sure that each received what was good for them according to their state of health.

Their tender care for their guests was not limited to the body alone but extended to the soul. Their palace was no place for lewd music and burlesque songs from the shows and whorehouse of the city; no ruddy-cheeked, luxuriously dressed, long-haired youths would frequent their table either (was there a sideway glance towards Emperor Manuel's more epicurean and Westernised court in the good bishop's oration here?). Instead, you would find black-robed, long-bearded monks, pale and gaunt from fasting, their ascetic forms and edifying conversation rendering the royal table a place of spiritual nourishment as well as physical one. Frequently, Anna lets us know that patristic texts of great complexity and depth would be read at the table (a standard monastic practice) at the request of the empress, who apparently had a knack for theology to equal that of her husband.

The palace itself had something of the character of a religious establishment. Situated next to the Church of the All-Holy Theotokos of Blachernai, it had been built over five centuries earlier by Empress Pulcheria on the site of an ancient spring of water (still extant today in the basement of the Greek Orthodox church) in the north-western corner of the city. The church, connected with a series of staircases to the palace, was the home of a precious relic and of a miracle-working icon. The relic was the maphorion, the veil of the Holy Virgin herself, which emperors would take with them on campaign to secure victory against their enemies. The icon was the Hodēgētria – She Who Shows the Way, depicting the Virgin Mary holding the infant Jesus with her left arm while pointing at him with her right hand. The icon was covered with a veil (not the holy relic). Every Friday evening the veil would lift slowly of its own accord and would stay up until the following night; in the rare cases it did not, it was considered a bad omen. Alexios would consult the icon as the ancient Greeks consulted an oracle.

The prevalent religious atmosphere was mainly the doing of Anna Dalassene, the emperor's mother and proxy whenever he was away on campaign. She had a great fondness for holy men and monks and had even attached one of her trusted monks, named John, to her sons Alexios and Isaac when they were still youths. Brother John followed the young lords everywhere and slept in their tent during campaign. Dalassene wanted to discourage misbehaviour and protect her sons from sin (with moderate to low success, if the stories told about Alexios' 'love for Aphrodite' are to be believed); the monk also made an excellent spy for his mistress, reporting back to her every discussion and every meeting his young charges would hold. His duty ended only when Alexios found a wife (or rather was allocated one).

For a modern child, or indeed for any child, the atmosphere during those dinners must have been dreary. But Anna tells us that she enjoyed listening to her father and her uncles as they reminisced about battles and heroic shenanigans throughout Alexios' wars against his numerous enemies, with some stories straight from myth and epic. Precocious children like nothing better than being around grownups. If the royal couple were tedious with all their religiosity (Anna herself, although clearly adhering to the religious spirit of her times, does not come across as excessively zealous about religion), at least Alexios and Eirene were good, kind, and modest. Tornikes states that for someone who did not know better it would be hard to believe they were the master and mistress of the palace, so approachable, simple and unaffected were they. 'They never sneered down their noses nor did they ever looked disdainfully upon those who were by birth and position situated lower,' Tornikes gushes in a rather surprised tone.

Alexios' simplicity of manner and approachability are confirmed by other writers of the era, which can only make us imagine what the general behaviour of aristocrats would have been. Tornikes also praises Anna for her graciousness. Indeed it would appear that the Komnenos-Doukaina couple were well-bred themselves and raised their children the same way. Being models of true Christian behaviour and spirit, they were the best parents anyone could have, Tornikes concludes. From them, for their living example, Anna was taught some of the virtues that would be hers later in life: temperance, moderation, modesty, generosity, magnanimity, and not least, sweetness of temper. That was her first education – or at least what Tornikes and his era thought of as a child's ideal education – and in no way does it foreshadow or explain what Anna would become in future: the most educated woman of her time, and a secular intellectual at a time when women authors of her calibre would be nuns and abbesses.

Maria of Alania and Constantine Doukas Porphyrogenitos

At the age of 7, Anna left her home to move into the household in which she was supposed to spend the rest of her life. She had been engaged practically since birth to the young prince Constantine Doukas, a Porphyrogenitos like herself, son of former emperor Michael VII Doukas and his empress Maria of Abasgia – or of Alania, as they somewhat disdainfully called her in Byzantium. As part of Alexios' actions to legitimise his coup, he had made young Constantine co-emperor (he was no more than 9 years old at the time). In the happy event of his betrothal to the days-old infant Anna, the two children were presented to the people of Byzantium as the heirs to the throne; from then on they were acclaimed and hailed as future emperor and empress, 'our names linked in acclamations.' Constantine was allowed to wear the royal red-purple buskins and diadems of an emperor, which proclaimed his position as designated heir (Anna would not rule; her husband would be the ruler). But this did not last very long.

Anna was 4 years old when her father's longed-for male heir arrived; there was no doubt in anyone's mind that Alexios would make him co-emperor and successor. Surprisingly, Alexios did not hurry to confirm his own son and heir for quite a long time, for which he was publicly and privately chastised, including by the metropolitan bishop (and later saint of the Orthodox Church) Theophylact of Ochrid, a protégé of Maria of Alania and tutor to young prince Constantine – which sounds rather disloyal of him. Alexios' delay has been a matter of speculation in his time and in ours; it would appear that he did not feel safe enough in his own right, engaged as he was in multiple wars immediately after his accession. But he felt strong enough to assert his own line after a decisive victory against the Pechenegs, a Turkish people ravaging his north-western border, in 1092. On 1 September of

religious education and their own preference for theology over science is well known. Anna mentions that sometimes at breakfast her mother would read St Maximos the Confessor, a profoundly philosophical Church Father. Young Anna was impressed and expressed her wonder at this, asking the Empress: 'How can you read such a high concept text? It gives me a headache even to consider it.' If Anna's comment strikes us as typical teenage critique of a parent's taste, Eirene did not take it that way: she praised Anna for being reticent to read such doctrinally complex texts (it might be a dangerous thing to do for someone inexperienced, for heresy was lurking everywhere). She promised her that there would come a time when such texts would taste to her as sweet as honey and she would never want to read anything else. The time did indeed come for Anna to engage with difficult texts and vertiginous concepts, with which she was particularly apt. George Tornikes recalls at length some philosophical conversations Anna held with the philosophers in her circle on subjects such as the Being, Providence, the Nature of the Divine and other such high concepts. But Anna's preferences was not so much for patristic texts as for ancient philosophers such as Aristotle, Plato, Proclus, and other pagans.

In the preface to her will, Anna states that her parents encouraged and helped her in her pursuit of knowledge. But George Tornikes tells a very different tale. Although her parents were themselves lovers of knowledge, he says, particularly that which was contained in sacred texts, they were not so keen on their young daughter indulging in the study of the profane or *thyrathen* (literally: from outside the door) education, by which they meant classical, Hellenic, or pagan. Why was that? The good bishop explains: 'They viewed pagan ("thyrathen") education with suspicion as a harmful thing, in the same way that a wise mother of many children often views matchmakers, fearing that they might introduce inappropriate desires into her virgin girls' minds.'

Obviously, certain parts of pagan philosophy were not only acceptable but admirable. For example, the study of logic, in which Anna's era included philosophy and natural sciences, was perfectly appropriate since in revealing the secrets of nature it would generate admiration for its creator. But grammar, which included literature as well as the study of language, was another matter. Poetry was particularly pernicious, what with its polytheism – 'atheism really' – and its myths of gods who were constantly involved in disgusting love affairs, 'ravishing virgins and kidnapping youths and committing all sorts of indecent exploits in word and deed.' Such stories were bad enough for men; but to virgins and women they were extremely harmful. In the parents' view, 'the ears and the eyes of a girl must remain virgin from such contact, for through them indecent longings flow into the soul;' correctly, they did not to want little Anna to endanger her purity by reading such tales which could inspire 'licentious loves'.

But, Tornikes continues, they had not taken into account the integrity and strength of their daughter's mind and courage. Like someone who finds out that an ambush is set up for them on the way home and there is no other way to get there but to take up arms and tackle the bandits with courage, little Anna armed herself well against those insidious fictions. Like another Odysseus avoiding Circe's potions and the chant of the Sirens, opening and closing her ears to their guiles with the help of rational thinking, she tackled grammar and poetry with a strong and alert soul. She was never in danger because she was strong, brave, and wise.

However, just to be on the safe side, she made sure to keep her studies a secret from her parents. All day long she had to stay by her mother and suffer the tediousness of the court. But in the evenings, when she parted from her mother to go to bed, she was free for a short time to pursue her own interests. 'Like a girl in love who has been eyeing her lover furtively through secret holes,' Tornikes writes, 'as soon as she was parted from her lady mother in the evening, she would dash to a tryst with her darling grammar, sacrificing the greatest part of her sleep and rest to the pursuit of her studies.' Away from the supervision of her parents, Anna read. We can imagine her eagerness as she immersed herself in the jubilant, irreverent myths and turbulent passions of Greek poetry, drama, and comedy after the dreary diet of pious texts and the solemnity of her mother's court.

Anna was not self-taught. Her teachers were educated eunuchs, old men who had been long in service at the palace, Tornikes informs us. Eunuchs were men who had been castrated as young boys, normally before they reached puberty. The destruction of their male reproductive system resulted in a specific appearance, devoid of male secondary sexual attributes; their faces remained hairless and smooth, their voice high-pitched, and their hair long; they were also taller than the average height and often blonde. They were unable to impregnate women, although they were not beyond having sexual relations and, judging by hagiographical texts, apparently they were often used as sexual objects by wicked masters; but generally eunuchs were deemed safe around women and for this reason they were employed as servants, guards, or officials in the women's quarters in the imperial palace, as well as in private mansions and homes.

In the Eastern Roman Empire (as in Imperial China), eunuchs were extremely valuable in imperial administration. Even though they often came to wield immense power in the imperial court through their knowledge, wealth, and connections, they were never a real threat to the emperor, as they would never be allowed to become emperors themselves. No one with a marked corporeal disability, such as missing body parts, was permitted to hold the supreme office – this is the reason why conspirators or dethroned emperors were so often blinded in Byzantium. Even though Byzantine law forbade its citizens to become eunuchs, many were imported as slaves from beyond the limits of the empire; but the law cannot have been very strict when it came to children of poor Byzantine families who envisaged a high-flying career in imperial administration. Anna Dalassene's pawn of a patriarch, Eustratios Garidas, was a eunuch. Tatikios, one of Alexios Komnenos' most trusted generals, was reputed to be a eunuch too, and was described as such with horrified fascination by the crusader chroniclers, as we shall see later. Tornikes makes sure to mention that Anna's teachers were eunuchs, as he wants to make it clear that she never risked her honour or her parents' by having strange men around her at that tender and perilous time of her life – 12 was the beginning of marriageable age for Byzantine girls.

Those furtive lessons at night, when everyone else was resting, cannot have been easy for a young girl:

'So many constraints in her education,' Tornikes exclaims,

> and yet look at her! Witness her love for Demosthenes and the sciences, see her amazing progress! Other students, boys and men, with all the opportunities she was denied, going to proper schools and with keen teachers at their

side to encourage and goad them, took so much longer to accomplish what she, a little girl living in the luxurious surroundings of the palace [and presumably with all sorts of distractions and counter-inducements to study], did completely on her own and without permission, never mind encouragement.

Writing in the 1150s, Tornikes belongs to a generation in which the genre of the ancient novel had come back into fashion, almost a millennium after they were first written in the second century CE. These were adventurous and rather raunchy stories of young lovers separated by their parents, enemies, or adverse circumstances including pirates, living entombment, infidelity, and violence, to be reunited at the end in a triumphant marriage. Interestingly, the heroines in those novels were feisty and daring, sometimes even more so than the heroes. In Anna's time, it would seem that such romances, distant ancestors of eighteenth and early nineteenth-century gothic and romantic novels, were just beginning to be written and recited at fashionable gatherings of the aristocracy or even at court.

Tornikes himself presents young Anna as a true heroine, armed with the strength of her will and rational mind, fighting with courage and conviction to overcome the obstacles that stand between her and the object of her love. Like many a protagonist in the romances which were so popular in Tornikes' time, Anna defied her parents, albeit in secret and never leaving their house, not for the sake of a lover, but of learning. Descriptions of Anna and her love affair with philosophy and science follow those pattern of forbidden love and final triumph and have something of their erotic overtones.

And Real Romance?

Whether Anna's parents knew of her secret nocturnal pursuits and tacitly approved or had no idea and would have been alarmed to find out, one thing is certain: for them Anna's purpose in life was not education but marriage. At the age of 12 it is certain that the discussion of a suitable match would have been one of the most pressing subjects in the Komneno-Doukas household. Alexios and his mother would have looked among the sons of Byzantine aristocracy as at that time foreign alliances were not envisaged for the daughters of the family, although the Komenos sons all married foreign brides, a tradition that continued in the next two generations.

In general, very few Byzantine princesses were given out to marriage abroad. Princess Theophano had married the German emperor Otto II in the late tenth century, bringing with her dowry the sophistication and luxuries of Byzantium (to the horror and consternation of the German clerics, she used a fork to eat and bathed frequently); but she was only a niece, not a daughter of Emperor John I Tzimiskes. A little later, the Porphyrogenita Princess Anna, sister of Basil II the Bulgar-slayer, married – against her will – Grand Prince Vladimir of Kiev, bringing about the Christianisation of the Kievan Rus. Such matches were still rare in Anna's time, though they would become much more frequent in later centuries.

Until her parents had decided on a suitable match for her, Anna would have to stay in the women's quarters, unseen by other men, at least in theory. Eleventh-century Byzantine general and provincial landowner Kekaumenos notoriously suggested in a handbook of good advice to his son that daughters should be kept firmly inside 'like convicts', or they would endanger the family honour by attracting amorous attentions and who knew what next. However, it is doubtful that the court was as strict as that.

Tornikes discusses Anna's two romantic involvements – which were both chosen by her parents for her and both highly suitable. He admits that the engagement to Constantine was desirable to all parties and perfectly natural: the young people were both children of reigning emperors, born in the porphyry room and made for each other. But God decided otherwise. Somewhat boldly, Tornikes considers the premature ending of that engagement as the work of divine providence. He agrees that the fiancé was perfectly eligible in every possible way, and he acknowledges that, had this engagement continued to marriage, Anna would have become empress, but this was neither her calling nor her heart's desire. God saw that this princess did not care about imperial power and that her true calling, her greatest passion, was to attain wisdom. Marriage to Constantine would place obstacles in her way; eligible and suitable as he was, he did not share Anna's passion for study and knowledge. Therefore, God in his ineffable wisdom took Constantine away early and put another in his place. That man would be of a slightly less illustrious family than Constantine's, but with far superior qualities to most men that ever existed, both physical and intellectual, and more to the point, a man who shared Anna's love for letters and wisdom. That man would be the perfect match for her and would help her to attain 'the highest summit of wisdom', as another historian would describe her achievement long after her death.

Chapter 4

A Woman's Lot

The world has never presented us with such a man, nor has history taught us that there ever was one such as he. For other men among the Greeks and the Romans may have achieved great things, some as orators, others as generals, others in letters, some in philosophy and some in poetry; but to have the same man be a general and a teacher of poets and a philosopher and a senator and a student of orators and in all that not to be lagging behind but to beat even those who were masters in each sector, that was not everyone's attribute but the Kaisar's alone.

(Theodore Prodromos)

Let them behold their children as young shoots of olive trees gathered around their table.

Marriage Service of the Greek Orthodox Church

A Girl of Marriageable Age

At 14 years old Anna was ripe for marriage according to the standards of her age. In the medieval Greek world, the usual marriage age was 12 for girls and 14 for boys – as soon as puberty hit and they were physically able to have children. Emperor Leo the Wise (r. 886–912 CE) raised the age limits by one year, and Alexios I, Anna's father, raised them even higher to 14 for girls and 15 for boys for legal marriage. But even though the Church frowned upon early marriages or even forbade them outright, marriages of pre-pubescent children were not unheard of. The horrific story of Princess Simonis (b.c. 1294), daughter of Emperor Andronikos II Palaiologos, married off at the age of 5 to 50-year-old Serbian King Stefan Milutin, is the most famous example of child abuse in Byzantine history; apparently the marriage was consummated when Simonis was only 7 and as a result she was never able to have children. But this appears to be a rare exception, thankfully, to the rule that legal age should be concomitant with biological pubescence.

Another option for girls and women was monastic life. But for Anna, such a path was out of the question. Her role in life was to marry, and to marry well in accordance with her family's wishes. Interestingly, in the prologue of her last will and testament, written when she was in her mid-thirties, Anna states that if it had been up to her wishes only, she would not have married at all but would have chosen 'the unyoked life', i.e. the monastic life (tellingly, the Greek work for spouse, syzygos, literally means 'together under the yoke'). But it is highly likely that this statement was only paying lip-service to the prevalent idea in Byzantine and generally in medieval society, due to a reading (or misreading) of St Paul, that the monastic life was of a higher order than marriage, which served the flesh (Corinthians I: 7-8). Anna's statement might just be a platitude and not the expression of her real desire: if that was the case, why did she not choose to become a nun directly after her husband died in 1136 or 1137, but only *in extremis* on the very last day of her life, over fifteen years later? At any rate, Anna lived at a time when marriage had attained a higher status in ecclesiastical ideology; sainthood was not hitched solely to the single, 'angelic' life of the monk or nun. Married saints become more common, and motherhood, already sanctified in depictions of the Mother of God together with her child, was glorified even more with a new emphasis on the bond of tender love between the two.

Living her restricted life at home, constantly at the side of her mother and as much out of view as it was possible for an imperial princess, Anna waited for her father's decision on her future. The choice of husband was the parents' prerogative, although at least formal consent was sought by the spouses-to-be. Romance was not a prerequisite for marriage in the Greek world, but if one was lucky, love would come after marriage.

In the meantime, she continued with her covert education. Tornikes, expressing the common view that girls, fit only for the home and for the distaff and loom, were vulnerable to vices such as vanity and love of luxury and fashion (an idea that seems to still hold sway among certain circles), admires Anna all the more for not caring for such things. For highborn young girls and particularly for those lucky enough to be born into the imperial family, life would be replete with all the good things money could buy: 'clothes decorated with pearls and precious stones, woven with gold

virtues. Tornikes, dazzled and awed before such a marvel, exclaims that in the whole of history there must have been just two or three women who reached the summit of all wisdom: Sappho (the famous poet from Lesbos), Theano (philosopher connected to the philosopher and mathematician Pythagoras), and Hypatia (the great philosopher and scientist from Alexandria). How and why a fourth one appeared in his own time he could not explain, but there she was: his late *basilissa* (the title given to princesses of royal blood and not just to reigning empresses), the fourth case of a wise woman in history. Anna was rare and as astonishing a phenomenon as a comet appearing on the star-studded literary firmament of twelfth-century Constantinople. As the only woman she appeared as a mythological creature, a phoenix giving birth to itself, rising from its own ashes, unique in the world.

If we modern readers are appalled by the misogynistic view of the medieval author that all the intelligent and wise women in the whole of history could be counted on the fingers of one hand, even making allowances for rhetorical exaggeration, we should also consider that by singling out Anna as one of those very few women, George Tornikes betrays his awe at her unique achievement. All the more so because, as he notes, she had all her duties as wife and mother of many children, and of a wealthy and powerful imperial woman with so many affairs, public and private, to tend to. It would seem that Anna entered all these roles to the full. She took her place in the palace as a young married woman, amid the ease and luxury of life there, but, Tornikes asserts, she was not tempted or weakened by the rich stimulants of the senses of taste and smell, the variety of dishes and the exquisite perfumes of Arabian wood. If anything, their very abundance reinforced her temperance. If she were to be found draped in purple silk embroidered with gold and silver, her neck almost breaking under the weight of lines of pearls and precious gems, her fingers and arms covered in rings and bracelets and long earrings hung from her ears, it was not because of her vanity. No, she was aware that such ornaments did not add any beauty or strength or health; but they made her think of the hidden virtues of the soul. In a sense, the external gems and precious stones reflected her inner qualities. This attempt by Tornikes to spin Anna's fabulous clothes and jewellery as somehow indicative of modesty and virtue reveals that he, like other intellectuals who have ever come in contact with the radiance and opulence of the extremely wealthy, was simply smitten, perhaps a little against his will and better judgement. However, there is no doubt that Anna, even though outwardly complying with the paraphernalia of her social position, was engaged in serious study.

We do not have very much direct information about the education of the majority of women (and even men) received in the Middle Ages and it is rather difficult to obtain statistical data about literacy in any pre-sixteenth century time. Knowledge of that source can only be gleaned obliquely from other sources – texts, visual arts, books, and manuscripts. For example, the existence of written Lives of Saints may indicate that enough people could read them on their own to explain their circulation, or it might mean that there were only a few literate people who would read them out loudly to smaller or larger audience of illiterate people and that some wealthy illiterates would buy them for their libraries as status symbols. Specific books and book titles were mentioned in people's wills as legacies. Not all of the books were sacred; in the mostly Greek-speaking Eastern Roman Empire, many were pagan texts from Antiquity, among them romances. These, known also as 'ancient novels', had been written mostly in the second century of the Christian era and were extremely popular prose works, replete with star-crossed lovers, gods and goddesses, pirates, supernatural occurrences, and all sorts of extremely enjoyable adventures, including a bit of surprisingly frank sexual content.

In the Christian era, the novels were abandoned in favour of Lives of Saints, which in a way continued in the same vein, although now the love affair was between the saint and Christ, and the sex scenes were replaced by horror in the form of the tortures inflicted upon the saints and martyrs (including some sexual content relating to demonic activity in the Lives of the Fathers – and Mothers – of the Desert). But interest in the ancient novels never quite went away. In the ninth century Photios, a bibliophile patriarch of Constantinople and later saint of the Orthodox Church, left a monumental work, aptly named *Myriobiblon* (*Thousands of Books*), in which he wrote what can only be termed as reviews of many of the books he had read, with summaries, extracts, comments on the content and style, and his personal opinion of them. Theological, historical, and philosophical works were there, and surprisingly, a number of novels; some of them have been lost and all we know about them is what Photios included in his reviews.

In the twelfth century, there was a revived interest in the ancient romances and they became very popular among the intellectual elites of Constantinople. In the relative stability and economic affluence achieved during the Komnenian years, which meant there was money for luxuries such as patronage of poets and writers, this revival of interest in the ancient novel resulted in the writing of new novels, some in verse and some in prose, 'historical' novels at that, set in the Hellenic past, clearly inspired by the ancient models. On the other hand, Homer and Greek tragedy and comedy, as well as the works of ancient Greek philosophers, historians, orators, and legal speech writers were still – and would never cease to be – main staples of the Byzantine, Greek-speaking educational curriculum.

Anna herself tells us that she studied the trivium and the quadrivium. This classical education involved the triple subjects of grammar, rhetoric, and logic, and the quadruple study of arithmetic, geometry, music, and astronomy. This was the basic education that prepared students for the more advanced study of philosophy. Anna mentions in particular the philosophical works of Plato and Aristotle. But her education appears to have included the whole spectrum of Greek letters. She quotes often and appositely from a wide variety of Greek works. Homer is a particular favourite; her quotations from the *Iliad*, in particular, are very frequent and from memory, sometimes slightly paraphrased, as if she knew the work extremely well but did not always have it at hand to check the exact wording. Perhaps she even felt she knew it well enough not to need to check. But Homer's influence goes more deeply: the *Alexiad* as a whole has been influenced by the ethos of the epic, setting up Alexios Komnenos as another Odysseus or Achilles. Even the naming of her work is in the epic convention, as are scenes of battles and presentation of characters in the book, from her family to other Byzantines and even some foreigners. Sophocles, Euripides, Aristophanes, Demosthenes, and Herodotus, are frequently mentioned and cited. Her historiographical method, as she explains it herself, follows Thucydides, the father of 'scientific' history.

How was this high level of education possible for a woman? Anna herself in the prologue of the *Alexiad* offers a quadruple set of reasons: nature, love for knowledge, God's assistance, and chance. In other words, she was aware of her own natural gifts and the opportunities with which her fortunate birth provided, but she too, like Tornikes, had a strong belief in her own willpower and purpose. In Nikephoros, she found a kindred spirit. That alone was reason enough to love him and to mourn him so bitterly when he was gone, as she so poignantly does in the Prologue of the *Alexiad*.

Great literary couples are not a common occurrence in history. Abelard and Heloise are perhaps the best-known example of passionate love between two intellectuals of equal calibre. But their situation and trajectory was very different from that of their contemporary pair, Anna Komnene and Nikephoros Bryennios. For one, Anna and Nikephoros were of almost the same age; he was only three years her senior; for another, it was not illicit love that brought them together but a carefully arranged match by their families, in which much more was at stake than the couple's happiness. What is more, Anna and Nikephoros' story did not begin as a passionate love affair but by all appearances it developed into one, even though they lived and had many children together, while devoting much of their lives to the service of Anna's imperial parents – all conditions which generally test romantic love to the limits.

Children

Anna and Nikephoros had several children, as she herself informs us in the extant prologue to her last will and testament. Some of them died very young, 'exchanging this life for a better one.' Of the surviving ones, her two sons, Alexios Komnenos and John Doukas, and her daughter Eirene Doukaina are mentioned in other sources. One more daughter is also reported but not by name, although the name Maria has been proposed for her, as it was the name of Anna's favourite sister. It is more likely, however, that the other daughter was named after her paternal grandmother, the mother of Nikephoros Bryennios, whose name does not survive at all. This is not entirely unique as we are even unsure about his father's Christian name.

In naming her children, Anna followed a convention among aristocratic families of giving precedence to her own family, since her husband's family was less prominent. The name of Bryennios was never associated with imperial titles. Nikephoros Bryennios the Elder had tried and failed to become emperor, beaten by young Alexios Komnenos back in the late 1070s; his name would forever be associated with that defeat, always giving way to the name of the winner. Modern Britain has had experience of something similar within its own royal family, when in the 1940s the young Princess Elizabeth, heiress to the British crown, married Prince Philip, whose own royal family, formerly of Greece, had been left without a kingdom after being unceremoniously ousted by the Greek people in 1922. If the displeasure of the royal son-in-law at not being able to bequeath his own name to his progeny has been recorded for posterity in the twentieth century, we can only speculate whether Nikephoros Bryennios had felt something similar back in the twelfth.

Anna never mentions her children in the *Alexiad*. For this she was accused of being a cold-hearted woman who did not care about her own children enough to include them in her book (conversely, had she mentioned them, she would have almost certainly been accused of being a sentimental mother and therefore not suitable for the august task of writing history). However, there are many good reasons why she would not bring her own children into a history of her father, as recent scholarship has argued. Apart from being irrelevant to the content and purpose of that work, in Anna's culture it was considered imprudent to discuss one's children, as if drawing the attention of fate on them. In a culture replete with myths of women who were horribly punished for bragging about their progeny, like Niobe whose six sons and six daughters were all slaughtered in cold blood because of the jealousy of the gods, one can see why this could be a bad idea. Anna does mention them in the prologue of her last will and testament; poignantly, she states that 'it was God's will' some of them died, and she expresses her heartfelt wish that she predecease her living children – and her husband, for Nikephoros was still alive when Anna wrote her will. She omitted them from her work not because she did not love them enough but because she loved them too well.

The Boys

Unsurprisingly, we know much more about Anna's boys, Alexios and John, than about her girls. We are told in various sources that both John and his elder brother were very handsome and intelligent with a bookish turn, which they must have inherited from their parents. Born into wealth and privilege and high rank, they lived easy, comfortable lives and had guaranteed careers in the imperial court. This was a time more than any other when kinship with the emperor, by blood or marriage, was generally the safest way into power; the few exceptions of men outside the family network who got there on merit alone confirm the rule. We can easily imagine the kind of lives Anna's children would have had. Here is a snippet from a court speech recited on the day of the two boys' wedding (they got married on the same day to two foreign brides from Abasgia), which offers a concrete image of aristocratic wealth and privilege:

> All the gifts that nature granted them, I mean beauty and swiftness and strength, and all that their readily absorbed education taught them, that is to ride and play ball with dexterity, to hunt skilfully, to command and lead armies nobly; and all the material luxuries, imperial clothes and silver and gold and all the rest that is valued by men, splendid houses, Arabian horses, high-born friends, for all these too contribute to good life, let your own eyes credit them with each; as for me, I admire them most for their modest and gentle manners.

While court poet Theodore Prodromos praises the boys for their friendliness and lack of affectation, the tone of social envy is unmistakeable. It must have been quite trying for poor scholars who depended on the patronage of the rich and powerful and who made their living by composing fawning speeches for happy (or sad) family occasions for their aristocratic benefactors to witness this display of fabulous privilege on a daily basis, particularly when they had to knock on doors and beg for commissions.

The eldest son, Alexios Komnenos Bryennios, was born in 1102. He must have been 16 years of age when his Georgian bride Kataë, daughter of King David II the Reformer, arrived with her entourage in Constantinople. On that very day his grandfather Emperor Alexios I Komnenos, after whom he was named, lay dying in the Palace of Mangana, and his maternal uncle John Komnenos Porphyrogenitos was hurrying to the Great Palace, anxious to secure the allegiance of the Varangian Guard and be proclaimed emperor instead of young Alexios' own father and mother. A contemporary chronicler describes the chaotic situation in the streets of Constantinople as the members of the foreign mission proceeded in pomp down the Mesē, Constantinople's main avenue, mingling with the frantic armed followers of John.

The wedding took place later, possibly in 1122. It was a splendid event, depicted in dazzling vividness by Theodore Prodromos, the most prominent of the court poets, in a speech addressed to Nikephoros Bryennios, the father of the bridegrooms. Such a grand occasion as this double royal wedding involved a series of events before and after the wedding ceremony. A speech would have been addressed in one of the after-ceremony banquets on the 'second day' of the wedding, where young Alexios and his brother were praised abundantly. Alexios was presented as the living embodiment of his grandfather of blessed memory, the emperor Alexios. 'Remember all ye that are present, the time of Alexios' power,' Prodromos urged the eminent audience,

> but lest tears spoil the occasion of the nuptials, only remember the best of his reign – the peace, the order, the great deeds in battle. Do not sigh, my holy queens [to Empress Eirene and Anna, the grandmother and the mother of the bridegrooms, who were present], do not sigh, but consider this festive occasion, and remember his mildness, his steadiness, all the other attributes of his grace.

In the same speech, Eirene was called the root from which such perfect fruit had sprung; Anna was addressed as 'the Fourth Grace, the Tenth Muse', her royal soul dressed in wisdom as her body was invested in the royal purple, the happy wife of the kaisar (Bryennios), the peerless, the one and only. And what a joy it was for the family to see the two young offshoots of such illustrious families join in matrimony with two young women of the best blood – two suns united with two moons! What joy for their father the kaisar to see his sons in such happiness, and what joy for their imperial grandmother, head of their house, and for the divine porphyrogenita (Anna) whose joy was equal to that of her master the kaisar, having seen her sons crowned the day before (reference to the Orthodox marriage ceremony during which the bride and groom are 'crowned' with wreaths or circlets or coronets) and acclaimed by the senate and the demes! What was even more important, they were led to the altar by their uncle the emperor, who had only just celebrated his own victory at war.

What joy also for the royal uncles and aunts present at the feast! But what joy especially for the young people themselves, the bridegrooms, and the brides, with their lovely and modest new sister Eirene Doukaina, sadly a premature widow! Undoubtedly Prodromos' rapturous speech would have hit the right note of flattery and interest with the imperial audience, but for the modern reader it can be a little tedious nevertheless.

This picture of opulence, joy, and familial harmony, which reads like the equivalent of today's publicity photos of royal weddings, offers valuable insights into the relationship between Anna and John, in view of the theory – prevalent for so many centuries – that Anna and her brother John were mortal enemies (of which more later). Had Anna attempted to kill her brother the emperor, would he have been the best man in her son's wedding? Would she have even been allowed near the emperor, never mind sit next to him in the joyful wedding event in a place of honour?

Some scholars have argued that the wedding took place after Alexios' death but before Anna's alleged coup; however, the mention of the war which John had just won places the wedding in 1122 CE, long after the supposed attempt, which would have taken place in 1118. On the other hand, there is an intriguing point in the speech, where Prodromos compares the wedding of Alexios and John to Kataë and Eirene, respectively, to the mythological wedding of Peleus and Thetis. Those readers who know their Greek myths will remember that during that wedding the goddess Eris, spurned and uninvited, threw the notorious golden apple of discord among the divine guests, making the goddesses fight amongst themselves for the title of 'The Most Beautiful' and eventually causing the Trojan War. The mention of Eris, or Strife, goddess of conflict and discord, is rather enigmatic here. In high-flown metaphor, Prodromos states that even Eris was invited to the wedding of the young princes, albeit not as an enemy but as a friend. Could this be an allusion to past conflict in the family, which was now happily resolved?. Prodromos concludes that the real weddings were much superior to that other wedding, in the same way that the affairs of the Byzantine court were much nobler and more distinguished than the mythological affairs of the gods. The Byzantine mind, used to complex extrapolation, would have made here a comparison between the outcome of Eris' intervention in both weddings, the mythological and the real one: in the former case the result was war among gods and mortals, in the latter peace and harmony in the imperial family. Prodromos, a highly experienced court poet, could have used this very oblique reference to very guardedly and politely praise the members of the royal family for resolving their differences and making peace in the end, unlike the gods and goddesses of Mt. Olympus.

The eldest son, Alexios Komnenos Bryennios had a brilliant career; he was close to his cousin Emperor Manuel, son of John II Komnenos, and served under him in military and diplomatic capacities. Even if there had been a rift between their parents, it did not seem to have affected their relationship. He was the principal Byzantine diplomat in the mission to Antioch in 1161 to negotiate the marriage between Manuel, at that time a widower with two daughters, and the beautiful Marguerite-Constance of Antioch, who was renamed Maria when she married Manuel. Alexios was also very highly praised as the praetor of Athens by the local bishop, Michael Choniates, the brother of the historian Niketas. Apparently Alexios was known not as Komnenos or Doukas, but as Alexios the Just, like Aristides of classical Athens, such was his integrity and sharp sense of impartiality and righteousness.

The second boy, John Doukas Bryennios, was born in or after 1103. He married a princess of Georgia, who arrived at Constantinople on the same day that his grandfather Emperor Alexios died. We do not know her Georgian name, but she was renamed Theodora on her marriage. She died young, probably in the year 1138. In a poem written for her funeral, our old friend Theodore Prodromos, readily provides consolation in sad times as he offered congratulations and rejoicing in happy ones, which also gives us an update on the status of family members. He begins with the imperial ladies. The deceased lady's grandmother-in-law Empress Eirene is now deceased. Her mother-in-law, the wise Anna, the white and red rose that bloomed in the porphyra who was so much like her mother in everything, is now covered in a black calyx, because the dearest kaisar is gone too ('o my heart, don't break!', cries Theodore in anguish, real or fake). Her husband, the 'good and sweet' John was away on campaign, as one of the cataphract rider-archers, with his master and uncle, Emperor John II, when his wife fell ill. As young John besieged and mowed down the barbarians, his poor dear wife was besieged and mowed down by an army of ailments, fever, and hot and cold shivers. In the eighth month of her illness she deteriorated and her husband had just enough time to return from the wars for one last embrace. Afterwards, poor Eirene put on 'the angelic garment' (i.e. she became a nun on her deathbed, exactly what her mother-in-law, Anna, would do many years later on *her* deathbed), changed her name to Katherine, and during sacred hymns she closed her eyes, arranged her arms on her lap and departed with God. Her surviving son Nikephoros, named after his grandfather the great Kaisar Bryennios, would always remind John of his dearest wife, the boy's mother.

Like his brother, John also had a brilliant career in the military and diplomatic service. He distinguished himself in a number of wars against the Italians, the Seljuks, and 'barbarians of the Caucasus'. He belonged in the inner circle of his cousin Emperor Manuel and intervened once in a fight between two of his first cousins, Manuel's son the Sebastokrator Isaac and future Emperor Andronikos. [Table 4] According to historian John Kinnamos, a heated argument between the cousins escalated and as a result John was wounded in the hand. By the looks of it, such fights were not uncommon in the highest of circles, often ending in brawls and physical violence. Anna herself narrates a similar episode in her father's generation: apparently, her father and her uncle Isaac quarrelled about Isaac's son John, Anna's cousin, who was accused of conspiring against Alexios. In that quarrel which took place in a family gathering, Anna's uncle Isaac threatened Adrian, another Komnenos brother, and was ready to grab him by the beard but was stopped in time, before the family quarrel escalated into a brawl. There is also a notorious scene of the altercation between her uncle George Palaiologos and the crusader Tancred, nephew of Bohemond; when the young insolent Norman showed disrespect to Alexios, Palaeologos grabbed him by the throat It is all in the *Alexiad* and it makes for very enjoyable reading.

The Girls

Much less is known about the two surviving daughters of Anna and Nikephoros. That there were two is made clear in the typikon (foundation charter) of the convent of Mother of God Full of Grace (Theotokos Kecharitomenē), founded by their grandmother Empress Eirene. In the typikon, the empress mentions them both as successors to the *ephoria* (governorship) of the convent, but only mentions one of them, Eirene Doukaina, by name. Eirene Doukaina was the favourite granddaughter of Empress Eirene; she was the daughter of her own beloved daughter and she bore her grandmother's full name. Eirene Doukaina the Younger is specifically mentioned several times in the typikon of Full of Grace, generally with the qualifier 'most dearly beloved'; the empress used qualifiers for all her children, calling them 'most beloved', but when it comes to Anna and her daughter, the wording is especially warm. It seems that Eirene the Elder had extraordinary confidence and trust in the younger Eirene's abilities as a manager, because she designated her as *ephoros* (governor) of the convent of Full of Grace after her mother's demise, together with her aunt Maria. After Maria's death Eirene Doukaina the Younger is named as the sole ephoros, bypassing her Aunt Theodora, Eirene's youngest living daughter, who is not even named in the succession. This has been seen as an indication of the empress' disapproval for her daughter's unseemly marriage (more of that later), or as a more sinister declaration of the deep rift within the Komnenos family – of factions according to their political stance regarding John's succession. As governor of the monastery, young Eirene would have the right to eat with the nuns if she so preferred but was advised not to take more than two or three women of her retinue with her when she did, as it would encumber the nuns financially.

Not much is known of young Eirene Doukaina's personal life. She was widowed very young, because at the time of her brothers' double wedding she was there as a young widow. Her husband's name is never mentioned; neither is his family name. No doubt it would have been someone important, but not more important than the Komnenoi (but then who was?). Eirene's only son was named Alexios Doukas, combining the imperial name and surname of his maternal grandfather and grandmother respectively.

George Tornikes addresses Eirene Doukaina the Younger in Anna's funeral oration and mentions – though it may only be a rhetorical flourish – that she resembled her mother, both in physical traits and in spiritual qualities. Eirene was to Anna as Anna was to her own mother, and would pay her debt to her mother for all the blessings she bestowed upon her in the same way that the Anna had paid her debt to her own parents. In a letter to the young princess, her mother's old friend praises her for being a true mother to her son, not only in body but also in spirit, because she took pains to educate him herself in all the virtues from a very tender age. It would seem that Eirene was hands on with her son's education in the same way that her mother had been with her, and her grandmother and namesake with the education of all her children. At least old George Tornikes says so; whether it was all an embellished, idealised image of the perfect aristocratic family or an accurate depiction of parents who cared enough for their children so as to be directly involved in their education, there is no way to know. Perhaps the truth is somewhere between the two.

Of the other sister, Anna's youngest surviving daughter, nothing at all in known, except for the fact of her existence. The further a girl stands away from the imperial throne, the easiest it is for her to sink into obscurity.

Chapter 5

The Power Factor

When I grew up and developed my rational abilities,
I unequivocally loved both my mother and my father. And
there are many witnesses to this trait of my character; in
fact, everyone who knows about my affairs; and it is further
attested by my many feats and labours and dangers in which
I put myself for their because of my love for them, without
sparing honour or money or my very life. For my love for
them burned my soul so that I would my life up for them
several times over.

(Alexiad, 6.8.2. l 11-20)

Lord Baelish: 'Knowledge is power.'

Queen Cercei: (ordering her guards to seize him and cut
his throat, then ordering them to release him): 'No. *Power*
is power.'

(D. Benniof, D.B. Wise, and G.R.R. Martin (writers),
A. Taylor (director), 'The North Remembers',
in Game of Thrones, HBO, 2012

A Family Affair

It has been proposed that the nuclear family in Byzantium was the
main unit of society and not that different from families in modern
times. The closely-knit (and at times rather dysfunctional) nuclear
family of Alexios and Eirene with their nine children has a tinge
of nineteenth-century modernity about it, not least because of the
extraordinary intellectual yet devoted eldest daughter. If Anna's life
was divided in phases according to its main focus, then the years

between 1097 and 1118 were definitely the family years. Anna raised her young family then, and more important to her historical legacy (for good or for evil), those were the years she devoted to the service of her father and mother and which comprise the main part of her narrative. They could also be called the years of power, with the exception of her very early childhood when she bore the imperial diadem and insignia with her fiancé Prince Constantine Doukas but was too young to have any proper understanding of her position or real influence. Those younger years were the nearest Anna ever came to power in the traditional sense of the word: executive power, domination, the ability of giving orders, and having them carried out. Power is at the centre of Anna's story as a historical character and as an author; it is also crucial in her reception in the ways she has been perceived by historians and later generations.

When it comes to the Komnenoi, family and power largely overlap. This was one of the most significant traits in Alexios I Komnenos' reign and a major shift in governance, born out of necessity. As a usurper, who could Alexios count on for support but his kin by blood or by marriage? Their help was crucial in obtaining the throne and fundamental to his continued occupancy. The examples of recent emperors – Michael VII who famously did not want to be burdened with relatives, and Botaneiates, who did not have extensive support networks – were cautionary tales enough. Anna's grandmother Dalassene was well aware of the importance of networks and laboured all her life towards building them; she had even yielded to the inevitable and accepted the Doukas alliance, a *sine qua non* in Alexios' success, as it turned out.

That is not to say that it was only family members that belonged in the inner circles of power during the reign of Alexios I, as some historians have claimed, starting with Zonaras. There were outsiders too, sometimes foreigners from East or West, men who had proven their abilities and loyalty to Alexios in some way (even if it did not always end well, as we shall see). Not all Komnenoi were made equal. As a modern scholar has observed, power in the Komnenian administration was distributed in ring-like formations around the emperor, the proximity and relevance of those rings increasing or diminishing depending on time and circumstances. Sometimes this ebb and flow of power was dictated by natural causes – people grew older, or died, or fell out of favour; younger people and newcomers filled the vacuum pretty quickly. But the chances were that these new people were mostly affiliated with the Komnenoi by blood or by marriage. All those daughters and sons and nieces and nephews, and their spouses and *their* families – the greatest houses of the empire and even some foreign ones, once the local pools were exhausted – continued the pattern in the next two or three generations of Komnenoi. When the dynasty changed from the House of Komnenos to the House of Angelos, it will hardly come as a surprise that this new dynastic line had risen to prominence after an initial marriage alliance with the Komnenoi.

Not all the members of Alexios' family championed him or were on good terms with one another. As any lawyer dealing in family law will confirm, there is nothing as acrimonious as feuds amongst members of the same family. In 1080–81, Alexios' brother-in-law Nikephoros Melissenos fought him to the bitter end for the throne and only recapitulated when most of the army had declared for Alexios. Even then he had to be bribed generously with the title of kaisar to accept the emperor and stop being a nuisance. Alexios' two brothers, Isaac and Adrian, had a big fight between them when the former's son John was accused of conspiring against his uncle Alexios. A family council was called, in which all the brothers and brothers-in-law were present. Isaac was mad with Alexios for believing 'gossip' he heard and furious at Adrian for spreading lies and calumnies, threatening to tear off Adrian's beard. Another brother-in-law, Michael Taronites, husband of Maria Komnene sister of Alexios, was sucked into the conspiracy of Nikephoros Diogenes and was punished with exile and confiscation of property; he was lucky not to lose his eyes. There are hints that perhaps even Alexios' own brother Adrian may have been implicated in the conspiracy. The strife continued in the following generations; the story of Anna and John's rivalry is central to Anna's reception, but there is an equally acrimonious story between John and his younger brother Isaac, which rarely makes the cut in the main modern historical accounts, or at least only gets a brief mention and certainly not the same emphasis as the story of Anna's attempted coup. The bones of the story are similar: sibling conspires against brother John II, the legitimate emperor; sibling fails; John forgives sibling in his great kindness; sibling ends up in exile in monastic foundation. In other words, there was no such thing as a large, happy House of Komnenos.

Not that Anna conveys any such impression in her history, quite the contrary if one reads carefully. Anna barely mentions her siblings in her history. She pays slightly more attention to the first three in order of birth after herself, Maria, John, and Andronikos, but she hardly dedicates any space to her other three surviving siblings, Isaac, Evdokia, and Theodora, except a mention in passing (Zoe and Manuel died as infants so there would be nothing to say for them). This has been explained in many different ways, mostly as the selfishness of a power-hungry woman who only cared about her own right to succession and tried to eliminate her siblings (particularly 'the impudent John', as the poet C.P. Cavafy put it) when she could, as in John's case. Viewed under the prism of power (her desire for which seems to be taken for granted), this makes sense. But what if Anna only has anything to say for those first three siblings because they were the ones she really knew before she left to make her home with Empress Maria?

The alleged tiff (or worse) between Anna and John must be seen in the general context of family feud, in my view. Power games are constantly played out in every family, particularly when there are questions of inheritance, be it of property or otherwise. This is probably the key to better understanding the relationship amongst the Porphyrogenita children of Alexios and Eirene. Anna's position in the family as the first-born was particularly charged: the eldest in a large family of children often occupies a space between parents and siblings; parents tend to be closer to the eldest than to their other children because of the time when this first-born was the only child, an experience that would never be repeated with the other children. On the other hand, the siblings, especially the younger ones, sometimes may see a parental figure in the eldest sibling, particularly when there is a considerable difference in age.

Brothers and Sisters

Relationships among the numerous Komnenoi siblings were, as it is always the case, unequal. Although before the age of 6 or 7 boys and girls spent their time in the women's quarters together with their mother and sisters and all the other female relatives who lived there with them, and of course under the care also of servants and eunuchs, after that age, boys and girls had a very different upbringings and daily lives and moved in largely separate spheres. The girls would stay in the women's quarters learning enough letters to be able to read the Gospels, Psalms and the Lives of Saints, although the education of upper class women could be of a higher order. The princesses would also be taught manners, morals, and the arts of 'the distaff and the spindle', by which in the case of the imperial girls we should understand all the necessary skills that would allow them to raise a family and supervise and run a household of their own. They would also be interested in clothes and makeup and jewellery and spend much time in such pursuits, as Tornikes mentions – in the context that Anna had no time for such frivolities so dear to girls and young women in general. Conversely, the boys would usually receive a more thorough education, as well as training in sports including polo – a particular favourite of Byzantine aristocracy – and hunting. In the art of war, they were taught both the basic martial arts of fighting in battle and single combat, as well as tactics and strategy.

Anna was much closer to some of her siblings than to others. Her sister Maria, nearest to her in age, was born in the Porphyry Chamber at the eleventh hour (i.e. about 5 o'clock in the afternoon) on Friday, 19 September 1085, a proper Friday child, 'sweet-natured and modest' in her sister's words. The two sisters would be close throughout their lives and many decades later Anna's health would collapse while she looked after her ill and bereaved sister. Maria was not as brilliant as Anna, 'second in birth as she was in graces', as Tornikes commented, somewhat unkindly. When Maria was 9, she became engaged to 16-year-old Gregory Gabras, son of the renowned doux of Trebizond (and later martyr of the Greek Orthodox Church) Theodore Gabras, who was seeking independence of his mountainous region of Pontos by the Black Sea from Byzantium. The boy had previously been engaged to another Maria, the girls' first cousin, daughter of their uncle Isaac Komnenos. Neither Theodore nor Gregory were keen on the alliance with House Komnenos, seeing it as a ploy by Alexios to keep them in the fold – which was probably true. Young Gregory, who was held in the palace rather more as a hostage than a fiancé, had something of his father's indomitable spirit and tried to escape several times and make his way back to Trebizond, but was caught and taken back into luxurious imprisonment every time. In the end, Alexios must have decided that there was no point in pursuing a match that was so obviously unwanted and let the young man go, or as John Zonaras brusquely put it: 'he ended the engagement when it pleased him and sending the young man away, he got another fiancé for his daughter.'

Whether Maria was aware of any of that drama at her young age is not known. Her new suitor, to whom she was eventually married, was another aristocratic young man, Nikephoros Euphorbenos Katakalon. He was the son of one of Alexios' most trusted generals, and the protagonist of one of Anna's delightful micro-episodes. In the war of Alexios against the Cumans, a northern Turkish tribe, Nikephoros Bryennios the Elder sent some soldiers to Alexios for help; both young Nikephoros and his father were part of the detachment. But they were ambushed by a Cuman band on the way and as they tried to escape, a Cuman warrior tried to cut them off. But Nikephoros, thrusting his long spear into the enemy, saved his father and the other men who escaped the ambush and joined Alexios. Interestingly, all the main named protagonists in that war – except the Cumans – were (or later became) members of the close or extended Komnenos family.

Anna liked Nikephoros Katakalon and was proud of him; whether this was because of her love for her sister or the man's independent worth can only be guessed. At any rate, she gives a glowing description of him: 'he knew how to wield the spear and the shield; the young man was truly a wonder, a gift of nature; to see him on horseback, one might think he was not a Roman but a Norman.' This was a great compliment, as the Normans were admittedly the best horsemet in the world – or what Anna and the Byzantines of her times knew about it. She also said that Nikephoros 'was most pious and amiable and gentle with everyone.' Maria herself seems to have been happy with him, but he died relatively young. Maria suffered additional losses in later life, when the sisters were in their sixties. Maria lost a child (probably one of her sons) and a grandchild. This broke her heart and her health. Anna who by that stage had amassed considerable medical knowledge – Tornikes is again our source – attended poor Maria in her illness. But as a result, she neglected herself and her own health and Maria appears to have died after Anna.

The next Komnenos sibling, third in order after his two sisters, is John. He was the long-awaited male heir, born on September 13, 1087. 'His birth was the perfect complement to the happiness of the imperial couple and made all their true friends rejoice with them,'

Anna wrote in her account of the early years in Alexios' reign. She then offers a description of her new baby brother: the baby was dark, with a wide forehead, thin face, a nose that was neither snub and wide nor aquiline and narrow but something in between, and very dark eyes, from the very first revealing a keen and curious spirit. In this sketch of an intelligent but plain younger brother, many historians have read the hatred that Anna allegedly nursed for the 'usurper', the little boy who would supplant her in her parents' affections and 'spell the end of her imperial dreams.' This description seen under a different context would sound rather neutral, and certainly not indicative of hatred; clearly such a reading can only be explained by preconceived ideas about the relationship between Anna and her brother.

Anna's portrait of John may not have been particularly flattering, if one compares it, for example, to her lyrical description of her young fiancé Constantine Doukas, whom she likens to Eros, the son of Aphrodite. But historian William, Archbishop of Tyre corroborates Anna's description of John as not exactly handsome, stating that John was short, ugly, and so dark-skinned that his nickname was 'the Moor'. Swarthy of skin, short of stature, John clearly took after the Komnenos side of the family. Perhaps Anna was not disposed to like a little boy of whom everybody made too much fuss; jealousy towards a younger sibling is not uncommon, and this may have formed her first strong impressions of the baby which she recalls many years later as she is writing. There is also a certain disagreeable tendency in traditional patriarchal societies, even today, to openly show a preference for male children that can rile an older sister, particularly one who has been the centre of attention until then (or at least has only just learned to share it with a baby sister). But to claim that such a description is proof of Anna's hatred is far-fetched. She does not even call him ugly. The idea that the description is even negative may have more to do with the racial prejudices of nineteenth-century historians who automatically associated the swarthy skin of the baby with ugliness, rather than with anything Anna actually said or intended.

John's nickname was *Kalos*, Good, or *Kaloioannes*, Good John or Beautiful John. Initially *kalos* meant beautiful, but later the meaning shifted to signify moral beauty only. Calling John 'beautiful' could only be a rather unkind joke – the sort of Roman humour that called bald Julius Caesar 'hairy'. But apparently 'good' was an epithet that

John deserved; even Edward Gibbon, who notoriously hated and disparaged the Byzantines, had good things to say for him, comparing him to the Roman philosopher-emperor Marcus Aurelius. John was merciful and good-natured, another Komnenos trait that John shared with his father. His foundation, the monastery of Christ Pantokrator, included a large hospital with wards for men and for women; the latter was staffed by women doctors, even though it was attached to the male monastery. John reigned for twenty-six years, from 15 August 1118 to 4 April 1143, when he died from a poisoned arrow that brushed against his finger in a hunting accident in the outskirts of Antioch. During his reign, no one was condemned to death, an admirable record and not only by the standards of the age, as Gibbon notes admiringly. Yet not all the stories his contemporaries tell about him are flattering, as we shall see later in the discussion on Alexios' death and John's succession.

The next boy, Andronikos, another September baby born on the nineteenth in 1091, is considered as Anna's favourite brother, mainly because she has dedicated a number of lines in the *Alexiad* to mourn for his death. By all accounts, Andronikos was a sweet-natured, kind boy who would grow up to be a general favourite with everyone. He married a Russian princess famous for her exquisite beauty, predictably named Eirene. This was not the name of her birth. Foreign brides marrying into Byzantine royalty always took another name; almost every foreign princess who married into the Komnenoi was named Eirene, which must have been confusing in family gatherings. A hasty reading of the *Alexiad* may have confused many readers into believing that Andronikos died in battle, mainly because Anna speaks of his bravery in battle and then straight away about his death, but without connecting the two. (Such careless readings and conflations of primary sources have led to other notorious misunderstandings, for example that Mary Magdalene was a prostitute). The truth is that Andronikos died prematurely not on the battlefield but from a fever-related illness that sounds like malaria, away from home, in 1130/31, while on military campaign against the Turks. The details of his death are given by Theodore Prodromos. So very popular was he, Theodore says, that everyone mourned for him at his death including the enemies against whom he was campaigning. His funeral was a public event in which all the inhabitants of the city went out in the streets in weeping masses to bid him farewell. The chief mourners followed the byre of the dead prince: his mother, the Dowager Empress Eirene, who had brought his body back from Asia Minor herself, his brother Emperor John, and his sisters Anna, Maria, and Theodora. The court poet compares the sisters to the daughters of Helios, the Greek Sun God, mourning for Phaethon, their prematurely lost brother who crashed his divine father's chariot. Andronikos' nephews, the sons of Anna, Maria and John were the pallbearers. Theodore offers a moving description of his horse, following the cortège 'with its head bowed down; feeling the absence of his beloved rider, now and then it neighed pitifully, woefully.' Anna mourns Andronikos with poignant words: 'O youth and prime of body and nimble jumps on horseback, where to didst thou fall into ruin?' At Andronikos' birth she had been 8 years of age, old enough to play with the new baby as if he were a doll and without the pangs of sibling jealousy. In her old age, as she wrote her history, she wept for Andronikos, 'my most beloved of brothers', his death one more of the evils she had to suffer in her life – so many evils that if the ancient myths ever came true, she would be transformed into a bird or a stone, like so many bereaved heroines of ancient tales.

While Anna was away from the family home living with Empress Maria, Alexios and Eirene had five more children. On Sunday, 16 January 1093, round 3.00 pm, Isaac Komnenos, Anna's third brother and fifth Komnenos sibling was born in the Porphyry Chamber. He would grow up to be an intellectual like his big sister Anna, and an adventurer, spending many years abroad in the East, 'wandering in the far limits of the East, living but as if dead' to his family and friends in Constantinople, as he wrote himself. Isaac was also a philanthropist. He established a hospital in his monastery of Kosmosoteira, Virgin Mary Saviour of the World, in emulation – or competition – with his brother John, whom he initially supported but later challenged, spending much of his life in exile as a result. He was perhaps a little eccentric: in the typikon, the foundational charter of his monastery, he stipulated that monks must change their outdoors shoes before entering the church to protect the marble floors.

Eccentricities apart, one aspect of Isaac's life and role in the history of House Komnenos that has not been given the attention it deserves is his several conspiracies against his brother John II Komnenos. If Anna was indeed a conspirator, she certainly was not the only one in the family: Isaac tried several times in the 1130s to make a bid for the throne against his brother (who by that time had reigned for well over a decade) and briefly against his nephew Manuel in 1143 when John died outside Antioch. What do modern books make of it? Isaac merits half a line in John Julius Norwich's very popular *Short History of Byzantium*, largely based on Gibbon: '[Manuel] also ordered the arrest of another Isaac, John's brother, already exiled *after previous conspiracies*' (my emphasis). Those 'previous conspiracies' passed over so casually were repeated and were much grander in scope than Anna's alleged conspiracy: in a long campaign Isaac tried to muster the combined forces of the emir of Kappadokia Gümüsthegin Ghâzi, the sultan of Iconium Masoud, the ruler of Trebizond Constantine Gabras (brother of Gregory, Maria's former fiancé) and the Armenian ruler Leo, unsuccessfully. He ended up an exile in Heraclea Pontica, known also from the poet Ovid's exile several centuries earlier. Yet Isaac's conspiratorial moves implicating foreign enemies do not seem to weigh with latter historians quite as much as Anna's attempt at the throne (if indeed any such attempt took place). Three contemporary sources (John Kinnamos, Niketas Choniates and Michael of Syria) confirm Isaac's several attempts to the couple that mention Anna's conspiracy (Zonaras only mentions Eirene and Nikephoros but does not incriminate Anna explicitly; Niketas Choniates is the only source that does). It almost feels like bias against the eldest sister; or is it just leniency towards the younger brother? At any rate, it is remarkable but not unexpected that such rivalries existed among siblings and heirs of an empire and that a sister was blamed more than a brother for the same type of behaviour

Two more girls were born to Eirene and Alexios. The unfortunate Evdokia came next, sixth child and third girl, born on 14 January 1094. Her father's choice of husband for her was a disaster. Michael Iasites, son of a distinguished family with connections to the Komnenoi (his father was a kouropalates and his mother's family had already been connected to House Komnenos by marriage) may have looked like the kind of imperial son-in-law Alexios was after. But instead of supporting and strengthening the house, Iasites proved thoroughly unsuitable. Simply put, he was a bad sort. His arrogance was shocking enough. He was abusive to his young wife and treated her with extraordinary conceit. When her mother the empress intervened, the silly young man antagonised her too. The clash between mother- and son-in-law continued for a while. When Evdokia fell ill, Eirene decided enough was enough.

The couple were divorced and Evdokia became a nun. Her mother had special rooms built for her in the convent of Kecharitomene (Mother of God Full of Grace), which she had just built and endowed. Evdokia died young, but not before she could nurse her father, along with her mother and other sisters, in his last fatal illness; she was there at his deathbed, holding him up so he could breathe and sprinkling his temples with rosewater to refresh him and ease his pain. Empress Eirene laments her daughter's untimely death in the typikon of Full of Grace. Had she lived, Evdokia would have been *ephoros* of that monastic foundation; her death made her sister Anna governor instead.

The last living daughter, seventh child of the imperial couple, was Theodora, born 15 January 1096 (January and September must have been great birthday celebrations in the Komnenos household and the kingdom, as most of the siblings were born in either month). Theodora married twice. Her first husband, Constantine Kourtikios, died early and left her no children; at her father's death, aged only 22, she was already a widow. Anna implies that Theodora was the one to provide a black dress to her distraught, hysterical mother, who sheared her hair and threw away her rich purple dress and shoes as soon as Alexios was gone. Theodora's second marriage was rather surprising: it appears that she married for love, or because of the strong physical attraction that often passes for love. Her new husband, Constantine Angelos, came from a family neither very rich nor particularly distinguished, from the city of Philadelphia, to the southwest of Constantinople. But he was extremely handsome and, according to the sources of the time, his Greek-god looks seduced the young princess. The marriage cannot have pleased her mother. Eirene snubbed Theodora doubly, first by excluding her completely from the governorship of the Convent of Full of Grace, and secondly by allocating fewer alms and prayers for her memorial service on the anniversary of her death, once that sad event took place (more of that later). Perhaps the reason for Eirene's displeasure was Theodora's marriage to a pretty boy who did not bring much to the family except Theodora's (apparent) happiness. In the event, Constantine did not prove as useless as one would perhaps expect; he served Emperor John and particularly his son Emperor Manuel with some success. On another account one might consider Theodora's choice unlucky for the empire, were one to believe Niketas Choniates. According to Niketas, the weak and inept Angelos emperors – the descendants of that marriage – who took over after the death of Andronikos I Komnenos (nephew of Manuel I) were to a great degree responsible for plunging the empire back into strife and civil war, just as it used to be before their forefather Alexios I Komnenos' time. The fatal blow of the capture of Constantinople in the Fourth Crusade (1204), in which Emperor Alexios IV Angelos was heavily involved, would be the last straw.

Of the last two Komnenos babies, Manuel and Zoe, born respectively in February 1097 and March 1098, nothing is known except that they must have died shortly after their christenings. Anna was already a married woman by that time.

Dutiful Daughter, Dysfunctional Family

> When I grew up and developed my rational abilities, I unequivocally loved both my mother and my father. And there are many witnesses to this trait of my character; in fact, everyone who knows about my affairs; and this is further attested by my many feats and labours and the dangers in which I put myself for their sake because of my love for them, without sparing honour or money or even my life. For my love for them burned my soul so that I would give my life for them several times over.
>
> (*Alexiad*, 6.8.2. l 11-20)

Of all the brothers and sisters and their spouses, it would seem that Anna and Nikephoros Bryennios were the ones closest to the imperial couple, or at least to the empress, during the reign of Alexios. In Anna's own words, she gave everything up to serve her parents: time, money, health, her whole life and soul. Later in her history, she asserts: 'And those of us who were loyal to the emperor worked hard and supported our *Despoina* and mother in guarding him, each one of us according to our powers, with all our souls and minds, sleeplessly.'

What exactly does this mean? Who were those 'we' that Anna says were 'guarding' the emperor and how did they support their lady mistress? This comment is embedded in a larger passage in which Anna discusses the war between Alexios and the Normans after the end of the First Crusade (1104–08). Eirene was accompanying Alexios in the campaign, although she was a very private woman and intensely disliked being exposed to public eyes. 'This has been written for those tongues who love to scoff and revile others, and always find fault where there is none and misinterpret everything that is done in good faith,' Anna added with some vehemence, which is perfectly explained when we read her statement as an answer to those 'wagging, spiteful tongues' that spread rumours of conjugal disharmony. Alexios took Eirene with him on campaign, they claimed, not because of any love or devotion, but simply because he did not trust her; following the maxim 'keep your friends close and your enemies closer,' he feared to leave her behind in the capital, unsupervised and unchecked in conspiratorial activity. Anna was well aware of those rumours but challenged them. In her version of events, her mother was simply devoted to her father and heroically overcame her own retiring inclinations in order to assist him in his imperial duties. Anna and Nikephoros would be near the empress to help and support her. At some other point in her book (14.7), while discussing her sources Anna states that much of what she wrote she witnessed herself; she assures her readers that she did not lead a pampered and protected life in the women's quarters at home but accompanied her parents on campaign. Perhaps she and Nikephoros funded themselves while they travelled with their imperial parents or contributed financially when and where it was necessary. Not much else is said on the matter, but it might explain Anna's allusions to her sacrifices for her parents including her own money.

This was not unusual; aristocratic women could be very wealthy in their own right. Anna tells us earlier in her account of the first years of Alexios in power, that her mother had contributed much of her personal wealth (being a daughter of the House of Doukas, she was rich in her own right) to finance the emperor's first campaign against Robert Guiscard and the pseudo-Michael VII, right after Alexios' coronation. Filial duty at least in Anna's case went far more than obedience to her parents; it was active service in their interests, which of course was the interest of the empire itself as they saw it. A life of ease and reclusion it certainly was not, for travelling and participating in military campaign, even for the imperial family, was not exactly comfortable. But Anna seems to have enjoyed the movement and freedom; she even mentions that during such a trip to Philippoupolis (today's Plovdiv in Bulgaria), they had time to visit the old city and observe the ancient ruins – much like nineteenth-century imperial British women abroad.

For Eirene's increased presence in Alexios' affairs (and Anna's history) to make sense, we need to take a look at the family dynamics in the imperial household at that time. It was now almost twenty years after Alexios had ascended to the throne of Byzantium, with the help of his close family by blood or marriage. He had successfully averted a number of direct challenges or conspiracies in the 1080s and 1090s, and managed major crises such as the Norman war and the First Crusade. While he was occupied in his various wars, his mother and his eldest brother held the fort in the capital; Anna Dalassene was invested with absolute executive powers by imperial chrysobull and ruled the empire while her son was out at war with the Normans and the Pechenegs; she was also helped by her second son, Isaac Komnenos.

But almost two decades later, the situation was different. Anna the Elder had withdrawn to her own monastery of Pantepoptes sometime in the late 1090s. Anna the Younger insists that her grandmother had never wanted to rule anyway, and that her main desire in life was always to retire in a convent and spend her final years in peaceful contemplation of God; only filial love and duty to the family had convinced her to accept the helm of the empire which her son had bestowed upon her. Zonaras' story, as usual, offers a less idyllic version of things. According to him, in the first years of Alexios' reign Anna Dalassene was the real emperor, her will enshrined in law; this was good for Alexios up to a point, as for every unpopular decision everyone blamed his mother and not him. But eventually he became unhappy with this arrangement as he felt he did not have any real power at all and would have changed it if his love and gratitude for his mother did not stop him. Anna Dalassene, a very intelligent woman, soon realised how things stood and decided to step down of her own accord, rather than be asked to go or, worse, sent away in an undignified manner. She died a few years later in Pantepoptes, at a very advanced age and in full royal honours. Her eldest living son, Isaac, died just over a year later. With these two deaths and his mother's demise in particular, something shifted in the balance of power in the family of Komnenos, which would also affect Anna Komnene's life. Alexios turned to his wife for the help and support he needed, even more so as he was getting on in years and also the first symptoms of an illness that would eventually carry him off began to appear.

Power Games

Eirene began to accompany her husband on campaign when Alexios was in his late thirties. Anna's first recording of Eirene and Alexios together out of the capital is in 1094, during the conspiracy of Nikephoros Diogenes. The former protégé turned conspirator had attempted to murder Alexios in his sleep, as he and the empress slept together in their tent. They had no guard around them, which possibly suggests that Alexios was extremely confident in his popularity or that indeed Tornikes was right to call the imperial couple approachable and unassuming. The only person there was a little servant girl fanning the mosquitoes away from the sleeping couple; her presence was enough to deflate Diogenes' murderous intent. From that time on, Eirene seems to be a steady presence by her husband's side in the military camps around the empire, wherever necessity took him.

Up to that time, Alexios' relationship with Eirene was not particularly cordial, in spite of the several children they had together and even though Anna paints a uniformly idyllic picture of her parents' marriage. But Zonaras, again, provides a rather more cynical version. At first, he states, the emperor was indifferent to his wife. He was not repulsed by her, but he did not care much for her either; he was given to sexual passions and was regularly unfaithful to her, which made the empress very jealous (understandably!). However, as he grew older and 'time blunted the fiery arrows of love,' he turned all his love to the *augusta* and they were inseparable. At the same time, he began to have pains to his feet and legs and joints, which made him increasingly more dependent on her. This is confirmed by Anna's statement that Eirene was the only one who knew how to alleviate Alexios' pains by giving him massages and looking after his health, and that the emperor only wanted Eirene to administer those treatments to him. It was obvious that Eirene was now the person closest to the emperor; as a result, Zonaras continues, she became all powerful and the emperor submitted himself to her will, to the point that people began to believe that after Alexios' death the imperial power would be transferred to her, and not to his son and heir John.

Roughly a decade after Nikephoros Diogenes' conspiracy, another plot shook the city of Constantinople. This time too a great number of high-ranking officials and wealthy aristocrats were implicated, including members of the Iasites family whose scion Michael had caused so much grief to Anna's younger sister Evdokia; but the main conspirators were the extremely wealthy John Solomon and the four brothers Anemas, who had served Alexios in the Norman and Cuman wars. The conspirators were careless though, involving all sorts of vain and silly people who could not hold their tongues. When all was revealed with the help of the sebastokrator (second-in-rank after the emperor) Isaac Komnenos Alexios' brother, still alive in the early 1100s, metaphorical heads began to roll (Alexios did not execute people that easily). Solomon's vast wealth was confiscated; his family was kicked out of their fabulously luxurious town-house, which was then gifted to Empress Eirene. Many aristocrats who were related to Komnenoi were exiled. The Anemas brothers were arrested and condemned to be publicly blinded. Before the execution of this terrible punishment, during which their eyes would be gouged out with hot knives, they were handed over to the mob for a ceremonial *diapompefsis* – a humiliating procession through the streets of the city. Michael Anemas, the man who would become emperor had the plot succeeded, was the main conspirator. He had certainly looked the part of emperor, tall, young, and handsome, but he and his brothers were now paraded through the streets of Constantinople riding oxen sideways – like women – their heads and beards shorn, dressed in burlap sacks and crowned with heaps of animal entrails, animal blood (and worse) streaking their faces, while people threw filth at them and sang derisory songs. It was a ghastly and heart-breaking sight. Worse was to come. The procession would end with their public blinding. As the procession passed in front of the palace of Blachernae, Anna and her sister Maria looked on from a high balcony. Michael Anemas turned his face up to face them, and raising his arms in supplication, begged with signs that they should cut off his arms from the shoulders and his legs from the buttocks and his head off his shoulders and end his troubles. 'Everyone was naturally moved to tears and cries of anguish, and we the daughters of the king even more so.

And I wanted to save the man from such an evil fate, Anna writes.'
She and her sister ran to find their mother and ask her to intervene
with their father to spare Anemas the terrible punishment. Eirene and
Alexios was at prayers in their private chapel. The girls hovered outside
the door, not daring to disrupt the service, while Anna made desperate
signals in the hope that her mother would see and catch on. Eirene did;
excusing herself, she slipped out of the chapel and asked her daughters
what was going on. Breathlessly, Anna explained; there was no time for
delay, they should do something quickly. Her mother had the ear of the
emperor and could intervene on Michael's behalf before the cortege had
reached the Hands – a gate at the palace, above which was fixed a pair of
bronze hands in supplication. Traditionally, it was the boundary beyond
which a sentence could not be recalled. If the procession carrying the
condemned man to his place of execution or blinding passed the Hands,
there would be no redemption for Michael Anemas. The people were
well aware of this and apparently took their time, hoping that reprieve
would come – Anemas was a popular fellow and everyone pitied the
loss of his youth and beauty. Eirene was moved to tears herself and at
once intervened with Alexios. The emperor was up on the ramparts and
gave the signal of pardon in the nick of time. Anemas' eyes were spared.
Instead, he was taken to prison in the Palace of Blachernai, in a tower
which would be hence called the Tower of Anemas.

Eirene's intervention with Michael Aneman was not the end of her
benevolence. Taking pity on the wife of John Solomon, who had become
homeless because of her husband's stupidity (he had been duped into
believing he would become emperor, and he had blabbed here and there
about the favours he would grant once he did), the empress returned her
house to the unfortunate Lady Solomon without taking as much as a
pin out of it. This episode, casting Eirene more or less in the role of the
Theotokos interceding to Christ her son for mercy on behalf of sinners
and granting gifts to the repentant, is more than the pious recollection of
a loving daughter – it is an indication of Eirene's clout and of her actual
power. It is also a nice contrast between her – and Alexios' – mercy and
the harshness of the sebastokrator, who, earlier in the episode, had made
Solomon confess under threat of torture.

As Eirene's power grew, and Alexios' physical deterioration made
him more dependent on her by the day, the star of the son-in-law, Kaisar
Nikephoros Bryennios, shone more brightly on the political firmament.

Eirene liked and trusted him, and probably not only because he was her favourite daughter's husband, but also because Nikephoros was popular and competent. We have the word not only of his fond wife, but of the more sceptical and harder to please John Zonaras. Nikephoros' popularity was connected to his learning but his wife was even more formidable than he was in this, writing in a perfect Attic language (Byzantine intellectuals at the time prided themselves in using classical Greek in their writing and not the common medieval Greek of their day). Additionally, Zonaras asserts that the wife of Bryennios had a very agile mind that could grasp and discuss difficult concepts. All this she had acquired by her natural intelligence and through extensive study, for she was engrossed in books and was attached to scholars and conversed with them in depth. Anna is presented as a very intelligent and educated woman who devoted her time to learning, books and discussions with other intellectuals. She is depicted as a great asset to Nikephoros, but at no point does Zonaras say that Anna wielded or desired political power; it was always Nikephoros and her mother who did. From Zonaras' description, it sounds as if Nikephoros' role within the palace was similar to a modern chief of communications, making all the important announcements to the senate and the people. But he did more than that; he judged cases and issued fair and balanced decrees, informed by his formidable education. For all these qualities, he was much in demand and soon became the epicentre of power. Things came together for the kaisar, as everyone sang his praises. Perhaps the House of Bryennios would get their chance to occupy the gilded throne after all. But to John, the emperor's son who was also co-emperor, this situation caused great despondency and anxiety. Nevertheless, he bore circumstances with remarkable patience and bided his time.

The Bitter Summer of 1118

Alexios suffered from an illness which affected his legs initially and later seems to have completely damaged his respiratory system. Anna, who among the many things she studied acquired considerable medical knowledge, attributes the beginning of his illness to an injury during a game of polo, when his old friend and comrade in arms Tatikios mistakenly hit him with a polo mallet. A chill which he caught during an event at the Hippodrome settled at his back, aggravating matters further. The medical team in charge of Alexios' health, among whom where the most famous doctors of the day, Nicholas Kallikles and Michael Pantechnes, prescribed cathartics to purge the ailment. This seemed to work for some time. But the coup-de-grace was administered by the long hours of work, irregular meals and all sorts of sacrifices concerning his personal well-being, including rest and comfort. He endured countless hours spent on negotiations, particularly with the Westerners who had no sense of moderation and talk well into the night, while the emperor listened to them standing up, in the ancient Roman tradition. His limbs, especially the legs, hurt so much that he could barely walk. From the precise description of his symptoms as Anna gives them, it would appear that he suffered from gout initially, although, as Anna correctly notes, this was strange because Alexios was an abstemious man. With the emperor's health in steady decline, preparations began to be made, at least in certain quarters, for his death. Of course, in theory at least, the succession had been settled back in 1092, when Alexios had made his first-born son (and third child) John co-emperor. But, apparently, now that Eirene was all-powerful at court, and with the favouritism she showed towards her son-in-law, the cards were being reshuffled and nothing was certain. Or at least John, the legitimate heir, seemed to think so.

In the summer of 1118, Alexios Komnenos took a turn for the worse. Anna overheard him complain to her mother: 'I don't know what is wrong with my breathing; I want to draw a deep breath and relieve the pain in my heart but although I try I can't relieve any of this crushing weight; and it's like I have an enormous stone on my chest which stops my breathing; and I don't know what is wrong with me, my love; do you have any idea?' Eirene called the doctors, and after they examined him they found problems in the circulation in his arteries but could not pinpoint the cause. It was certainly not his health regime; he was always a frugal military man who ate like an athlete. The weight of all his cares and worries inflamed his heart and affected his whole body, was the verdict for his ailment - modern medicine also considers stress as one of the causes of heart disease.

Alexios' health quickly deteriorated. He was so ill that he could scarcely breathe unless his wife held him up. He could hardly eat; his stomach was swollen, and later his oesophagus and gums too.

Eirene and their daughters, Anna, Maria, Evdokia and Theodora, were constantly at his side, trying to alleviate his suffering, while his team of doctors consulted together, considering what treatments could be profitably applied at this stage, when the patient was exhausted and in too much pain. Anna participated in those councils as an umpire since the doctors often disagreed among themselves; her medical knowledge and connection with the emperor entitled her to do so. The treatments, consistent with the cutting edge of medical progress of their time, purgatives, cauterisations and bleedings, must have weakened the poor patient's constitution. They tried a potion with pepper, which initially did some good but made things worse in the longer term. The best his wife and daughters could do, alongside with his doctors, was palliative care. Eirene spent days and weeks on end giving him massages and holding him up so that he could breathe; upright on his pillows was the only position in which he could sleep. Movement seemed to help him somewhat (Georgina Buckler, the first scholar to have written a monograph on Anna and a nurse during the Great War, comments that this is true of asthmatic patients), so they added wooden poles to his bed and carried him from one room to another in the five-floor palace, seeking better air. By that time the sick emperor had been moved from the Great Palace to the Palace of Mangana, which used to belong to Maria of Alania. It was somewhat ironic that his life ended in the same palace where Maria had died – she who had been such an important part of his life back when he was on the ascent to power.

What was Alexios' illness? According to a twentieth-century doctor:

> gout, then renal disease with thickened arteries, a big heart, hypertrophy (that is the cause of the weight he felt in his chest). Then either oedema of his lungs or water in his pleural cavities (the symptoms would be much the same to an ordinary observer), and this would give all the symptoms of 'air-hunger' from which he suffered. Then he gets all the troubles which arise from an enlarged heart which is beginning to fail and getting dilated, dropsy, ascites [water in the abdomen] ... with uraemic symptoms, the ulcerated palate and swollen tongue. Quite probably his swoonings may have been slight uraemic convulsions, but they may have been really only faints from the failing heart.

On Thursday, 15 August, the great Feast of the Dormition of the Mother of God, Alexios' symptoms took a turn for the worse – experiencing diarrhoea, vomiting and fainting fits. The emperor was collapsing. 'We were distraught and did not know what to do,' writes Anna. They moved him to a top-floor room with a northern, uninterrupted view, so that he could at least have an illusion of breathing more freely. The three principal doctors of his team, Nicholas Kallikles, Michael Pantechnes and the eunuch Michael of Libos were present. It also appears that many of the Doukas family members were there to support Eirene, pressing her to have something to eat before she herself collapsed. But Anna's mother, with bloodshot eyes, weepy and hysterical with grief, fell on the floor and wailed, hitting herself on the head, her meltdown probably a result of not having slept for several nights in a row. This made the poor emperor forget his own woes and express his concern for her; he and their daughter Evdokia tried to calm her down, but she was helpless with grief. Alexios, in a lucid interval, ordered her to stop her lamenting over him and grieve for herself and her own troubles instead. The god-fearing emperor probably meant, in a spiritual sense, that she should look after the state of her own soul. The daughters tried to relieve their mother by taking her place next to the sick bed, so that she could get some rest. Anna was constantly by her father's bedside, taking his pulse and consulting with the other doctors who tried to be optimistic and fed the family with false hopes. But Anna would have none of this. She could clearly see that Alexios was getting worse, alternately fainting and gaining consciousness. Maria, Anna's beloved sister' tried to give him some water to drink from a beaker, but his tongue and pharynx were swollen. She sprinkled his temples with rose water and massaged him with essence of rose oil to bring some comfort. When he regained consciousness, Alexios told his daughter to sprinkle some on her mother as well – a touching solicitude for his wife at the very end of his life.

Eirene had her eyes fixed on Anna, waiting for her pronouncements as if she were an oracle. '[M]y lady Maria, my beloved sister, a jewel among women, the steady soul, the abode of every virtue' administered her father's palliative care, her long sleeves screening the emperor's suffering from their mother's view. The emperor was drawing the very last of his breath. From their high windows at the top of the palace the women could hear the city centre churning with unrest. The empress, wailing, cast her purple mantle and shoes on the floor and said,

'Let it all perish – crown and kingdom and power and throne!' and her daughters wept with her. Finally, Anna could sense no more pulse. She let go of his cold hand, put her face in her hands and walking backwards, wept. This was the signal: Eirene let out a long and piercing shriek and the other daughters began their loud wails and laments. Anyone who has ever witnessed death in a Greek house, even today, will know this loud and vociferous type of mourning, which has very ancient roots and is attested in Homeric epics and classical tragedy. If Eirene seems to have been somewhat self-centred and performative in her grief to modern readers, we need to bear in mind that mourning was not just an outlet for the mourner's feelings; it was a public expression of duty towards the dead and the living. This is the reason why she did not 'keep it together' while Alexios was still alive and gave way to extreme expressions of sorrow. It was important that she showed him proper love, honour and respect and that he and everyone else should see it.

'How to represent this disaster for the whole world, how to weep for my troubles?' Anna writes, reliving the scene. Her mother requested a razor and when she was handed one, she took off her royal headcover and sheared 'her beautiful locks' to the skin. She threw away her dark red buskins and requested plain black shoes. She asked for a black dress, but there was not one to be found until Anna's third sister, Theodora, widowed by her first husband Kourtikios, brought one of her own dresses for her mother. Eirene wore the black dress and covered what was left of her hair with a plain black veil. 'And so the emperor surrendered his sacred soul to God, and my own sun set,' Anna concludes her narrative of her father's death. Alexios Komnenos, the emperor, the husband, the father, was dead. But where was the son and heir?

Undutiful Son

John Komnenos, Alexios' eldest son, was not in the room when his father let out his last tormented breath. Aged 31, John had already been long married to the Hungarian princess Eirene (formerly Piriska or Piroska, daughter of King Ladislas of Hungary) and was the father of many children. Anna mentions the birth of his first two – the twins Alexios and Maria – and the joy their birth gave her own parents. The imperial couple and, presumably, Anna and her husband who were accompanying them, received the happy news in Serres, in the midst of preparations for an anticipated invasion of the Norman Bohemond, and hurried back to Constantinople to celebrate the birth of the new heirs of the dynasty. John lived in a separate palace with his family and did not share with his sisters the task of looking after their sick father. It would have been to his credit if he had, but it was not so out of the ordinary that he had not, since caring for the sick in a family was traditionally the duty of the women. However, he would have been expected to be present for his father's very last hours on earth. But on the night of 15 August, as Anna somewhat sniffily declares, 'the heir to the throne' (not 'my brother' or 'John') was not there with his mother and sisters (and presumably some other relatives). He 'had been and gone' and learning of his father's death during the night, he hurried to the Great Palace, instead of going to Mangana to pay his respects. It should be noted that the manuscript is very corrupt at this point, with several lacunae, and missing words may or may not change the meaning drastically. But from what we can glean from its current state, John was already on his way to the Great Palace while his father lay dying in Mangana. Anna does not mention John any further.

So, where was John and why was he not there to support his mother and sisters and honour his dying father?

Our two primary sources who cover this story besides Anna are John Zonaras and Niketas Choniates, whom we have encountered several times until now. While Anna gives a frame-by-frame description of what happened inside the chamber of the dying emperor, the other two sources offer their own slightly different versions of events inside but also show what was happening on the outside, in the streets of the capital 'churning with unrest.' More interestingly, they elaborate on Anna's terse phrase 'the heir to the throne … hurried to the Great Palace.' Our third primary source, Anna's faithful George Tornikes, also has something to say about John's unseemly absence from his father's deathbed.

John Zonaras' Version

Zonaras' version agrees with Anna's on several points. Firstly, he agrees with the locations where events took place. The emperor was taken to the 'great eastern palace' and attended by doctors there, but was soon moved to Mangana for its more favourable air. Secondly, Zonaras agrees with the treatments given; he mentions the cauterisation with a hot iron which apparently removed Alexios' abdominal fluid, but does not linger much on the medical side of things, not having Anna's personal interest and technical knowledge. He also concurs that the doctors were not telling the patient or the family about the imminent end, adding the interesting information that some monks were prophesising that it was not the end because the emperor would not die before he arrived at Jerusalem to worship at the Holy Sepulchre and lay aside his royal crown there. Alexios believed them, 'because it is easy to believe whatever agrees with our wishes.' But the Jerusalem he reached was the one in heaven, where he had to lay his crown aside not by his own will. Interestingly, Anna does not mention any monks or priests being present at the scene of Alexios' death at all, although she speaks of his medical team several times. Thirdly, Zonaras gives the same date and describes the same people in the room as Anna did: the fifteenth of August of the eleventh indiction (1118 CE), with the empress there and her dear daughters gathered around her.

> It was getting late in the day and the sun was already drawing west and the emperor's son is told that his father is about to go. So he [John Komnenos] went into the palace where his father lay dying, not with the purpose of lamenting the one who was about to depart, but to make sure with his own eyes that he was dying. And as soon as he saw him, he went out, and mounting his horse he left Mangana with his entourage. For as he was leaving the palace, many went along with him. As soon as he was out of the Mangana enclosure, he met the Abasgians; these were the envoys bringing the girl [princess] from Abasgia who was going to be the bride of the eldest of the Kaisar's [Nikephoros Bryennios' and Anna's] sons. On encountering [John], they hailed him with loud voices and made obeisance. At that point they say that the empress with violent emotion told the dying emperor that his son had left. But he said nothing, either because he did not want to or because he could not, but raised his hands high; I don't know if he was praying for blessings for his

was asking forgiveness from God for any wrongdoing. But the woman undoubtedly thought that her husband was glad because of what he'd heard her say; and as all her former hopes were dashed and all the promises overturned, she let out a deep sigh and said: 'O husband, while you were alive you excelled in all sorts of lies and your words were always contradictory to your thoughts; and now as you are leaving this life you are exactly the same as you were before.' These were the worlds attributed to her.

Niketas' version of how John got hold of the Great Palace is slightly different and more violent than Zonaras'. John showed the guards the ring which he had 'stolen' from his father but they needed more proof, so John and his followers stormed the gates and entered the palace, where they barricaded themselves for a while. Alexios died during the night. The date was 15 August. He had reigned for thirty-seven years and four-and-a-half months. At dawn, the empress sent for John while the body of his father was taken to the monastery of Philanthropos for his funeral. But John refused to go; not because he was neglecting his duty to his mother or out of disrespect for his father, but because he was afraid for his newly established power and feared his opponents. Therefore he clung to the palace 'like an octopus to a rock' and left his father's funeral to his relatives, most of who attended, even though the son and heir did not.

John was now the emperor and one of his first tasks was to appoint the most important men in his new administration. His brother Isaac became sebastokrator, nominally the second-in-command right after the emperor himself, but in reality the most important man was John's childhood friend, John Axouch. He was a 'Persian', i.e. a Turk, who had been John's companion since childhood. He had been captured as a boy of 10 by the crusaders during the siege of Nicaea and given as a gift to Alexios, who then gifted him to his son John, because they were of the same age. Of all his companions, John loved Axouch the most, and the boys became inseparable. Their friendship would last throughout John's life and when he died, Axouch looked after the interests of his son Manuel, whom John had appointed as his heir despite being the fourth son. But this belongs to a different story.

One year after John's tempestuous coronation, trouble was stirring again, according to Niketas. Many members of the emperor's family, apparently dissatisfied that they had to pay deference to Axouch, joined the party of Bryennios:

> [They] offered him the kingdom, because of his education and of his regal appearance and because he was in the highest rank of royal connections. As we have already said, he was married to the sister of the king, the Kaisarissa Anna. She had a great interest and experience in philosophy combined with knowledge of all sciences. Soon they made their move at night with murderous weapons against the emperor who was staying in Philopation, not far from the land gates, easily accessible. They corrupted the gate keepers with generous gifts. But the enterprise against the emperor failed because Bryennios, who was usually somewhat dull and slack, broke their agreement and stayed in the city, and thus the ardent purpose of the conspirators was quenched. It is said then that the Kaisarissa Anna, disgusted with her husband's sluggishness, was cut to the quick as if suffering a great deal, and cast blame upon nature, because it had given her the wide and hollow genitals and Bryennios the long and balled member.

This astonishing, sexually explicit language is completely out of character for Anna, a very prim and proper lady, who refused to mention in her book what exactly the German emperor's men did to the pope's envoys 'because it is not appropriate for a woman and a princess to even utter such things.' It sounds more like the kind of gross language used by men gossiping about a woman whom they see as behaving outside her gender norms. Niketas continues with a morality tale, to showcase the men's superiority over this transgressive sister:

> They were all arrested within days but none of them was maimed or tortured. But the property of every single one of them was confiscated, although a little while later it was returned to most of them. The emperor first showed his

philanthropy towards the very mastermind of the plot, the Kaisarissa Anna. Things happened more or less as follows: the kaisarissa's property, gold and silver and and rich clothes and wealth of all sorts were all collected in one building; Emperor John inspecting it said: 'How has the order of things been reversed in my case! My family is my enemy, and strangers are my friends. So this wealth needs must flow towards those who love me.' And he ordered that everything should be taken to the Grand Domestic [John Axouch]. Axouch thanked the emperor for his great generosity and asked permission to speak. When this was granted, he said: 'O king, even though your sister caused all those problems and treated you so unfairly, and with her actions swore off the family connection, she did not sever the tie of nature; as long as she is the sister of a good king, repentance will bring back the feeling of love which she lost in her madness, with nature's help. O master, spare your sister who challenged your power, and let her punishment be the acknowledgment on her behalf that she was beaten by your virtue. Give her all these things that lie before us now, not because she deserves it, but because you want to. It is only fair that she should have them and not I, since it is her patrimony and will pass on to the family.' The emperor, convinced or rather moved, acted upon this exhortation, saying, 'I would be unworthy of ruling, if you were judged to be more charitable and above any unnecessary and opportunistic gain than I and my family.' Hence, he returns everything to the kaisarissa and makes peace with her.

And what was Eirene's role in all this, according to Niketas? She was never found guilty of any involvement in the conspiracy but apparently kept her distance from the whole affair throughout, remembering that after all John was her son: 'It is said that she issued forth the following wise maxim when she found out about the plans: "It is permissible to look for a king when there isn't one, but not to remove him once he is in place."' She also said: 'The murderers of my son caused me greater anguish than I experienced when I was giving birth to him; at least birth pangs were working to bring my son to the light, while the others came from the deep vaults of Hades and would cause me eternal sorrow.'

If indeed Eirene said such a thing, it is impossible that the murderers were Anna and Bryennios: she would have surely disowned those who were out to cause her 'eternal sorrow'. But her love and good opinion for them continued even stronger after Alexios' death. Niketas' story sounds like a set-piece or morality play – or at worst a jumble of gossip from various conflicting sources that 'grew in the telling', as J.R.R. Tolkien would say, and as such reached Niketas several decades later.

George Tornikes' Version

Anna's obituarist comments on the events surrounding Alexios' death and John's succession without giving a detailed account, which would have been outside the scope of his text. He is not writing a history or chronicle, like the other authors, but a very different kind of genre, on which decorum and speaking well of the dead are placed in certain constraints, but also allow certain liberties. If any events on the deceased's life are incriminating, an obituary is not compelled to include them; on the other hand, the requirement for a positive presentation of the deceased does not equal a licence to lie. Tornikes chooses to include the event of Alexios' death because it demonstrates one of Anna's main virtues, if not the most prominent one: her love for her parents. She nursed Alexios all through his illness, consulting with his doctors and supplying her own medical expertise; she served her father 'with her own two hands as if she were a servant and not a princess' even though she was not in very good health herself at the time; and she supported her mother, who never left the emperor's side.

Tornikes begins his account of the last hours of Alexios' life by comparing Anna to one of those brave men on a sea voyage during a tempest who encourage pilots and sailors with their loud voices and apply their art to saving the boat from going down. Similarly, Anna worked along with the doctors, cheering them on or occasionally threatening them, in a rather manly style, gladly giving her own soul in exchange for her father's life (as Anna herself claimed in the *Alexiad*).

Anna Komnene. Original
painting in the Byzantine style by
the Greek master iconographer
Vassiliki Argyropoulou.
(Author's private collection.
Used with permission.

Mother of God with Baby
Jesus (Theotokos of Vladimir).
Reproduction of twelfth-century
icon. (Author's private collection)

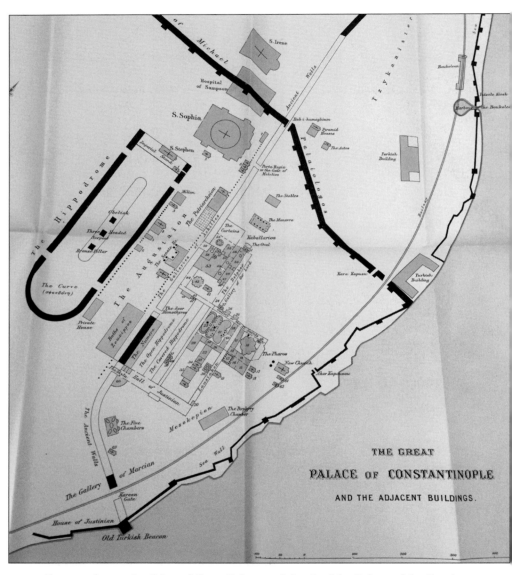

Above and opposite: Map of Great Palace and detail of the Palace of the Porphyra.
(By permission from the University of Glasgow Library Special Collections)

Obelisk

Three Headed
Serpent

onze Pillar

The Augustaion

The Patr...

The Senate Ho...

The Galleries

...of Achilles

The Manavra

The
Curtains

Kaballarios
The Oval

59

54

55   551

58   57   56

52   50

53   49

48

47   Gallery of Our Lord

46   The Delphar

44   43   42   24   27   26   25

The door
Monothyros

40   45   41

Private
ouse

Baths of
Zeuxippos

The Numera

The Open Hippodrome

The Covered Hippodrome

23   22   21   Gallery of the XI. Saints

28   64   11   10   65

29   30   31   12   The Pharos

32   13   14

34   33   16   15   17   New Chur

35   36   18

The Skyla

Hall

60

of Justinian

Lausiakon

19

61   62

20

Mesokepion

The Porphyry
Chamber

The Five
Chambers

The Ancient

63

Wall

Empress Evdokia Makrembolitissa and Emperor Romanos IV Diogenes.
(By permission from the University of Glasgow Library Special Collections)

Facsimile page from the Typicon of Theotokos Kecharitomene (Convent of Mother of God Full of Grace) with the signature of its author Empress Eirene Doukaina, wife of Alexios I Komnenos and mother of Anna Komnene. (By permission from the University of Glasgow Library Special Collections)

Facsimile of the autograph signature of Empress Eirene Doukaina's from the Typikon. It reads: 'Eirene in Christ the God faithful empress (basilissa) of the Romans the Doukaina.' (By permission from the University of Glasgow Library Special Collections)

The Mother of God and host of angels surrounded by priests, monks, kings, laymen and laywomen. Reproduction of illumination from Byzantine manuscript. (By permission from the University of Glasgow Library Special Collections)

ANNA COMNENA READING THE ALEXIAD.

Anna Comnena (Anna Komnene) and her parents Emperor Alexius Comnenus (Alexios Komnenos) and Empress Irene Ducas (Eirene Doukaina), characters in *Count Robert of Paris*, historical novel by Sir Walter Scott (1832). Illustration from nineteenth-century edition of the novel. (Author's private collection)

View of Constantinople from the Asian shore in the eighteenth century (Ottoman period). (By permission from the University of Glasgow Library Special Collections)

Why did the son and heir, already pronounced co-emperor by his father for a very long time, feel the need to act in such a surreptitious and even undignified manner? What is the role of Eirene in all this? How much was Nikephoros Bryennios involved? Zonaras pits only Eirene and John against each other, whereas Nikephoros appears only as something of an instrument in Eirene's plans and Anna is mentioned only as his wife, including, incidentally, a snippet of information about her high education, beautiful writing style and wide knowledge. And let us not forget that Nikephoros was the grandson of that other Nikephoros, Alexios' former rival; but for a throw of the dice, as the Byzantines would say, the Bryennios dynasty would have been established on the throne, and Nikephoros, not John, would have been the legitimate emperor. As for Eirene, the Doukai and the Komnenoi had a past of their own, beginning with the succession of Emperor Isaac I by Constantine X Doukas and not by John Komnenos, as we saw in chapter 1; not to mention the sustained rivalry between Anna Dalassene and the Kaisar John Doukas, and the hatred between Dalassene and the then young Empress Eirene. It is quite possible that Alexios' death was an opportunity for all those old grievances to be aired again, for one last time, as it is often the case with dysfunctional families around the not-yet cold body of the *pater familias*.

A Burial Fit for a King

Anna may not mention any priests present at the deathbed of her father, but it is highly unlikely that there would not have been any; the Christian tradition of the last rites was certainly followed. Alexios would have made his last confession, if he were in a position to speak at all, and he would have received communion for the last time. A family member – possibly one of his daughters, Evdokia or Maria, would have closed the dead emperor's eyes and crossed his arms over his breast, placing an icon of the Christ between them. The body would then be washed and shrouded. Empress Eirene, now a widow, cut her hair short and put on black clothes; the whole family would dress in black for the forty days after the king's death. Only his son John, the new emperor, would wear white, which was the colour of mourning that an emperor wore for a dead parent (or spouse, child or grandchild); on the ninth day this would be changed into yellow, until the end of the mourning period.

The accounts of Zonaras and Tornikes about the night of Alexios' death tell us that there was no one there with the dead emperor except his wife and daughters – though Tornikes adds two of his sons-in-law, the husbands of Anna and Maria, and his grandchildren. But everyone else had gone to follow the new emperor. Whether this is true or pure gossip, it is certain that once the official announcement of Alexios' death was made, the patriarch and the priests from Hagia Sophia would sooner or later proceed to the Palace of Mangana, followed by the senate, the palace officials and the noblemen of the city, dressed in black or grey, to pay their respects to the dead emperor and offer their condolences to the bereaved empress and to the rest of the family. John should have been there to receive them. The fact that he was not would have been enough for his mother and his eldest sister to be displeased and critical of him. Family feuds have started for less. It was a serious breach of the duty by a son whose father had cherished him all his life. Zonaras thought so too, hence his melancholic observation that Alexios was lucky in life but unlucky in death; his son, who owed everything to him, had dishonoured him.

When the time for the funeral arrived, the patriarch and clergy would have sung funeral prayers over the body, and then a palace official would have stood in front of the dead emperor, calling out loudly three times: 'Come forth, King, the King of Kings and Lord of Lords is calling you.' This was the signal for the officers of the imperial guard to lift the bed and exit the palace. Then the body would have been carried to the church where the funeral service and burial would take place. In older times, the imperial mausoleum was the Church of the St Apostles (which has not survived). The cortege would have made its way on foot to the church from the Great Palace through the Mese, the main avenue of Constantinople. The patriarch and two rows of clergymen would have headed the procession, holding lamps and chanting, the members of the family walking behind them, just in front of the coffin. If the new emperor had been present, he would not have worn his crown as a sign of deep mourning. The officials and senators and all other authorities would have followed, dressed in their official attire, holding candles and singing praises to the departed, while the crowds would have watched from the roadside and from high windows and balconies (weeping, if the dead emperor had been popular).

Once inside the church, the body would have been placed on a dais for the duration of the funeral service. When that was over and it was time to lift the body and place it in the imperial sarcophagus, the same palace official as earlier would stand in front of the dais and call out three times: 'Enter, King, the King of Kings and Lord of Lords is calling you.' He would then shout: 'Take the crown off your head.' The crown would have been removed and a simple silk imperial purple headband would have been placed on the head of the dead emperor. Finally, the body would be placed inside the sarcophagus and the emperor would pass into eternity.

At the time of the Komnenoi the burial place of the emperors had changed; most of the emperors in that dynasty chose to be buried in the monasteries which they had founded. In accordance with the general turn of the imperial style from the ceremonial and public to the less formal and private which characterises that era, the emperors adopted a much more modest style of departure from this world. Alexios was thus buried in the monastery of Christ Philanthropos (Lover of Humans), next door to the convent of Kecharitomene (Mother of God Full of Grace). He would thus stay near his wife and daughter, who had loved him so much and were now desolate at his passing.

Chapter 6

The Contemplative Life: Writing the *Alexiad*

The Convent of Theotokos Kecharitomenē – Mother of God Full of Grace

In the northwest side of Constantinople, in the neighbourhood of Defteron (Second), not very far from the Palace of Blachernai, two monasteries stood, one next to the other, ringed by high walls that separated them from the world and from one another. These were the convent of Mother of God Full of Grace and its twin, Christ Philanthropos (Lover of Humans), founded by the imperial couple Empress Eirene Doukaina and Emperor Alexios Komnenos, extreme Byzantine examples of 'hers and his'. Full of Grace was for women, Philanthropos for men. In Greek Orthodox monasticism there are no orders of monks and nuns with established rules as in Roman Catholicism. There is not even a separate word for men's and women's monastic foundations; they are all indiscriminately called Monē (monastery). Each monastery has its own set of rules, set down on its foundation charter which is called a typikon. The typikon set out in detail everything that pertained to the foundation's structure, government, property and income; its liturgical life; its offices and elections; clothes and food for the monastics, their occupations and expected proper behaviour; their days of fasting and of feasting and what should be served at table; how the church should be illuminated; how specific rites should be carried out. In short, there was no detail great or small that was not set out clearly in that charter, which had the status of a binding, legal document and of which a working copy was always at hand to help resolve matters as they arose in daily life.

Of the two twin monasteries founded by Eirene and Alexios neither survives today, although there is a much later monastery also called

(once a month for the healthy nuns and as often as the doctor prescribed for the sick ones, as baths were believed to be healing in Byzantine culture), what prayers they will say, what services they will attend, and what kind of priests will be best for them; unsurprisingly, she stipulates that these should be 'eunuchs of godly life'. A very interesting feature in Eirene's typikon is her provisions concerning the lighting of the church: there are at least three regulations concerning the lighting of candles and lamps. Eirene specifies their number and position in the church and the duration of lighting, where her standard is an equal measure of splendour and economy. Eirene was such a manager that she even made provisions for the maintenance and repair of cisterns and water pipes, and she was proud of having managed to install 'ever-flowing (i.e. running) water in my monasteries', by which she means her own Full of Grace and its male twin Christ Philanthropos, under the auspices of her husband. Both 'his and hers' monasteries seem to have been much more comfortable places to live in than the majority of private homes in that era.

Remembering the Dead

One very interesting aspect of the typikon is Eirene's detailed provisions regarding the commemorations of the dead. Services and prayers for the repose of the souls of members of the empress' family would have been held daily, as well as on the specific anniversary date of the death of each of them. These commemorations (*mnemosyna* in Greek) were, and still are, a very important part of the Orthodox tradition. In the Middle Ages praying for the dead (and for the living) was an important function of monastic foundations in East and West; the monks and nuns were to pray for the founders and donors of their establishments, as well as for the whole world. According to the typikon of Full of Grace, there were to be special all-night vigils and memorial services on the anniversary of the deaths of Eirene's husband, children, parents, siblings and in-laws. Those anniversaries would be treated as feast days. The church would be amply illuminated. The nuns would be granted a feast and would eat fish and shellfish on Saturday if the anniversary fell on a Lenten day. For context, it should be added that unlike the Roman Catholic Church where eating fish is considered a privation suited to the solemnity of Fridays, in the Orthodox Church, which is much stricter, monastics are normally vegetarian and everyone is vegan on a Wednesday and Friday. Throughout Lent (and there are three Lenten periods in a year, not just the one), fish is considered a great indulgence and only allowed twice during the pre-Easter Lent, on the Feast of the Annunciation and on Palm Sunday. For the memorial service, the nuns would prepare kollyba or kollyva, boiled wheat grains mixed with nuts, honey, raisins and pomegranate seeds – an ancient Hellenic tradition of mortuary offerings predating Christianity; this nourishing food would be subsequently distributed to the poor, along with alms in coin since almsgiving was also a part of the offerings on behalf of the dead.

Eirene's detailed catalogue of the persons for whom commemorations would be celebrated includes all the member of her close family, living or dead; it is also an interesting index of Eirene's personal values and feelings towards them. For the living, the commemorations would begin after their death 'on whatever date it is that they shall die.' Eirene uses formulaic designations for her family members; except for her husband, who is 'my most mighty emperor Lord Alexios Komnenos', she uses the form 'the dearly beloved [son / daughter / son-in-law, etc.] of my majesty [title] [name]' and then she details the logistics of each commemoration – church service, illuminations, food and alms for the poor. For her son John, for instance, who is mentioned third in order, right after his father and herself, she stipulates: 'Let the mnemosyna of the beloved son of my majesty, the Porphyrogenitos and Basileus Lord John take place on whatever day it is that he shall die, and let there be abundant illuminations and special treatment for the nuns; let there be distributed at the gate loaves of bread to the amount of five modioi and coins to the value of six trachea nomismata.' This was a very generous offering, amounting to about 88lbs of bread; one trachy nomisma would buy about 14lbs of wheat. The offerings to the poor for her husband, Emperor Alexios, would be double of those for her son: ten modioi of bread (about 180lbs), plus eight measures of wine and twelve trachea nomismata in coin were to be distributed to the poor on the day of his commemoration.

The order in which Eirene mentions her dearly beloved may be significant: first comes Alexios and herself, then her son the Basileus Lord John and his wife Despoina Lady Eirene, then her son Sebastokrator Lord Andronikos, her son-in-law Kaisar Lord Nikephoros

(Bryennios, Anna's husband), her son Kaisar Lord Isaac, her son-in-law Panhypersebastos Lord Nikephoros (Euphorbenos Katakalon, her daughter Maria's husband), her son-in-law Pansebastohypertatos Lord Constantine (Angelos, husband of her daughter Theodora). She does not distinguish between sons and sons-in-law, but orders them in accordance to their court titles; also she puts them first, before the daughters and daughters-in-law. Intriguingly, the enumeration of her female relatives begins with her granddaughter and namesake Eirene Doukaina:

> Let the memorial services of my dearly beloved granddaughter, lady Eirene Doukaina, the daughter of the Porphyrogenita Kaisarissa Lady Anna, be celebrated on the anniversary of the day on which she shall die, and let there be copious illumination and distinction of the day for the nuns; and let there be given away at the gate bread of four modioi and four nomismata *trachea* in small coin.

Then follows the 'dearest' Kaisarissa Anna herself, followed by Eirene's daughters Maria and Evdokia, her daughters-in-law the Sebastokratorissa Eirene (wife of Andronikos) and the Kaisarissa Eirene (wife of Isaac), and finally her youngest daughter Theodora. All of them were alive at the time Eirene wrote the typikon, which dates it before 1118 (partly, in any case; as we shall see, there is an addendum). It is slightly confusing that all the daughters-in-law of the empress were named Eirene and we are grateful for their titles which help to distinguish them; they were most probably foreigners – we know that at least John's wife was Hungarian – who changed their names on marrying their Byzantine bridegrooms and adopted the name Eirene with its auspicious meaning (peace) in honour of their mother-in-law, and perhaps for the significance of the name itself. The pool of names for Byzantine high-born ladies was about as wide as that of Tudor England and the Eirenes, Annas, Marias, Evdokias and Theodoras are the distant sisters of the Elizabeths, Annes, Marys, Catherines and Janes many centuries later

After her own family, Eirene mentions her parents and her parents-in-law, and finally her siblings. As we look at the provisions Eirene made for the repose of the soul of all her dearly beloved family members, we can detect something of the dynamics in the imperial family, at least as far as Eirene's personal attachments are concerned. Judging by the alms and rites prescribed for each family member, Eirene does not generally differentiate between her children, who get the exact same treatment, with the notable exception of Theodora, her youngest daughter, who is classed with the lesser daughters-in-law. There are variations among the sons- and daughters-in-law as well. For example, the younger Empress Eirene (John's wife), Nikephoros Bryennios and the other Nikephoros (Katakalon, whom Anna liked as well) are treated exactly like her own children, but fewer alms will be distributed for Constantine Angelos (Theodora's husband)' and for the other daughters-in-laws' souls. Obviously, the offensive Michael Iasites is not even mentioned. The mention before her daughters of her granddaughter Eirene Doukaina, child of her own favourite child Anna, may show some personal special attachment to the girl who bore her name; but the offerings to the poor on her future mnemosyna are set at four modioi of bread and four nomismata of coin – less than what is allocated to the empress' own children, but more than what is granted to the not-so-favourite son- and daughters-in-law and even the youngest living daughter.

Should we read anything in the fact that when it comes to her redoubtable mother-in-law, Eirene cannot bring herself to mention her name at all? She only states: 'my sanctified [i.e. died as a nun] lady and mother-in-law' but does not mention Anna Dalassene's name. Would we go too far in imagining pursed lips and a sour expression on Eirene's face as she considered the woman who had made her life so difficult in the first years of her marriage and would have happily caused her divorce and disgrace? Perhaps there is a simple explanation for the omission of Anna Dalassene's name and the reference to her only by her family connection (Eirene gives her own mother's both names, the secular Maria as well as her monastic name, Xenē). Perhaps Eirene forgot, or she thought Anna Dalassene was too well-known to require it; still, hers is the one name in the litany of relatives' names that is not set on paper in the typikon, and one might think as one pleases.

Anna and Eirene

'My dearly beloved', 'my most beloved (*potheinotatē*) daughter the Kaisarissa Lady Anna', on the other hand, is mentioned several times in the typikon. The strongly affectionate language used by Eirene

Anna and the Philosopher's Circle

In the leafy and peaceful surroundings of Full of Grace, in the comfort of her luxurious apartments, Anna entered a period of vigorous intellectual activity, of which writing history seems to be only a fraction. Tornikes would be introduced to her and become part of her circle there sometime in the 1130s. A considerable part of his funeral oration describes Anna's literary salon, which he would have frequented from the early stages of his career as a teacher in the Patriarchal School of Constantinople. He was one of the many notable philosophers, churchmen, scholars, poets, and orators who sought Anna's company and patronage, most of whom were probably connected to the church of Hagia Sophia and the university, and probably unmarried (they have been compared to the Oxford and Cambridge fellows, who were compulsorily celibate until 1878). For her, it was an opportunity to enhance and deepen her learning in philosophy, astronomy, geometry, rhetoric and poetry. Such works were presented, read, discussed and commented upon during the meetings at her apartments in Full of Grace, while on the other side of the wall the peaceful life of the monastery continued, unaware of the hub of intellectual activity next door. In his funeral oration Tornikes hastens to reassure the readers that only approved texts were studied that did not go against the orthodox doctrines of the church. He compares Anna to Jonas, submerged in the sea of pagan learning but emerging triumphantly intact from the belly of the whale, because she sought knowledge not as an excuse to stray from God but as the means to come nearer to God.

Philosophy, and in particular the natural philosophy of Aristotle, was the focus of Anna's attention. Her patronage was crucial in the renaissance of Aristotelian studies at the time, bringing into the fore texts, mostly relating to natural history, anthropology and zoology, which had rarely or never been studied before. She studied Plato and the Neoplatonists as well. Interest in pagan philosophy was not unique in her family; her uncle Isaac had converted the works of Neoplatonist philosopher Proclus into Christian teachings. But for Christian thinkers, Aristotle was always the safer option; Plato's theories of re-incarnation and the world of Ideas were a tad too exotic and had led other philosophers astray before. Additionally, Anna was genuinely interested in more positive, rational approaches to the world. As Scottish author Naomi Mitchison wrote: 'Anna was much more scientifically minded than either of her parents …

she was always much interested … in any sort of technical achievements of peace or war that came her way.' Mitchison imagines Anna 'most happily talking to the experts, handling their things, looking at plans and recipes.' Anna commissioned annotated editions of Aristotle from scholars in her circle, and Tornikes confirms that he heard one of them complain that his eyes were damaged, dried out from the heat of the candles, as he had to stay up all night for several nights in a row to finish the commissioned work.

Anna's approach to philosophy was to mix pagan and Christian teachings 'in the same way that the most accomplished doctors smear the rim of a cup of a bitter medicine with honey, or mix a honeyed potion with an astringent.' Tornikes goes on to compare her to a bee that picks up only the sweet nectar and ignores the poison. This reflected the eclectic style of twelfth-century philosophy; it also echoes the great Cappadocian fathers of the church, whom Anna very much admired. One of them, St Basil the Great, fourth-century Bishop of Kaisareia (or Caesarea, now Kayseri), who had studied in Athens, had used the same metaphor in an oration addressed to young students. In this spirit, Anna admired Plato for the elegance of his style but rejected the outlandish theories (most notably reincarnation). Tornikes goes on for a long time relating Anna's specific ideas on the nature of the soul, the connection between reason, destiny and providence, the origin of the world and the role of God the creator. It is apparent that such discussions were commonly held in Anna's salon; further than that, it sounds as if they not only discussed and commented on philosophical works but actively tried to construct a philosophical system themselves.

Tornikes reminisces fondly of Anna's words and opinions, referring to her more than once as 'my own basilissa', 'my dear basilissa'. To make sure that no one could accuse 'his dear basilissa' of being unwomanly with her interest in philosophy, he hastens to assure us that she used it as a means to sustain herself through the difficult times of her life, and to remind us that she had the feelings of a woman (despite her unfeminine penchant for abstract thinking). She never neglected her womanly duties, and like a dutiful daughter she was her mother's mainstay during the empress' old age and final illness, although she too was getting on in years. She was almost undone when she lost her mother, to whom she had been very devoted. Just like with her father's illness, Anna was hands-on with her mother's care, 'doing the manual work of a servant.'

That should appease anyone with fears that the princess encroached on masculine behaviour with her philosophers and her editions of Aristotle.

One of the most intriguing pieces of information in Tornikes' funeral oration is that Anna was a great and prolific letter-writer. None of those letters survives, or at least none has emerged so far – who knows what treasures lie hidden in manuscripts tucked away in library archives and private collections? Until the happy day that a letter we could attribute to Anna emerges, we will have to take Tornikes' word for her style and content. He states that Anna's epistles were a continuation of the lively and productive discussions held in her circle, but on paper with those who were away. They were a testimony to the strength and quality of her writing, with their harmony, propriety, beautiful concepts and important ideas. Tornikes makes the perceptive observation that although letters are written for private consumption, letters of such literary quality as Anna's were destined 'by nature' to enter the public sphere. They were to be Anna's legacy to the world, but not for her personal gratification – oh no; her words were offerings, in the same way as her alms to the poor in the various hospices around the city for the repose of the soul of her parents, her own 'sacrifice of praise'. Anna is one of the many women writers who honed their literary skills in letter writing, although one of the very few to do so in her era. The close connection between epistolary writing and women writers and the recognition that it was a valid literary form exercised by women was made several centuries later. It is interesting that Tornikes makes the connection, and after his lavish praise of her epistolary skills, he introduces Anna's greatest achievement, at least in terms of posterity: the writing of the *Alexiad*.

The *Alexiad*

The idea for a history that would give an account of Emperor Alexios, his rise to power and his long reign was not originally Anna's. Empress Eirene had proposed it to her son-in-law, or rather ordered him to write it. It is not certain when Nikephoros began working on the project; possibly sometime near or after Alexios' death in the late 1110s or 1120s. His narrative proper begins with Romanos Diogenes in the 1070s, after a quick overview of the Komnenos family starting with the first Komnenos of note, Manuel Erotikos and his two sons, Isaac, Alexios' uncle, later

Emperor Isaac I Komnenos and John, Alexios' father. When Nikephoros fell ill and died sometime between 1136 and 1138, his account had just about reached the time before Alexios' coup. Nikephoros modestly called his work *Material for History*, stating in his introduction that his writing could not do justice to his subject, which demanded the skill of Thucydides and the eloquence of Demosthenes (the top historian and orator of classical Athens no less). He pointed out that he was collecting the material for some other, better historian to work with. Did he have his wife in mind as he wrote this? Was she even considered at the time as someone who might one day write a history of the calibre and power of the *Alexiad*? It is not impossible, but it is interesting to note that despite her great love and esteem for her daughter, Eirene asked Nikephoros, not Anna, to write it. Anna herself mentions that her father discouraged her from writing history and suggested that instead she ought to write melancholy poetry, elegies and dirges, to mourn his many trials and tribulations; he said the same thing to the empress when she ordered 'scholars' (Anna does not specify whom) to write his history. Perhaps Alexios though that a woman should only be writing emotional poetry; perhaps he was being modest about his own achievements, or perhaps he was just grumpy and in pain, as he was already seriously ill at the time.

As it turns out, Anna did write some poetry. We know only of two poems possibly, both with religious themes. One is a description of an icon representing Christ as a child; she playd with the antithetical concepts in Christ's nature – a young child but existing before time, motherless in the beginning fatherless in the end – and admires the art of the painter who can represent both the divine and human nature of Christ. The other, which is dubious, is a conversation between a golden reliquary enclosing a bone from the wrist of St John the Baptist and someone who is looking at it; the reliquary was supposed to have been in her own possession with the verses written on it. Women writing religious poetry were not unknown in Byzantium – the great poet and hymnographer Kassia was such a case.

There is no other historical work written by a woman in the medieval Greek canon. One other Greek female historian is known from late Antiquity, Pamphile, of whom only a handful of fragments survive and those mostly cited in other people's work. But the *Alexiad* survived whole (if a little battered, especially in the last chapter) and in several manuscripts, which means that its worth and importance were recognised almost immediately; the oldest extant codex is dated in the mid-to-late twelfth century, almost contemporary with the author herself. There are many reasons for its popularity. Hailed as one of the masterpieces of Byzantine literature, and the first historical work of that magnitude in length as well as style and composition written by a woman, the *Alexiad* is the history of Anna's father, the emperor Alexios Komnenos in fifteen volumes. The faithful Tornikes thought that Anna was motivated to write it by her 'zeal for the truth' and her desire to immortalise the deeds of her father and her mother. Interestingly, he is one of very few – if any at all – to include the empress in the scope of the work next to the emperor. Obviously, Tornikes considered the *Alexiad* a 'sacrifice of praise' to the memory of her parents, alongside her other writings. But Anna herself offers a much grander and unforgettable statement of purpose in the Prologue of her work:

> Time flows unstoppable and ever-moving, and in its movement it takes and carries away all things that come into being and sinks them into the depths of obscurity, some of them insignificant, others great and memorable; and as it is says in the tragedy [Sophocles' *Ajax*], it reveals what is hidden and hides what has come to light. But the science of history becomes a powerful defence against the current of time and stays somewhat its irresistible flow and holds up all that it can grasp and holds them tight and does not let them slip and perish in the depths of oblivion. I have noted these things, I, Anna, daughter of Emperor Alexios and Empress Eirene, born and bred in the Porphyra, not without my share of education, but on the contrary having thoroughly studied Greek and rhetoric, and being very well read in the arts of Aristotle and the dialogues of Plato and shielded my mind with the quaternity of knowledge (for it is necessary to declare – it's not for bragging – what nature and the study of science and God above has granted and opportunity has brought about). And with this work of mine I wish to give the account of my father's deeds, those he achieved when he took the sceptre of imperial power and those he did before he wore the crown serving other kings; these deserve more than to be surrendered to silence or to be taken at the flood of time as if in a sea of forgetfulness.

This powerful image of time as an endless stream and history as the dam that stops the flow to retain what is worthy of commemoration is cleverly counterbalanced by the equally powerful image of the author who has the confidence, knowledge and skills to construct this bulwark. It is as if she is challenging the world, asserting that she is up to the task. Perhaps we should not wonder that so many historians mistook Anna's intellectual ambition for something more than just authorship and saw her desire to halt the stream of time and rescue her father's memory as the desire to change the course of history itself by taking her brother's place, or rather her father's.

The *Alexiad* is a peculiar work in linguistic terms, its peculiarity part and parcel of the tradition of Medieval Greek historiography. It is written in Attic Greek, a form of the Greek language which was spoken in classical Greece but survived in writing for many centuries. Medieval (and not only medieval) writers considered Attic Greek superior to all other forms of spoken or written Greek, because many of the greatest works ever to be produced by Greek culture were in that dialect: Plato, Aristotle, Thucydides, Xenophon, fifth- and fourth-century tragedies and comedies. Only highly educated people in Anna's time wrote in that form of Greek, and it was high praise indeed to be able to do so. Another peculiarity is that it combines various genres; as well as classical historiography, there are echoes of the epic (Homer's *Iliad* and *Odyssey* were another great influence, as the title *Alexiad* suggests), biographies, eulogies and laments. Its composition and scope draws on rhetoric and is permeated by Aristotle's *Poetics*. According to Aristotle, poetry (by which he meant fiction, i.e. epic poetry and tragedy, and would have surely included novels, if that genre had existed in his time) and history both tell the truth about life and the world; but poetry is more powerful than history, because it speaks of universal truths, whereas history only deals with limited events. Anna, who played a major part in the revival of Aristotle in the twelfth century, commissioning new editions and discussing them with the leading scholars of the age, applied Aristotle's observations on the composition of the best poetic works to her own historical work. Unity of plot was one of them; vivid depictions of characters was another. These traits of the *Alexiad* have been noted and praised. Whereas other historical works of her time are disproportionate and unwieldy, the *Alexiad* has a definite narrative arc, focussed on Alexios as the protagonist, on a quest to save the empire and his own soul. Characterisation is achieved via showing the protagonists in action; no wonder that modern literary theorist Julia Kristeva has called the *Alexiad* 'a historical novel'.

If Anna's history seemed to overemphasise some events or rearrange their order, for example the second Norman war, certain episodes in the First Crusade, or Alexios' 'war' against heresy, it was because the narrative arc and the requirements of the 'plot' (i.e. Alexios' progress and development as a character) were much more important than historical sequence. In fact, it is more or less accepted now that history is much more than a sequential narrative of events and that there is always some editorial process in the writing of it: the mere act of choosing what to include and what to omit out of the immense pool of non-stop, round the clock events, acts and words, implies that choices are made to which some kind of principle or rule of composition is applied.

Authorship and Critique

One of the most striking features of the *Alexiad* is Anna's consistent interest in military matters and all things technical. Anna clearly delights in such descriptions; for example, she digresses from an account of skirmishes between Byzantines and Normans in order to describe the Norman crossbow (*tzangra*); she offers plenty of details regarding tactics and deployments in descriptions of even minor battles. Indeed, her explicit and frequent references to warfare led a modern scholar (as late as 1995, and not in the 1950s as one would suppose) to claim that Anna could not have written the *Alexiad* herself, because a woman would not be interested in or have any knowledge of military subjects. All she did, the scholar claims, was edit her husband's work; Nikephoros Bryennios was the real author of the *Alexiad*, not Anna. This proposal has been successfully refuted and Anna proven beyond doubt to be the true writer of the Alexiad. Anna, diligent student of Aristotle and of the quadrivium (music, arithmetic, geometry and astronomy) was indeed a keen observer and analytical thinker. Furthermore, male historians of the time did not actually write about war and battles from experience either but followed a stylised narrative that suited to the genre as it had been established by the great historians of Antiquity.

It has been pointed out that Anna's work has always been viewed as 'exotic and controversial' because of its female authorship. This is one of the questions to be asked: had it been written by a man, would the *Alexiad* be viewed differently? Possibly. But had it been written by a man, the *Alexiad* would not have been the same book. The author of such a book would have had nothing to prove, except that he was impartial towards his father (supposing it would be a son who wrote it). But partiality or impartiality is the least of the reasons for which scholars like Gibbon disapproved of it; it was the author's character, as they perceived it, that grated on them. A male author's 'display of knowledge' would have been taken as a matter of course; the imaginary male author would not have to talk about his education and credentials quite as much as Anna does, and he would not have to lament his (real or imaginary) woes in order to appease the readers for writing history in the first place. Criticism of Anna's history was largely a criticism of the woman herself, which is quite often the case with women writers. Science fiction author Joanna Russ wrote about this in her powerful essay *How to Suppress Women Writers*, citing a list of common disparagements against women's writing: she did not write it herself; it is not good enough; it is too personal; it is not important. Critics of Anna Komnene's *Alexiad* have used them all.

Gibbon disliked Anna Komnene for what he perceived as her character; perhaps also because she was an aristocratic and royal person and he was writing from a perspective of critique of the aristocratic class within the context of the Enlightenment. Women are more likely to be criticised for their social class – high or low – than men, as modern scholars have noted. Poet Sophie Collins has pointed out how women's authorial personas (i.e. the voice of the narrator) are usually taken as indications of the author's real character. There is no doubt that Anna does speak with her own voice in her work, inserting herself in the narrative so to speak, but the reader is advised to be careful how to read this voice. Anna, like all classical writers or those who write in the classical tradition, *adopts* an authorial persona which is appropriate for the narrator of history. As a woman, she cannot easily convince her contemporary readers to accept her as a writer of history. She needs to do two contradicting things: to flaunt her qualifications (high education, imperial birth and therefore access to sources) and at the same time to appease the readers with suitable humility, reminding them that she was

an unusual plague of locusts had fallen upon the land; they did not touch the grains of wheat but only devoured the vineyards. The oracles explained this mysterious portent in the following manner: the locusts were the incoming hordes of the Kelts (Anna's name for the Westerners); the wheat, good and wholesome, represented the Christian populations; the vineyards, whose produce can lead to intoxication and all sorts of debauchery, signified the 'barbarian Ishmaelites', by which she meant the Seljuk Turks who had overrun Anatolia and Syria. The message of the prophecy was unmistakeable: the armies of the West would not harm the Christians but would destroy the infidels. Clearly, Anna misunderstood Islam, which forbids the consumption of alcohol; furthermore, she stated that the Persians (by which she meant the Turks) and the Hagarenes (Muslims, Saracens, descendants of Hagar; the Byzantines also used the term Ishmaelites, descendants of Ishmael, the son of Hagar and Abraham) worshipped Astarte, Astaroth and Khobar and were slaves to Aphrodite and Dionysos, to lust and wine, which suggests that she conflated their religion with the pre-Islamic pagan religions of the Middle East. This image of the East as a location of sex and debauchery is an Orientalist stereotype by which the West would perceive and describe the East for many centuries to come.

And so it happened that a plague of locusts would appear just before a new army from the West arrived; Anna adds that after clouds of locusts appeared a few times in a row, people knew to expect a new surge of Frankish soldiers.

'A Cairn of Bones'

In the late spring of 1096, the first wave of crusaders reached Constantinople. They were led by a man named Peter the Cuckoo or Peter the Hooded – Anna uses the Greek name Koukoupetros, the first composite of which may mean cuckoo, *koukos,* or monk's hood, *koukoulion* in Greek. This man, Anna tells us, had previously set out to worship at the Holy Sepulchre but suffered much at the hands of the Turks and Saracens who ravaged the area. Unable to bear his failure, Peter meant to return to the Holy Land but did not dare set out on his own again. Therefore, he conceived a prudent plan: travelling all over Europe, he preached the largest pilgrimage the world had ever seen.

'A divine voice has ordered me to proclaim to all the counts in France that they should all depart from home and go on pilgrimage to the Holy Sepulchre and unite to deliver Jerusalem from the Hagarenes.' Astonishingly, he succeeded.

It is practically impossible to know the exact numbers of those armed pilgrims; for Peter's first wave, Anna offers an estimate of 80,000 foot-soldiers and 100,000 riders, probably an exaggeration. At any rate they were numerous enough to cause alarm and consternation in Byzantium. It must have been quite a shock to see them arrive at the outskirts of the Queen of Cities: a motley crowd of noblemen, clerics and monastics, soldiers, peasants and camp-followers, men, women and children, wielding palm branches and bearing stitched crosses on their shoulders, low in provisions but high on religious fervour. Many of them were destitute and dependent on the richer pilgrims' kindness for their sustenance; most expected the emperor to provide for them, while eyeing his wealth with covetous eyes.

Alexios did not want this particular plague of locusts anywhere near his capital and his palace. Prophecy or no, he had been a soldier all his life and knew very well that a large crowd of hungry people would not distinguish between Christians and infidels if it came to that point. He was also well aware that if faith motivated most of the pilgrims, there were many among them with less exalted motives, ambitious younger sons of the aristocracy and mercenary desperados of all sorts. In hindsight, judging by the horrific accounts of atrocities committed by crusaders in the Western chronicles, including the massacre of the Jews in the Rhineland, Alexios was right to worry. At the same time, he made sure that the pilgrims could buy food and other necessaries for their sustenance. Anna asserts that the emperor organised 'abundant markets' for them and instructed his soldiers and officials to receive them with courtesy, albeit with a vigilant eye. It is not certain if Peter had a personal audience with the emperor, but either in person or by proxy Alexios offered Peter good advice; he told him that he should wait for the armies of the dukes and counts before he moved further east. Constantinople was the rendezvous point for all the contingents of the First Crusade. But Peter was in a hurry to move on and did not heed the sagacious emperor.

He and his army of pilgrims passed across the Bosporus to the Asian side and set camp in Elenoupolis, a small town not far from the ancient walled city of Nicaea, which was now the capital of the Seljuk Sultanate of Rum. There, 10,000 Normans detached themselves from Peter's ragtag army and took off for Nicaea, where they ravaged the area, committing most savage acts; they cut up and roasted babies on spits and tyrannised the elderly (a not infrequent accusation hurled against enemies in war, more like a literary commonplace to signpost their cruelty than a true account, although there is evidence of cannibalism in the First Crusade, as we shall see later). The locals tried to push them back but failed; the Normans took Elenoupolis and then Xerigordon, another small town. The sultan sent forces against them and managed to take Xerigordon back, killing and capturing many Normans; at the same time, he put a rumour around in the pilgrims' camp that the Normans had taken Nicaea and the locals were paying them tribute. The sultan knew how much the Kelts loved money, Anna sneered; when they heard the words 'tribute' and 'money' they rashly took the road to Nicaea. But lacking military experience, discipline and order, they were ambushed by Turkish forces near Drakon and piteously slaughtered. So many of them were put to the Ishmaelite sword, Anna continues, that when they heaped all their bodies together, they made 'no hill nor mound nor watch-tower, but more like a high mountain of considerable depth and width; and so high was the cairn of bones, that later some men of the same race as the massacred barbarians built a wall mixing the bones of the dead with the mortar, so the whole city was as a tomb for them. It is still standing as I write,' Anna says, 'a city surrounded by a wall of stones and bones.'

The Second Wave

On 15 August 1096, Feast of the Assumption – for the Byzantines, Dormition – of the Blessed Virgin Mary the Mother of God, in the faraway northern city of Regensburg, another large army of knights and soldiers, accompanied by non-combatants and beasts of burden and carts of provisions were setting out for the Holy Land via Constantinople. According to Anna, their numbers were 10,000 riders and 70,000 foot-soldiers. This crowd was very different from the previous motley crew that had already reached their midpoint destination by that date. Here the men were a proper fighting army, with suitable equipage, many of them with amazing war-horses which everyone admired.

Among the many richly-clad knights, two were most prominent, the leaders of the Lotharingian contingent: Godfrey of Bouillon the duke of Lorraine, and his brother Baldwin of Boulogne.

Anna tells us that Godfrey was the first to heed 'Cuckoo-Peter's' preaching of the pilgrimage. Consequently, he sold his lands and set out for Asia. Godfrey was of a great family; his mother apparently was a descendant of Charlemagne (most great families in Europe at the time boasted of a descend from Charlemagne). Godfrey has survived in literature, in the epic cycles of the chansons, in Torquato Tasso's hugely successful and influential epic *The Liberation of Jerusalem* (1580) and in later countless historical dramas and novels, as the one true leader of the First Crusade; in reality the expedition was too complex to have one leader only. One reason for this may be that Godfrey was considered otherworldly and truly pious, not in it for material gain; when he was offered the kingship of Jerusalem, he refused it, saying that there was only one king in Jerusalem, meaning Christ, thus cementing his high reputation. Another reason could be that he looked the part. Anna's short but vivid portrait of him describes him as a man of a great family, rich, brave and very proud of his exalted ancestry. Additionally, Godfrey was tall, blonde, and handsome – and looks were as important in the Middle Ages as they are now. He must have made a visually striking pair with his brother Baldwin, who was also very tall but dark, and equally brave and aristocratic in appearance. Baldwin, like many other crusaders, took along his wife and children, which implies that he intended to stay in the Holy Land. For many noblemen this expedition was an opportunity to conquer and establish their own territories, once they had taken them from the Turks. Anna believed that as far as the higher-placed pilgrims were concerned, this was their one and only true motive; the liberation of the Holy Sepulchre was only an excuse behind which they hid their avariciousness.

Godfrey and Baldwin with other kinsmen and noblemen from Lorraine and Germany took the same route via Hungary that Peter and his pilgrims had taken earlier. Another brother of theirs from a different mother, Eustace III, chose to go south and depart with a different contingent alongside Robert of Flanders and Robert of Normandy (William the Conqueror's son), who were to travel east via Italy. Perhaps Eustace made the right choice, as this time the populations on the overland route were not so welcoming to the armies on the pilgrimage as they had been before.

The memories were still fresh of the passage of the previous wave of pilgrims and the mayhem and destruction they had caused on their way. It would seem that the Hungarian King Coloman and his noblemen were every bit as wary of the crusaders as the Byzantines and with very good reason. The Hungarians demanded hostages from the Lotharingians, including no less than Baldwin and his family, as a safety to guarantee the good behaviour of the rest. Once the armies were peacefully and safely – for the local population – out of the country, the hostages would be freed to join them. The Hungarian king and his local officials made sure to assign the pilgrims specific places where they would be allowed to camp and in general took care that the crossing of this enormous army, the second within a few short months, would not be as disastrous and chaotic as the first one.

While Godfrey and Baldwin were crossing Hungary on their way to the Balkans and to the northern Byzantine frontier, their brother Eustace and his comrades-in-arms the two Roberts (Flanders and Normandy), Count Stephen of Blois, and Hugh of Vermandois, the younger brother of the king of France Philip II, were on the way to southern Italy. The rendezvous point was Bari, the port in Apulia where the northern forces would unite with the southern forces of Bohemond and the Italian Normans. Hugh went ahead of the others and sailed first from Bari in October, aiming to be the first of the Western princes to reach Byzantium.

Anna relates in detail the episode involving Hugh of Vermandois, who seems to have rubbed the Byzantines up the wrong way. It is not clear if she knew that in Latin sources Hugh was called Magnus (the Great; an unfortunate, probably phonetic, translation into Latin of the French *moins né* or De Mesne, which means something like younger son, or of lesser birth), but she was having none of what she perceived as his arrogance, no doubt viewed by the equally arrogant Byzantines as presumptuous pretension. With all the disdain which her own aristocratic Byzantine birthright gave her, she introduces him as 'a certain Hugh' who was the brother of the *rex* of France, 'as conceited as Nauatos' – a rather obscure character, third-century heresiarch who was extremely proud, pride of course being the root of the evil of heresy. It must also be noted that Anna uses the title rex and not basileus for the king of France. Although both words mean the same thing – rex is Latin for king, basileus is Greek– they did not have the same weight. In Byzantine usage a rex stood lower than a basileus.

The reason for this inauspicious introduction of Hugh was an irritating message that apparently Hugh had sent to the emperor, asking for a special reception in accordance with his high title as 'the king of kings and greater than the sun'. On receiving this rather bizarre message, Alexios alerted his nephew John, the doux of Dyrrachium (son of Isaac the sebastorkator who had caused a quarrel among the Komnenos brothers ten years earlier). John was to look out for Hugh's arrival and notify the emperor at once; in the meantime, John was to receive Hugh with all appropriate honours. At the same time, admiral Nicholas Mavrokatakalon (Black Katakalon) was to be on the lookout for any disturbances at sea. Who knew what Hugh, who had announced himself with such assurance, was like? It did not help that once in Italy, Hugh sent ahead twenty-four ambassadors, in full armour compete with golden plate and greaves, with Count William Carpenter of Melun and a renegade Elias from Thessaloniki in tow; these exalted personages informed John Komnenos that Hugh was the leader of the whole Frankish army and was bringing with him the golden standard of St Peter from Rome.

With all this hype, which Anna emphasises on purpose only to achieve a better dramatic twist later, the Byzantines waited for a very splendid arrival indeed. However, never was the dictum 'pride goes before destruction and a haughty spirit before the fall' more apt than in this case. A terrible storm broke between Bari and Dyrrachium and sank all Hugh's ships but the one he had boarded, which was washed ashore between Dyrrachium and a placed called Paloi. Two guards belonging to the patrol that had been set to look out for his arrival found him there, a humble survivor of a shipwreck rather than the magnificent leader of the Franks he had advertised himself to be. They rushed to assist him and when he asked for a horse, one of them courteously jumped off his steed and offered it to him. Hugh was then taken to the doux John Komnenos, who had prepared a splendid banquet for him, offering him all the appropriate honours as if he had arrived in state.

Alexios was notified, and sent a trusted man to take Hugh to Constantinople, as something between an honour guest and a prisoner. It was clear that Alexios did not trust to have Hugh out of his sight for a moment; he meant to keep all the Western leaders away from one another as much as possible. To sow discord among them and, if possible, to broker separate deals with each one of them was a way to deal with the multiple dangers; so many wary friends and allies could easily turn into nasty enemies. But Hugh was quite easy to deal with: Alexios lavished gifts and honours upon him and it was a matter of time before Hugh became his man, taking the 'customary oath among the Latins', which means Hugh became the vassal of Alexios declaring him his liege. His role now would be to convince the rest of the Western princes to take the same oath to the emperor of the Romans. According to the modern scholar Georgina Buckler, Hugh became Alexios' tame leopard; the first to take the oath, he was used to persuade the others, voicing the Byzantine view of the crusade.

Meanwhile Godfrey and Baldwin were escorted through Thrace to the Propontis. On 12 December 1096 they arrived in Selymbria, in the outskirts of the Constantinople. It was not a peaceful arrival; from the first moment there were skirmishes and conflicts between Godfrey's armies and the locals. One Western chronicler attributes the riots to the crusaders' wrath when they found out that Hugh of Vermandois was the prisoner of the emperor. The situation was tense. As winter set in fast and provisions became more precious and harder to source, two contradicting things happened: Alexios realised that his power over the crusaders lay greatly in his ability to control logistics and billeting, while the crusaders became more aggressive with the confidence inherent in large numbers of armed people. Tensions between the Byzantines and the Westerners grew. It did not help the situation that while Godfrey's large contingent was about to arrive and camp in the environs of the capital, more bad news was on the way from the West: an old acquaintance was crossing the Adriatic Sea, leading another large army on the way to Jerusalem via Constantinople – a man that Alexios had met several times on the battlefield and would have been happy never to see again: Bohemond, prince of Taranto.

Shenanigans on Pirate Ships

A decade after his last bitter war against them, Alexios was expecting the Normans as supposed allies and the leader of the Italian Normans was none other than Bohemond, son of his old nemesis Robert Guiscard. Bohemond himself had fought against the Byzantine army in Larissa and had shown himself to be a chip off the old block.

Bohemond arrived on the coast of Dyrrachium about two weeks after Hugh's misfortune. He was closely followed by other crusader warriors and their armies, which were 'countless' according to Anna.

Her descriptions of their passage are a joy to read. In a style redolent of classical historiography, in the model of Herodotus the father of history, Anna abandons the description of the bigger picture in order to focus on particular episodes which excited her interest. Modern historians use this technique quite often as well; in these microhistories, apart from the entertainment factor, the reader can often learn more about the reality of existing in the past and connect with the people of that age in more direct manner. For example, in her account of the passage of the crusader armies from Italy to Greece she focusses on the story of one Prebentzas (identified as either Richard of the Principate or Richard of Brabant), which reads like an episode from a picaresque romance and is probably the kind of story she would have been told by one of the soldiers who were present. This man Prebentzas, Anna writes, paid 6,000 golden 'staters' (Anna uses the ancient coinage term anachronistically to refer to a golden coin of very high value) to hire a small fleet consisting of a three-mast pirate ship with 200 oarsmen and three smaller vessels. His aim was to cross the straits of Lombardy without being seen by the Byzantine navy, which patrolled the area; for this reason he took the route further down south towards Chimarra. However, the Byzantine spy network was very efficient; the admiral of the fleet, Nicholas Mavrokatakalon ('Black Katakalon' – a relative of Anna's brother-in-law Nikephoros Katakalon), had asked his second-in-command, who was shadowing the pirate vessel in his own galley, to light a torch over the water as soon as the pirate ship had unfastened its moorings. On seeing the signal, Nicholas sailed to meet Count Prebentzas: 'suddenly the sea was alive with ships, some in full sail, others like millipedes on the water with their hundreds of oars,' Anna describes. When the skipper of the hired pirate ship saw them, he took them for enemies come all the way from Syria to kill them (his geography must have been rather shaky); Prebentzas and his men prepared for sea-battle. It was the Feast of St Nicholas (6 December), traditionally considered as the protector of sailors and seamen, and the sea was perfectly calm, illuminated by a full moon that made the night so bright as if it were spring.

As the pirate ship stood still on the dead calm water, ready for the attack, the son of the admiral, Marianos Mavrokatakalon, who spoke Latin, boarded one of the lighter boats and approached Prebentzas' galley. When he was near enough, he called out to them not to be afraid and not to fight against men of the same faith, but one of the Latins onboard hit him with his crossbow, 'a real invention of the devil' (here Anna makes a short detour from her story to describe the crossbow in detail; she seems impressed and appalled in equal measure by its efficacy as a killing machine). By extraordinary luck, the arrow glanced off Marianos' helmet and did not harm him at all. The young man retaliated by shooting an arrow at Prebentzas, which pierced his hauberk but did not kill him. This was the signal for full-on battle between the Byzantines and the Latins. One Latin priest onboard Prebentzas' ship in particular was so aggressive and unstoppable that when he ran out of arrows, he began to throw stones at the Byzantines (Anna digresses again to explain that Latin priests were nothing like Greek Orthodox priests, who observed the teachings of the Gospels and refrained from carrying weapons or participating in battles; but Latins, she points out, were as much devoted to war as they were to religion, barbarians that they were). The martial priest threw a stone at Marianos with such force that it broke Marianos' shield into four pieces, then landed on his helmet and knocked him out cold, 'just like Hector hit by Ajax's stone.' When Marianos came to, he resumed fighting, shooting arrows at his opponent three times. The Latin priest finally ran out of stones and arrows, and 'twisting and frothing and raging like a wild beast,' he began to hurl loaves of barley bread from a sack of provisions he found onboard. One of the loaves hit Marianos on the face, grazing his cheek. Finally Prebentzas and his crew surrendered to the Byzantines force and meekly followed them to shore. Once they were out on dry land, the bellicose priest searched for Marianos among the crowd; as he did not know his name, he tried to find him by his dress. When he finally located his erstwhile opponent, the priest embraced and kissed him, all the while bragging: 'You'd be all dead by now if I'd been fighting against you on land.' Then he gave Marianos a valuable gift, a silver goblet worth 130 staters, and dropped dead.

Anna's history is alive with such vignettes, in which something of the spirit of those times is captured and transmitted to the reader several hundred years later. Whether factually accurate or invented or, even more likely, embellished by the witness' memory and by Anna's own storytelling verve, interesting or funny episodes like this reveal the power of her writing. They also demonstrate Anna's ability to amalgamate facts, cultural observations and microhistories into a coherent and interesting whole, in the tradition of the great historians of Antiquity.

Skirmishes on the Walls of Constantinople

Godfrey and Baldwin reached Constantinople shortly before Christmas, but as with the first wave of pilgrims a few months earlier, their armies were not allowed to come inside the city. The presence of these better equipped and armed soldiers of the cross was even more worrying for Alexios. They camped northwest of Constantinople, outside the enormous walls, near a place called Kosmidion, not very far from the Palace of Blachernai. Would young Anna have seen the distant tents and heard the din coming from the camp from a terrace high up in the palace? Speculations about their intentions must have been part of the daily discussions in the palace and Anna must have heard many of them at the family table, as her father would certainly discuss the situation with her uncles, his brother the sebastokrator Isaac and his brother-in-law George Palaiologos. Meanwhile, more bearers of the cross arrived in droves from the West by the day, joining the huge army that was already installed outside the walls, until the whole countryside must have looked like an endless campsite.

The people of Constantinople too would have anxiously watched the barbarian hordes. They were a cosmopolitan lot and were used to foreigners, who were part of the life of that great metropolis, adding to its vivacity and robust economic and cultural life. Tall blonde Varangians guarding the emperor and the wealthy aristocrats, sturdy Slavs selling furs and amber, vigorous Turkish mercenaries, short and stocky like their war ponies, politely diplomatic Venetians merchants, Amalfitan and Genoese sailors, solemn Arabs and scholarly Jews, some mingling with the Greek population, others keeping apart in their own communities, they were all intrinsic part of the colourful mosaic that made the Queen of Cities so fascinating. But large armies were a different matter. They must have triggered terrible memories of sieges in the past and fears of mortal danger for the future, especially since there were always prophecies about the eventual doom of the Great City.

The danger looked real enough when Godfrey's soldiers began to loot and ravage the countryside and even attacked the north-eastern walls, setting fire to buildings and churches. An immense crowd of armed men billeted near the world's most fabulously wealthy city in winter time, when the cold and the wet, as well as hunger and poverty for a great number of them, made the contrast even more intense between their own miserable situation and the Greeks' ease and affluence, was surely going to cause mischief. Even if their leaders wanted to contain them, there would have been times when they were uncontainable. We need to remember that this was not an organised army in the modern sense – there was no strict discipline or hierarchical chain of command in the same way as it is understood today, nor was there a central authority to issue orders and except them to be obeyed by all. Peter the Hermit had learned this lesson to his chagrin (and to the pilgrims' detriment) a few months earlier. When some of the pilgrims destroyed buildings and robbed the copper from the roof of churches outside the walls of Constantinople in the winter 1096–97, it is doubtful that Godfrey condoned this behaviour, but there was not much he could have done to stop it.

The crusaders attacked the walls of the city, 'not with siege machines', Anna writes, 'for they had none, but emboldened by their sheer numbers.' Anna describes the terror-stricken reactions of the populace inside the walls when they saw smoke rising from the gate right beneath the palace of Blachernai; the attackers had set fire to the church of St Nicholas there. 'They moaned and wept and shrieked, useless with fear.' Soon the alarm reached the imperial circles. 'They feared this was the time for retribution for what they had done fifteen years ago,' notes Anna, remembering that time when the armies of the Komnenos brothers entered the city and wreaked havoc in the city in their bid for power on a Maundy Thursday (15 April 1081). It was again the same holy day, Maundy Thursday (2 April 1097), the most solemn day in the Christian calendar. Anna's chronology may be confused – and confusing – at this point. Other chroniclers state that the troubles caused by Godfrey and the accompanying princes' forces began at Christmas time, while she implies it was Easter. Perhaps the two different settings of these separate events with their common theme have been conflated in her mind as she writes, several decades later. Or perhaps during the long months of waiting for the rest of the armed pilgrims to arrive, the impatience of the crusaders suffering the cold and the hardship of winter and the anxiety of the Byzantines as the crowds outside the walls increased, led to flare-ups of hostility and conflict that took place in many disparate moments but in memory they all merged into one great episode. Or it could have been Anna's desire for narrative symmetry in setting both on the same holy day.

The emperor sent his own son-in-law, Nikephoros Bryennios, 'my own dear kaisar', ahead of a troop of select archers, to shoot arrows at the Latins (it is obvious then that Anna, age 14, was already married, or engaged to be married, to Nikephoros by the end of 1096 or early 1097). Alexios instructed Nikephoros to shoot but not to kill; he hoped that the sheer number of arrows would make the attackers think again, but he did not want bloodshed on such a solemn holy day. But in spite of the emperor's wishes, bloodshed was sadly unavoidable.

Anna's description of the battle around the walls is strongly reminiscent of Homer's *Iliad*. The young Greek archers led by her beloved kaisar were like Teucer, the Greek hero of the Trojan war, but her kaisar was much better than Teucer and the two Ajaxes, he was 'like Apollo himself and like Hercules.' Even though he tried not to kill with his arrows, in the end there was no avoiding it. Incensed by one 'impudent and shameless Latin' who not only shot arrows against the defenders of the walls but also hurled abuse at them, young Bryennios aimed and shot: the arrow pierced the man's shield, hauberk and arm and hit him on the ribs. While shouts from both sides, in triumph and dismay, rose to the sky, 'he lay on the ground speechless,' Anna quotes from Homer. The Latins were eventually driven back and dispersed by the combined efforts of archers, cavalry, and the emperor's personal guard.

Oaths

The emperor now needed a guarantee from the Western princes that they would offer their loyalty and services to him, in return for his continuing logistical support. Initially, the Western princes were resistant to this idea and unsure of how to proceed. They could not deny that they needed Alexios' assistance, without which they would starve; but they feared the tricks and traps of the 'cunning Greeks' and were sceptical about the emperor's gifts. The famous phrase from the *Aeneid 'Timeo Danaos et dona ferentes'* ('I fear the Greeks even when they bear gifts') was known to educated Latin prelates and chaplains, and First Crusade chroniclers Robert the Monk and Ralf of Caen frequently quote from the *Aeneid* to advise their princes. The Byzantines, on the other hand, were suspicious of the Westerners. They mistrusted their warlike nature and battle skills, tested in the relatively recent Norman wars. There were also those Western mercenaries employed in the service of Byzantium who sometimes went rogue and turned against the emperor and the state,

The city was very important to the Byzantine Empire; it was the gate to the East and the third great city of the empire after Constantinople and Thessalonika. As the pilgrim armies arrived outside Antioch on 21 October 1097, they saw a populous, wealthy city built on the rocky sides of Mt Silpius and practically unapproachable from that side. To Albert of Aachen it looked formidable with its 'three hundred and sixty towers' and protected on all sides by unconquerable double-walls. With large orchards and gardens inside the first circle of walls and with the seaport of St Symeon just down the road, it was a city that could withstand a long siege provided there was always an open way for provisions to get inside the walls. It was obvious that Antioch would make a splendid prize for a covetous prince, if it could be conquered. But it would not be easy.

The Romans of the East had lost Antioch first to the Muslim aggressive expansion in the seventh century, reconquered it in the late 900s and lost it again in the 1080s, in the aftermath of Mantzikert. Now it was ruled by the Turk Yaghi Siyan, who sent out for help immediately as he saw the countless armies setting camp just outside his walls. So began, according to modern historian of the crusades Thomas Asbridge, 'one of the most brutal, gruelling and prolonged military engagements of the Middle Ages', which lasted until 3 June. Interestingly, Anna says that the siege lasted 'three lunar periods' (i.e. lunar months) only. Oxford Professor Peter Frankopan in his commentary to the *Alexiad* suggests that she may have intended to 'diminish the difficulties encountered and the very heavy losses sustained' by the crusaders This makes sense in view of what happened during the siege of Antioch – the turning point for the relationship between the emperor and the princes on the armed pilgrimage, the point where all the tensions of mutual suspicion and mistrust flared up and erupted.

According to the Latin chroniclers, encouraged by their victories in Nicaea and Doryleaum, the crusaders hoped for a continuation of their successes. But there were disagreements in the council of the leaders as to the tactics; most of the Latin princes proposed a close siege, while Byzantine general Tatikios who was accompanying the crusade as the representative of the emperor, basing his views on the successful Byzantine tactics of reconquering Antioch from the Arabs a century earlier, proposed first capturing strategic points at some distance from the city so as to completely isolate it and thus force it to surrender when no provisions or support of other sort could come to its aid. The leaders, however, voted for a close siege, and it began in late October. Soon it was winter, and hunger begun to torment the Christian camp. Provisions coming by boat to St Symeon (known also as Soudi – the port town of Antioch) were not enough, and the crusaders had imprudently ravaged the countryside when they first arrived without thinking of a long-term stay. The weather turned very bad with incessant rain. Food became very expensive. Anna and Albert both agree on this: an ox-head cost three golden coins, a small loaf of bread that previously cost a penny now sold for 2 shillings; there were many stories of profiteering by the local populations who sold goods to the crusaders at extortionate prices. As a result, the poor starved and many of the relatively well-off now became impoverished. Many of the 'people of God', non-combatants and soldiers alike, were killed daily while they foraged for food or did the washing or bathed in the river, or even as they sat in orchards and gardens (Albert tells the story of a knight and an aristocratic maiden who were thus assaulted and murdered); equally, many soldiers were killed in skirmishes with Turkish parties bringing provisions to the city. At the same time, rumours circulated that the sultan of Khorosan would soon be coming to the aid of the besieged city with an enormous army. The situation looked hopeless for the Christians. No one was coming to their aid. Where was the emperor who had promised to protect and help them? Some of the crusader lords abandoned the siege, most notably Stephen of Blois, whose decision to leave had fatal consequences for the relationship between the emperor and the crusaders, as it turned out. Tatikios said that he would seek aid himself and return with provisions. He left in February, leaving his tent and his staff behind. He never returned.

Albert, Raymond of Aguilers and the anonymous author of the *Gesta* explain Tatikios' desertion by simply stating that he was a treacherous, double-dealing coward. But Anna has a different, much more sinister explanation, which she very likely heard from Tatikios himself. There was treachery and villainy involved, but not on Tatikios side. The old adversary, Bohemond, was behind this; Bohemond, who had already begun to set in motion a plan for conquering the city. Just like Alexios back in 1081, when he had tried to find a way to enter Constantinople during his coup, Bohemond too got friendly with one of the defenders of the wall: an Armenian guard on the tower opposite his camp. He 'tamed the man like a dog,' Anna scoffs, and with many promises convinced him to let himself and his Normans climb up the wall with ladders and take the tower. He made sure to keep this a secret from the other crusaders, initially. As soon as the rumours reached the camp that Kerbogha, the ruler of Khorosan, was coming with tens of thousands of soldiers to aid the besieged Turks in the city, Bohemond knew he should act fast. But knowing that Antioch ought to be surrendered to the emperor in accordance with the oaths they had taken, he conceived an evil plan to force Tatikios to leave, so that he could keep Antioch for himself. He took Tatikios aside and told him: 'I want to reveal a secret to you because I care about your safety. There is word amongst the counts that the emperor persuaded the king of Khorosan to march against them. This has upset them greatly and now they are scheming against your life. I have done my duty and warned you; it is up to you now to protect yourself and your troops.' Bohemond's words alarmed and upset Tatikios, understandably; he also took into account the fact that the crusaders were starving and he believed they would soon give up on the siege. Therefore he and his troops took a Roman ship from the port of St Symeon and sailed off to conquer Cyprus instead. Bohemond then got the counts and dukes to agree that whoever could take Antioch should keep it for himself instead of handing it over to the emperor. The others, despairing, accepted this; and so Bohemond, with the help of the Armenian man (whom other sources name as Firouz) scaled the walls of Antioch with his men and, opening the gates to the rest of the crusaders, conquered the city with stealth and stratagem.

The crusaders entered Antioch on 3 June 1097, almost a whole year after the conquest of Nicaea, but it was not the end of their troubles. The citadel of Antioch, a fortress inside the city on its highest peak, was still held by the Turks even though their ruler, Yaghi Siyan, had fled. Soon the city was surrounded by Kerbogha's troops. The situation for the crusaders inside Antioch was thus much worse than before - hunger and disease took their toll in far greater numbers. Although Tatikios had left, some of his men must have stayed behind (the Latin chronicles agree), because Anna continues her account until the end of the siege.

Anna's narrative more or less agrees with other contemporary accounts, although she confuses a name or two. For example, in her version of the events surrounding the finding of the Holy Lance, she writes that at the height of misery and despair among the now besieged, hungry Christians, their spiritual leader bishop Peter made them undergo a ritual of penance, and then told them to look for the Holy Nail – and not the Holy Lance, which was in Constantinople and had been kept there for many centuries since St Helena had found it and brought it back – under the stone floor in St Peter's old cathedral. Anna seems to have mixed up three different people into one: this Bishop Peter, she says, was the same Peter who had been defeated in Elenopolis; she obviously means Peter the Hermit, or 'Cuckoo Peter', who had led the first wave, the 'People's Crusade'. However, Peter was of too lowly standing to be of any material authority in the 'Crusade of the Princes'. The bishop and spiritual leader, as a stand-in for the pope, was Adhémar (also spelled Adémar or Aimar) Le Puy (or of Monteil), the aristocratic papal legate, who indeed had chastised the crusaders for their sinful living during such a holy pilgrimage, although that had taken place during the initial phase of the siege of Antioch, when the crusaders were still the besiegers. Peter the Hermit appears in the Latin accounts, but only as an emissary from the Christian army to Kerbogha.

But there was indeed a Peter involved in the finding of the Holy Lance: that man was Peter Bartholomew, who was a cleric according to some sources, or a peasant according to others, but either way he belonged to the Provençal contingent of Raymond St Gilles. Anna's testimony about the finding and the adventures of the Holy Nail is not very detailed and focuses mainly on the first part of that controversial episode of the First Crusade. The narrative is rather typical of miraculous findings of relics: a divine message ('divine voice') indicated where they should look, in this case to the right of the altar; the magnates among the counts went to look for it but failed the first time and only found the holy relic after a second effort. It was then handed over to St Gilles ('Isangeles'), because he was the purest of heart; he took the holy relic out to battle against Kerbogha, rushing out of the gates, and with the help of the Holy Nail and by divine power defeated the Turks, who ran away in terror despite their much greater numbers. Thousands of the enemy perished in the deadly whirlpools of the river, their dead bodies in the water so thick that those who fled stepped on them as on a bridge.

Interestingly, Anna does not mention anything about what happened afterwards, when some of the crusaders considered that the Holy Lance ('the Holy Nail' to Anna) was a fraud and put Peter Bartholomew, the man who 'discovered' it, through trial by fire. Peter Bartholomew died soon after from the wounds inflicted during the ordeal. The discovery of the

170

Holy Lance was seen by some as a ruse by the Provençals to assume a spiritual advantage over the other contingents; some saw the smearing of Peter Bartholomew as a plot by Raymond's enemies to discredit him. Whatever this may look like to modern readers, for the medieval participants in the crusade the power of a holy relic, especially one connected to Christ himself, was very great and real. That there were political considerations behind the story can be supported by the fact that the chronicle which most believes in the genuine status of the Holy Lance is the one by the Provençal Raymond of Aguilers, and the most critical ones are the *Gesta Francorum* by an anonymous author in the army of Bohemond and the chronicle of Robert of Clari, a monk who more or less copied and embellished the *Gesta*. Fulcher of Chartres also condemns the find as fraudulent, and he was closer to Bohemond, as a cleric in the Norman army of the North. Whatever the truth of the story was, Anna did not know or did not care about the aftermath; for her narrative, 'Isangeles' was the bearer of the Holy 'Nail', and as such he was instrumental in gaining that victory over the Turks.

This is how Bohemond became prince of Antioch. The principality was to remain in the possession of his descendants for over a century; the Byzantines would try for a long time and would eventually force the prince of Antioch to recognise their authority under Emperor John II Komnenos in 1138 (by that time Bohemond had been long dead). Anna's personal history at that time became closely linked to Antioch. Her husband contracted his last illness during his brother-in-law's military campaign to re-affirm the Byzantine dominion of the principality of Antioch. Anna's and Nikephoros' second son, Alexios, also participated in that campaign; his uncle the emperor sent him to fight against the Seljuks in Cilicia. Nikephoros died of his illness a few months later. The death of Anna's brother is also connected to Antioch: John died on 8 April 1143 en route there. He had been hunting in the mountains of Cilicia when he was wounded, accidentally or not it is not clear, by his own poisoned arrow.

Jerusalem

The conquest of Jerusalem, or liberation according to the epic cycles of song, poetry and drama it inspired, itself was not of a great importance for the Byzantine Empire. Anna dispenses with this event, which was the main focus of the First Crusade, in a few lines: after their total victory over Kerbogha, she narrates, the Kelts offered Bohemond the city, as they had agreed before its capture, and marched on to Jerusalem, taking many castles on the shoreline in their way, but leaving those of them that were well-guarded in their hurry to reach Jerusalem. Once there, they set siege to the city and took it in a month, after relentless attacks, killing multitudes of the Saracen and Jewish inhabitants. Having defeated everyone, they gave the rule of the city to Godfrey of Bouillon and named him king (rex).

Even though the pilgrimage had achieved its goal and the crusaders had now worshipped at the Holy Sepulchre, the crusade was not over. The leaders continued to expand their dominance in Syria and Palestine; indeed for some of them, Bohemond and Tancred in particular, it would seem that Jerusalem and the pilgrimage were, if not the last things on their minds, at least very low on their list of priorities. Bohemond did not even take part in the siege itself. Holding on to their possessions in Antioch and the surrounding region, uncle and nephew had to contend with the other crusaders and with the emperor, who was not happy with the loss of that imperial city whose ideological importance was great for Byzantium. The last straw was when Tancred besieged and captured the important port city of Laodicea, which Raymond St Gilles had taken first and handed over to Alexios as agreed. Clearly Bohemond and Tancred were now waging war on a Byzantine city.

The Fatimids of Cairo had become involved in the war at the time of the capture of Antioch, alarmed by the progress of the crusaders. Their relations with Byzantium at the time were neutral, if not friendly, but they would naturally react to the presence of the newcomers from the West. Anna tells a story according to which the Egyptians captured several knights in Ramleh (Ramel), the place of St George's martyrdom. The emperor bought them all out paying a very high ransom, because it caused him pain to see such strong and handsome and well-born men become captives in a foreign land. Anna praises her father's paternal care for those knights; Alexios' act of mercy shows clearly, Anna implies, that he was keeping to his oath of loving and protecting his vassals. It was not mere philanthropy, but a strong message that Alexios was doing his duty by the knights, as opposed to Bohemond who was not doing his duty by his liege, as he had sworn that he would. Although this episode took place a few years later, the fact that Anna inserted it here is not an indication that she was a confused old lady who mixed up her dates. What she does is rearrange her material to suit her narrative, which is not a linear account of events, but a titanic conflict between her father and his archenemy. This is part and parcel of historiography; all historians must choose and order the events in their narrative out of the multitude of events and chaos of reality, even though only some are accused of it by those who would overlook exactly the same in others.

Bohemond's Challenge

As we have seen, at the beginning of the crusade the relations between Alexios and Bohemond were cautiously friendly. Indeed, at certain points it would appear that there was a special relationship between the two. Bohemond was an old acquaintance, he spoke Greek, and knew the emperor better than any of the others – as the emperor knew him. Even as a former enemy he must have been comfortingly familiar, an anchor of sorts amidst the chaos and turbulence of the crusading crowds. Bohemond actively worked for Alexios, encouraging the other princes to take the oath of fealty or to act upon the emperor's wishes, and Alexios appeared to trust him more than any of them, as modern historian Jonathan Shepard points out. But in Anna's narrative there is always a tension between the two, a game of cat and mouse, in which the protagonist Alexios and the antagonist Bohemond are watching each other and waiting patiently for the move that will set them pouncing. Bohemond's reception in Constantinople with its episodes of mutual mistrust, which are not devoid of a certain comedic character, was characteristic of that tension between the two. The situation turned for the worst in Antioch, where Bohemund pulled one over Alexios by tricking his representative, Tatikios, into abandoning the siege and then refused to hand it over once he had taken it – in a way that somehow echoes Alexios' capture of Nicaea earlier (Alexios had advised his representative to make haste and raise the imperial banners on the walls after Nicaea's surrender, pre-empting the crusaders' move to do the same. This was not very well received in the crusaders' camp).

The last straw was when Tancred was sent by Bohemond to take the city of Laodicea (Latakia), although it was already occupied by the Byzantines after St Gilles turned it over to them, and brazenly ousted its

Byzantine governor Tzintziloukes. Acrimonious and openly challenging letters were exchanged between Alexios and Bohemond, in which the one accused the other of breaking the oath; this, the author of each epistle said, 'absolves me of any responsibility towards you.' Alexios' angry letter to Bohemond accused him of breaking the oath of fealty and asking him to hand over Antioch now. Bohemond's response was equally sharp, blaming Alexios for not helping the Christians in their hour of need and his henchman Tatikios for abandoning them in the siege. He concluded with the insolent assurance that he was not going to hand over what he had shed so much blood and sweat to win.

The next step in the escalating conflict between Alexios and Bohemond in the *Alexiad* takes place in 1104, one year after Tancred took Laodicea. An attempt to reach an agreement of peace with Bohemond failed. Bohemond, who 'being the same old Bohemond had not learned to make peace,' rejected the friendly overtures and sent Alexios' envoy away with threats: 'You should be grateful I am letting you go without chopping your limbs off,' was the purport of his insolent response. Eventually Alexios sent his general Kantakouzenos to besiege Laodicea by sea and another Byzantine general, Monastras ('who was half barbarian'), with an army overland. Knowing the deceitful and rebellious nature of that formidable man and his machinations, Alexios took no chances. The Byzantines laid siege to the city, erecting earthworks around it. When Bohemond asked Kantakouzenos why this was being done, the Byzantine general reminded him of his unkept promise and of his broken oath to the emperor: 'Since you did not deliver the cities to the emperor as you should,' he said, 'I am here to take them for him.' 'And how do you hope to do this, with iron or with money?', Bohemond asked, obviously angling to see if there was any scope for profit. 'The money went to our own allies for fighting with spirit,' responded Kantakouzenos smoothly. Bohemund was filled with anger: 'Know then that you won't even get a small fort without money.' He then rode with his cavalry all the way to the gates of the city. From the walls Kantakouzenos' men responded with a shower of arrows, but Bohemond and his men managed to get into the citadel; he then sent away the Kelts who held it and installed a new guard, for Bohemond was suspicious of the count who guarded it until then, and of the count's men. He then had all the vineyards around the city ripped out so as not to obstruct the Latin cavalry that was going to come and help the men holding the citadel.

Bohemond, the Coffin and the Dead Rooster

Having taken all these measures to hold Laodicea, Bohemond returned to Antioch, Anna continues. But as Kantakouzenos and Monastras were tightening the noose, eventually taking back the whole of Cilicia, Bohemond finally felt it tighten around his own neck, surrounded as he was from land and sea, and with no army or navy to speak of. And what did he do? He conceived a very sordid but extremely cunning plan: he let rumours spread of his own death, so that the whole world believed that he was gone, while he was very much alive. The rumour that Bohemond was dead flew faster than if it were carried by wings. When he was satisfied that everyone believed it, he laid himself in a wooden coffin with small holes that allowed him to breathe, and by his order the coffin was placed 'with its content of the living dead man' on a ship with two rows of oars (a bireme) which set sail from the port of St Symeon to Rome. All the 'barbarians' surrounding the coffin wept and wailed and pulled their hair, while he lay inside like a dead body. There his similarity to the dead ended. When they were out at sea, those in the know opened the lid to give him food and drink and then took up the fake wailing and lamenting once again. In order to make the whole enterprise completely believable (and to discourage any curious bystander from opening the lid of the coffin to take a look at the renowned hero), a dead rooster was placed inside the coffin with him; after four or five days, it began to stink. The stench convinced everyone that indeed Bohemond was dead. 'And he was enjoying his ruse all the more,' Anna writes, 'although I cannot help but wonder how he could bear the siege on his nostrils.' 'But that's the barbarians for you,' she concludes, 'stubborn and willing to suffer any self-inflicted hardship once they've made up their minds; this was the first and only case of such a ruse devised by a man whose only purpose was to destroy our empire, and no one has heard of anything like that before or will hereafter.'

When the ship reached Corfu, a safe distance from the emperor and proximity to his own land, Bohemond was let out of the coffin. The description of his release from his wooden confinement place eerily echoes the *Odyssey*, when ship-wrecked Odysseus wakes up in the very same island geographically; but the sinister and macabre episode also has black-legend overtones. Anna plays with the words Corfu (in Greek Koryfo) and *koryfe* (high point, peak). Corfu is the high-point from which Bohemond shouted out his ambition to the world: 'He rises from the glorious dead and leaving his death-carrying casket he fills himself with sun and clean air.' He then wandered into town. There, the inhabitants saw his foreign and barbaric attire and asked him, in true Homeric manner, where he came from, whither he went, what brought him there, and who he was. Bohemund paid no attention to anyone but looked for the governor of the island: he was a man (aptly) called Alexios, recently moved there from the east province of Armeniakon. In a solemn manner Bohemund stood in front of him and in 'totally barbaric language' launched his formal challenge to the other Alexios:

> I am that Bohemond, son of Robert, whose bravery and force you and yours have known for a long time; you and your army have done much evil to me and filled me with bitterness, since I took Antioch and the whole of Syria with my own spear for you; you kept feeding my hopes and had me engage in countless wars with barbarians. But know now that even though I was dead I have now risen and I slipped out of your hands and I fooled you all. And now, living and breathing the air of Corfu, I am sending some bad news your way: I have left Antioch to my own nephew Tancred, who is equal to fighting against your generals; I am on my way to my own country, very much alive and planning many evils upon you, for I shall raise an army of Lombards and Germans and Franks, all men of Mars, and I will fill your towns and country with murder and blood, until I strike my spear at Byzantium [Constantinople] itself.

Bohemond's (imputed) speech makes him sound like a super-villain in a modern-day Marvel film; Anna's only comment to it, which we can assume sums up Alexios' response, is a dry seven-word phrase: 'Such was the insolence of the barbarian.' The anticlimactically short Byzantine response makes Bohemond's long-winded speech somewhat ridiculous, for all its threatening posture. It also foreshadows how this affair ended. In classical Greek drama, a temporary madness or folly (atē or ata) makes the hero so arrogant that he is blinded to his own limitations and commits the unforgivable sin (hamartia) of displaying his excessive arrogance (hubris); this is followed by tisis, retribution, and nemesis, downfall. Or to put it in less highbrow terms, there is no heroic action film worth its salt in which the insolent, threatening super-villain can win. By launching such an arrogant challenge, Bohemond sealed his own fate.

While Alexios and Bohemond are both preparing for war, the tone of the *Alexiad* changes. This is the time in Alexios' life when Eirene makes her presence felt as his inseparable companion. She accompanies Alexios in the campaign against Bohemond and is active in protecting the emperor from attempts against his life nearer to home; she is also a force for good, introducing the 'feminine' virtues of charity and spirituality, as a balance to the 'masculine' tones of violence and conflict. It is also a time when Alexios begins to appear less of a military hero and more of a spiritual guide and leader, as modern scholars have noted. His physical decline has begun, and although he is at least a decade away from death, the symptoms of his gout are debilitating, exposing him to the ridicule of his enemies. Alexios bears everything with patience and fortitude, as opposed to the almost maniacal Bohemond.

Bohemond's campaign in the West played mainly on the religious differences between Greek and Latin Christianity. Bohemond called Alexios a pagan and an enemy of the Christians. Judging by the tone of certain chronicles of the First Crusade, such as the *Gesta Dei per Francos* (*Deeds of God through the Franks*) by the French abbot Guibert de Nogent, which was written retrospectively at the time of Bohemond's crusade or soon after, he succeeded. Guibert (who did not participate in the crusade himself, builds an image of the Eastern Roman Empire as an alien land with very little connection to the true faith, where the emperor is a fiend, his mother is a sorceress, and every family in the kingdom is forced to yield a daughter to prostitution and a son to become a eunuch. That kind of sensationalist writing has always been effectively used in propaganda. But Alexios was not idle, and he significantly addressed Bohemond's mendacious campaign by using a very different approach.

Anna narrates an event which may or may not be a repetition of something she has said before: after the defeat of the Latins in Ramel by the Fatimids of Egypt, Alexios had taken pity on the knights who were captured by the Egyptians and paid their ransom. Anna expands on the episode (or describes a new, similar one, it is not very clear): 300 knights had been captured at the time the countless numbers of Kelts had passed from Europe to Asia and fell like a plague on

Antioch and Tyre and the surrounding lands. They were kept in chains in a terrible prison like those of old (this is an intriguing little aside, which may imply that prisons in Anna's time were much improved). The emperor was heartbroken about the knights' tribulations and send his man Niketas Panoukomites with a letter and money for the ransom to the sultan in Babylon (this is the Byzantine name for Cairo). The Egyptian sultan received Panoukomites, read the letter, and agreed to let the prisoners go without accepting the money. There are echoes of Homeric hospitality when the emperor received the newly freed knights and 'shed hot tears' on hearing the tales of their horrible imprisonment, then offered them money and clothes and baths and did everything in his power to help them recover from their ordeal. He is not just being kind to them because he feels sorry for them – he is actively good towards people who wronged him. For, Anna points out, these men were his former enemies who had broken their oaths and promises to him; but now they enjoyed his hospitality and recognised his great forbearance. As Penelope Buckley points out, there is a note of Christian charity and saintliness in Alexios' character here. The narrative of his life subtly begins to shift from epic to hagiography, and this tone will become gradually stronger as the story of his life draws closer to the end.

The freed knights stayed with Alexios for some time, but as Bohemond's propaganda spread and he was telling all and sundry that Alexios was a pagan who aided pagans, the emperor had to send them back home to counter his lies with the truth of their experience. Anna hurries to reassure the readers that by that time the knights were nostalgic about their homes and wanted to go anyway. They duly went and confronted Bohemond's lies, sometimes doing so even to his face – not that it changed him a bit.

In the spring of 1106, a comet appeared in the sky, a portent that something important was about to happen. Anna does not exclude the possibility that strange and important events may be heralded by signs in the sky, but asserts her belief that ultimately everything has its explanation in the natural world. The student and later friend of Eustratios of Nicaea and the Aristotelian philosophers could have not believed any different. Her stance towards astrology is also underwritten by her philosophy which is basically a combination of Aristotle and Christianity. Astrology has helped to understand how to observe the position of the stars, she states, but otherwise it is pernicious to believe blindly in the power of the stars. Of course, Anna learned how to draw horoscopes, but like countless other curious and slightly mischievous spirits, her excuse is that she did it for research, 'not – heaven forbid! – to predict the future.' She *was* interested in the prediction of the future though and she speaks at some length about the most famous practitioners of divination in Constantinople during Alexios' reign. One of them predicted the death of her father twice and both times was almost right: there were indeed two deaths in the palace very close to Alexios, although not the emperor himself: the first time it was the palace lion, king of animals (they had a menagerie in Blachernai), the second time it was his mother. At any rate, the comet that appeared in the sky, travelling from west to east, burning bright for forty days and nights, was a clear omen of the Norman invasion.

On 9 October 1107 Bohemond landed on the Adriatic coast and headed for Dyrrachium with an army of 34,000. When the messenger arrived with the news, Alexios was just returning from the hunt with his dogs. Everyone gasped on hearing the name of Bohemond, but Alexios, undoing the leather strap of his boot, said calmly: 'Let's go eat now; we'll deal with Bohemond later.' Anna's use of short, snappy (and somewhat snarky) observations in response to Bohemond's bluster is effective in dismantling his pretentions. By the end of the following week, Bohemond and his forces besieged Dyrrachium. Alexios went to Thessalonika to spend the winter and left them to it; the best ally of a general is the winter, as many other invaders have found to their chagrin in the course of history. The winter is always a bad time to lay siege, and often the attackers fare worse than the besieged. In the spring of 1108, Alexios made his move, blockading Bohemond's army. His intention was to starve them out. He used certain ruses that would be considered 'dirty'; for example, he forged and put in circulations some letters, purportedly by one of Bohemond's closest companions, 'revealing' that they lives had betrayed Bohemond. He also secretly approached other Norman leaders in the camp, offering them money. The way Alexios – and Anna – saw it, tricks and stratagems were better than the loss of life. War had to be won by any means, and the fewer sacrificed the better for all concerned.

His plan worked. In September 1108, negotiation for surrender began and a month later, on 5 October Alexios and Bohemond signed the Treaty of Devol. By the terms of the treaty, Antioch and the rest of Syria would remain under Bohemond (and Tancred, who was in place) but as vassals to Alexios; Laodicea and all Cilicia would be returned to the Byzantines and stay under direct rule. The Latin patriarch of Antioch would be replaced by a Greek and Bohemond would make sure that the rest of the 'Latins' complied with the terms. Anna cites the whole document in detail. Her husband had played a great part in the negotiations, managing to bring Bohemond round where others failed. Interestingly, John Komnenos, Anna's brother, was also included in the treaty alongside Alexios, as co-emperor to whom Bohemond would now owe his allegiance. It was probably during that time that Anna had the opportunity to take a good look at that notorious Bohemond and write her famous description of the man, which has stirred so much speculation among historians, novelists, and readers.

Bohemond and Anna

Anna's portrait of Bohemond is one of her finest; she conveys the man's masculine beauty, presence and character tinged with a thrilling sense of danger verging on the erotic. As such, it has led to speculations on the nature of Anna's feelings for Bohemond: was she sexually attracted to him? Gibbon seems to hint at it: 'Some moderns have imagined that her enmity to Bohemond was the fruit of disappointed love,' and modern scholar R.D. Thomas has seen 'repressed desire' in her description. Taking their cue from historians, novelists made much of this. For example, Greek novelist Maro Douka has depicted a 14-year-old Anna spying on the crusader-princes behind a curtain in her father's palace and falling in love with Bohemond. She then has a dream in which he is in love with her, and on waking up makes plans to obtain her father's consent to their marriage so she and Bohemond could rule the whole world together. But Anna's father decides she is to marry Nikephoros Bryennios, much to her resentment and disappointment. Obviously artistic licence allows many liberties to novelist that are forbidden to historians.

As for scholarly insights into Anna's supposed erotic feelings for Bohemond, Penelope Buckley correctly notes that the historians who spoke of Anna's desire for Bohemond did not seem to take into account the conventions of the romance genre, which eroticises the male protagonist through a description of his athletic body. It must also be noted that Anna probably did not see Bohemond for the first time during the First Crusade (although it is not impossible) but in 1108. Anna was 25 at the time, married and mother of young children; Bohemond must have been at least 60. Who knows if the elderly Anna writing the *Alexiad* could have ever harboured such thoughts and feelings? Her fascination with Bohemond has plausibly been attributed to his similarity with her father in bravery, resourcefulness, and trickery; as another scholar points out, both Alexios and Bohemond 'acknowledged one another as fellow aficionados of the artful ruse.' Furthermore, with her fine literary instinct Anna builds up the character of Bohemond, 'her villain hero', as Georgina Buckler aptly put it, into such epic proportions so as to match the greatness of her father the emperor. And yet, it is an intriguing speculation to wonder if there were something more in her 'loving to hate him' attitude, given the length and vividness of Bohemond's depiction, which interestingly is given at the very last episode in which Bohemond participates.

Here is the description of Bohemond in Anna's own words:

No man like Bohemond had ever appeared before in the land of the Romans, neither barbarian nor Greek. He was dazzling to see and terrible to hear. Let me just describe his traits one by one. He was so tall that he exceeded by almost two inches even the tallest of men. He was slender of hips and belly, broad of chest, well-build of arms. His whole body was neither skinny nor fat, and everything on him was in perfect proportion, the harmony, I would say, of the Canon of Polykleitos [the famous sculpture of a naked man by the renowned Greek sculptor]. He had strong hands, steady feet, well-built neck and shoulders. To careful observation he appeared a bit bent, not that there was anything wrong with the vertebrae in his back, but perhaps there was a slight bend by nature. He was pure white all over his body [how did she know?] and only his white face was tinged with rose. He had reddish blonde hair which did not fall to his shoulder as was the case with the other barbarians – the man was not obsessed with hair – but it was cut to his ears. Regarding his beard, I cannot say whether it was reddish blonde or any other colour – the razor had passed and rendered his skin shinier than marble – but it was probably reddish blonde too. His blue eyes were expressive, at the same time bold and deeply thoughtful. His nose and nostrils breathed in the air freely, his nostrils broad to match the broad chest, nature giving free vent to the air from the heart to the nose. There was a sweetness to the man, but it was undermined by something threatening in his presence; he looked merciless and feral, perhaps owing to his huge stature or his look; it seems to me that even his laughter caused terror. Such was he in body and soul that he had spirit and passion in him, and they both inclined him towards battle. His spirit was agile and cunning, able to escape any grip. His words were measured and his answers always ambivalent. Only one man could beat an adversary such as Bohemond: the emperor. And he [Alexios] achieved this aided by luck and also with his eloquence and all the other gifts that nature had bestowed upon him.

Anna follows her literary idol, Homer, in the way she depicts Bohemond, an enemy and her father's rival, with objective admiration for his beauty, his presence, and his strength. Homer did the same with the two fighting sides in the *Iliad*, presenting Greeks and Trojans in equally heroic terms and attributing the final victory of the Greeks not to superiority but to chance and their use of stratagems. Alexios and Bohemond were set up thus as equals and their conflict of heroic proportions; its final ending with the defeat of Bohemond made his presentation as a worthy adversary to Alexios all the more necessary. This literary 'necessity', as Aristotle would say, in Anna's epic narrative of her father could explain the awed portrait of Bohemond much better than any personal attraction she may have felt. On the other hand, Anna admired beauty – Georgina Buckler attributes this to the natural love of Greeks for beauty – and has depicted portraits of other beautiful people in her history, including her beloved, unlucky first fiancé Constantine Doukas and his mother Maria of Alania. Ekphrasis, the rhetorical genre of the laudatory description of a beautiful natural or artificial object – person, landscape, work of art – is one of the staples of classical and post-classical literary writing, and Anna is adept in that as well as in other forms of literary expression. Perhaps her supposed sexual attraction for Bohemond is nothing but an exercise of style.

The *Alexiad* and the First Crusade

In the assessment of the *Alexiad* as a source for the First Crusade, it is important to remember why Anna wrote about it: it is not the event per se that interested her but the impact it had on her own world, on her father the emperor and on his empire. In her writings, she does not much care whether the crusaders captured Jerusalem, and perhaps this is the reason why she only dedicates a few lines to it, as an almost incidental affair. Although she recognises that the simple people were motivated by a true desire to worship at the Holy Sepulchre, she does not believe that the leaders were in it for the same reason at all: she appears certain that it was because of their greed and desire for personal profit. Other chroniclers, like Albert of Aachen, support this view, at least in the case of specific knights. Anna constantly emphasises the love of money of the Kelts in general and Bohemond in particular, whose venality is emphatically highlighted at every opportunity.

Much has been written about the *Alexiad*'s value as a source for the First Crusade, positive and negative. The assessment of the *Alexiad* in this case is as much victim to Western prejudice as the actions of Alexios and the Byzantines themselves at the time the events were taking place.

Military historian John France gives the following assessment of Anna as a historian of the crusade, which more or less sums up the negative views:

> Anna Comnena's *Alexiad* is informative, but it is also the most mendacious of the sources. She presents the Crusade as some natural disaster which fell upon the empire, never admitting that her father had asked for Western aid and she never admits his debt to its success. Her whole account, written forty years after the event, is coloured by hindsight and in particular by the question of Antioch, which would so concern Alexius and his two immediate successors. Anna is contemptuous of the barbarian Franks whom she denounces as untrustworthy while at the same time praising her father's cunning tricks. If her attitudes were widely shared by the Byzantine upper class one can perhaps understand the deep hostility to Byzantium which was generated in the ranks of the crusaders.

France has interestingly left Anna's assessment at the very end, even after the Armenian and Syriac accounts of Matthew of Edessa and Michael of Syria, which he admits have very little to add to our knowledge of the crusade. His use of the rather strong words 'the most mendacious' sounds rather unfair, considering that crusade chroniclers generally offer biased accounts depending on their provenance and support of this or that crusade leader. It is possible that Anna did not know about Alexios' letter to Pope Urban or about the mission to Piacenza; she was only 13 at the time and even to the most intelligent child of that age it is unlikely that this sort of thing would have been of interest. And even if she knew of it, who can deny that the passage of hundreds of thousands of crusaders through the empire, with their unruly behaviour and attacks on local populations, did somewhat resemble a natural disaster? It was certainly nothing like the orderly troops Alexios would have envisaged, and the simple people of the empire must have looked upon the crusaders with trepidation and even fear, even those who profited by the passage of so many armies.

Positive assessments of the value of Anna's account, on the other hand, highlight how unique and vivid it is. Peter Frankopan has pointed out that as the only text that gives an account from the Byzantine point of view, it stands alone, opposite a large group of Western accounts taken together; its chronological blunders and criticisms of the Franks are put under a magnifying lens, while Western chroniclers' bias and disparaging views of the 'deceitful Greeks' are accepted as a matter of course. According to Frankopan, the *Alexiad* is 'a source which contains an excellent supply of high-grade information, evidently drawn from a number of sources and eye-witnesses.' If it is problematic at certain points, owing mainly to the fact that Anna's sources were scant after the Byzantines left Antioch, as we have seen, the text as a whole is 'not the unreliable and untrustworthy work which modern scholars would have us believe.' Anti-Greek bias, which is a long tradition in Western sources and commentaries, as well as misogynistic suspicion towards the female author, as Gibbon demonstrates, played their part in putting down this text. And ironically, as Frankopan concludes, on close examination the critical views of Anna's work prove to be more biased and prejudiced than the text itself.

Chapter 8

The Death of Anna Komnene

I will first reveal this to the world, and let the sleepless eye [of God] be my witness, that I was very much loved by my parents and emperors ... and that during all the time I have lived with my parents I have never disobeyed them or done anything against their will and wish, unlike some children who, flattered by their parents' love for them, often do.

(Anna Komnene's Will)

Her Last Will and Testament

Anna wrote her last will and testament (at least the one that survives) sometime between 1118 and 1123, or even possibly as late as 1133, when her father was dead and her mother still alive. Her husband and her (four attested) children that reached adulthood were also living at the time. It would be a wonderful insight into Anna's daily life and interests if the whole document had survived. The catalogue of her books alone would have been a wonderful thing to see (Byzantine testaments often include books – a valuable possession at the time). Sadly, only the prologue remains from Anna's will. Although this document was found among the papers of Michael Italikos, an orator and intellectual who belonged to the 'salon' of Eirene and Anna, it is proven beyond doubt that Anna is the author and not Michael Italikos or even a nameless scribe – redactor of wills. The text has too many similarities of style to the *Alexiad* to be the work of anyone else.

Anna informs us that she wrote her last will and testament at the suggestion of her mother, and that she was still young and in good health when she wrote it. She believes that it is a very good idea to do this early in life, while one's mind is still strong and one is still articulate, before death grabs one like a lurking thief. She presents herself in a manner very similar to her self-introduction in the prologue of the *Alexiad*: 'I, Anna born, in the Porphyra, not without my share of learning, having studied thoroughly the divine words and not neglectful of classical education.' Her choice of words, in particular the use of *litotes* (expressing an affirmative by the use of the negative of its opposite, e.g. not bad instead of good) may seem strange to modern readers who are taught to think that a simple and direct style is best. But we must bear in mind that in Anna's culture directness of expression was seen as completely inappropriate, overbearing and rude. A woman in particular should not presume to speak (or write), and if she did, she ought to appear suitably humble and self-effacing. On the other hand, Anna needs to prove that she can and supports her claim with explicit reference to her extensive education, albeit in a somewhat self-deprecating style. 'I am not without a share in education' does not sound the same as 'I have a very extensive education,' but ultimately both statements describe the same fact. Anna's self-introduction in her will is the same necessary mixture of assertion and humility that we have seen in the Prologue of the *Alexiad*.

Anna goes on to give a short overview of her life, a feature in common with other Byzantine wills. She tells us that throughout her life she has been a good daughter who loved and obeyed her parents in everything and that they loved her back very dearly. Eirene's tone about Anna in the typikon, as we have seen, corroborates this statement as far as the mother is concerned. One proof of Anna's love for her parents and of her perfect obedience as a daughter was that, although she herself would prefer the 'most pure, unyoked (unwedded) life', i.e. the life of a monastic, 'and although that's where my inclination lay,' she married, because this was her parents' wish. 'And so I have served the flesh', she says, but goes on to imply that it was worth it:

> I could not blame marriage for parting me from my preferred singlehood; for it was the cause for the very best things that ever happened to me: the best and most divine man under the sun since time immemorial, who was most fortunate in birth and in virtues of body and soul, Kaisar Nikephoros, attached to the House of Bryennios; and the best and most beautiful children of both sexes, some of whom have quit

this perishable life – it was God's will– and some are still alive and may they stay so – Christ my King! – with their father the Kaisar, and would that I were delivered to earth first and would that I never witness – O Sun! – my lord and master the Kaisar's – but how could I speak the horrible word [funeral]?' – nor that of any of my children, for my life depends upon them all.

This highly emotional and artfully inarticulate passage evokes classical tragedy. The mere thought of her beloved husband and children's death renders her unable to form proper sentences. Anna's resignation to the death of some of her children, her refusal to contemplate the end of her husband and remaining children, and her wish to die before she sees such things happen again mean to convey her strong attachment to her family, her pride in them and her fear for their safety, as well as her stoicism at the face of past tragedies. Despite the rhetoric there is real pathos here; for a moment Anna Komnene, the proud princess, the formidable intellectual, the famous historian is only a woman who contemplates her own powerlessness in the face of death, especially the death of her loved ones. Despite a prevailing belief that medieval parents did not bond with their children as much as we modern people do because of high rates of child mortality, this was not actually true. Texts and icons ('books for the illiterate' as ninth-century Byzantine monk St John of Damascus called them) tell a very different story. One of the best-known icons of the Komnenian era, the Theotokos of Vladimir [Illustration 2], depicts a tender embrace between mother and child: sweet-faced, pensive Mary hugs her infant son, who kisses her sweetly on the cheek, his little arm round his mother's neck as he looks up at her with adoration. Poor Michael Psellos wrote a heart-breaking funeral oration for his daughter Styliane, who died age 9, probably from smallpox, his anguish palpable and true in the text beyond any rhetorical embellishments.

But after these emotional effusions, Anna gets back down to the business at hand. This is a pattern that Anna will establish in the *Alexiad* as well, where a passage of lamentation is almost always followed by a brisk return to business:

I will now turn back to the emperors, for everything in my life has been connected to them. My very breath and substance and existence, body and soul; additionally, objects of gold and silver and veils woven in gold thread and bales of silk cloth; also houses and plots of land and – to put in in legal terms – all my moveable and immoveable property and everything that is mine to dispose of, all these things I consider as coming from my parents' hands; and the purpose of the present charter is to arrange their management.

Anna adds that in taking this measure she is obeying her mother's instructions. This was possibly connected with the fact that Eirene had been making her own provisions regarding the convent of Full of Grace. With a new emperor on the throne, Anna's family as she knew it from birth and childhood until roughly at this time (her own marriage, rather than take her away, brought a new member into the Komnenos family) did not exist anymore. Alexios' death changed everything in its dynamics; John was now the head of House Komnenos.

Unfortunately, the rest of the document is lost. But this short teaser gives us some idea of the wealth Anna must have possessed by the mention of such valuable objects as gold, silver, expensive fabrics of silk and other woven with gold, not to mention the plots of land and houses. The description of the moveable objects echoes the treasure that Alexios had prepared for Bohemond when he arrived at Constantinople in the First Crusade. As an imperial princess from a wealthy family, married into one of the most powerful and wealthy aristocratic houses, of course Anna was very wealthy. But unless by a happy coincidence the rest of that document – which must surely be a hefty one – is ever found among a pile of neglected manuscripts in some storage room of an ancient university library or among the hidden treasures of a private collection, we will never know precisely how rich she was, nor what books she had in her library.

A Princess Servant of Asklepios

Thanks to Tornikes' obituary, we have a fairly good picture of Anna's final days and death. Although by that time he had been appointed metropolitan bishop of Ephesus, some 350 miles to the south of

Constantinople, Tornikes would have returned to the city from time to time and would have visited his 'dear basilissa'. He rather hated his post in the provincial city, which must have felt like an exile. The conditions in his seat do not sound ideal either; in a letter he complains that as he was celebrating a service in the cathedral church of St John the Theologian, parts of the plaster peeled off the ceiling and landed on his head. Back in his beloved Constantinople, he would also receive updates about his friend from other common friends and from members of her family and from servants in her household.

Among Anna's many accomplishments was the study and practice of medicine. According to Tornikes, this was her greatest accomplishment of all; but because as a woman she was confined in the domestic sphere, the general public did not know this. Interestingly, at the same time it is known that in her brother's hospital established in his monastery of Christ Pantokrator there were provisions for two or three women doctors who would look after women patients – even though Pantokrator was a male monastery. This provision indicates that there were other women who practiced medicine and that Anna was not the only exception in the male-ruled profession, although there was no question of her practising in public. Short of mixing the medicine and dress the wounds herself, Anna practiced the art with the best of the servants of Asklepios, Greek god of medicine and healing. She was also an expert in pharmacology, with a formidable knowledge of mixtures, combinations, and dosology of remedies according to the patient's individual case and needs. She was taught by the best doctors of her day, both in the theory and practice of medicine; we saw her at her father's bedside, participating in the consultations of the medical team attending to her father and even putting her weight in when there was a stalemate in differing opinions. In the *Alexiad* she describes the symptoms and discusses the various courses of treatment administered to her father; in her personal life, she loved to tend to her family – parents, children, relatives, servants; illness or accident, the kaisarissa was there to help.

When Nikephoros Bryennios after a rather short illness died in 1938, it is fair to assume that Anna was presiding over the council of doctors as she had done with her father twenty years earlier. Anna mentions her husband's death in the very prologue of the *Alexiad*, displaying her usual medical matter-of-factness when she gives an account of his illness and its causes. He returned ill from a long campaign alongside her brother the emperor (John II Komnenos – another instance of their harmonious terms) with a 'tumour in his internal organs due to his laborious toils.' In the Hippocratic tradition, Anna attributes Nikephoros' fatal illness to internal causes – the patient was 'anxious by nature and never ceasing in his toils [a workaholic?]' and 'endlessly worried about his family' – as well as external ones – 'intemperate climate and noxious air', 'infinite troubles', 'frequent commanding army campaigns'. Although he was anxious to finish his manuscript of *Material for History*, 'we [presumably Anna and his team of doctors] did not let him, for fear that his wound would open if he continued with his narrative.' Anna must have looked after Nikephoros both as devoted wife and capable doctor.

In the end, Tornikes implies that it was her dedication to helping others that indirectly caused her death. We know very little of Anna's constitution. She hints that she may have been suffering from an undisclosed ailment at some point in her narrative, stating cryptically that whatever her constitution was, the women in the palace knew very well (sadly they cannot tell us). Tornikes also vaguely alludes to an illness or weakness, which sounds temporary. At any rate, she was now in her late sixties and indomitable as always. Much had happened in her life by that time. She had lost many members of her family: her parents, husband, her brothers Andronikos (a favourite) and John, her young daughter-in-law Eirene, her son-in-law the husband of her beloved daughter, another Eirene. Not to mention the children she had lost as infants, whose loss she faced with resignation in her will. But now she was helping her bereaved sister Maria at a time of deep affliction.

Maria Komnene had recently lost a son and a granddaughter within a year and these two terrible blows played some part in her unnamed illness; she refused food and drink, which perhaps suggests that she suffered from some form of depression after so many losses. Anna nursed her favourite sister personally, but in her effort to encourage her sister to eat and drink, she did not pay attention at all to her own diet or rest. As a result, she fell ill, but owing to the pressure of her sister's situation she ignored the initial symptoms of weakness and fatigue.

Yet she became steadily worse and had an episode – possibly a stroke? Tornikes does not specify, though she seems to have completely lost her voice after that episode. But she recovered after a treatment of phlebotomy or bleeding – a standard pre-modern medical procedure of extracting blood in order to restore the balance of the 'humours' of the body; leeches were used for the purpose. This treatment was used until relatively recently in rural Greece. I have very vivid personal memories of witnessing a leeching as a child. The healer placed a couple of black leeches on the patient's arm, on the inside of the elbow. The creatures latched on to the skin and began to suck, quickly bloating with blood. When they had swollen up to three or four times their size, the healer would unlatch them carefully, one by one, and would roll them in a large dish covered in ashes, squeezing their sides at the same time. This made the leeches vomit out the blood and return to their original size. The healer would then latch them back on again and the process was repeated, until she was satisfied that enough blood was extracted from the patient. Whether it was the leeching or, as Tornikes piously affirms, the efficiency of Anna's prayers, she regained her senses and speech soon after. In her temporary improvement, she examined her own condition as a medical woman and issued the prognosis: she would not recover from that illness. Her medical colleagues who were in attendance sadly agreed.

Anna Dies

Perfectly resigned to the fact that she was dying, and as Tornikes put it, 'bearing it all with a divine magnanimity that surpassed Socrates' own, preparing not for the end of life but for a change of life, for a move from the world of temporary and visible things to that of the eternal and invisible', Anna took control of her situation. Once she was certain of her imminent death, she settled her worldly affairs, which probably meant that she revised the will she had made years earlier, which we have discussed; as her mother's heiress she possessed all the property in Full of Grace. One more thing that she had to take care of was her spiritual wellbeing; leaving the world behind, she was ready to dedicate herself solely to divine and spiritual things, by 'becoming the bride of Christ and putting on the habit of perfection.' By that Tornikes simply meant that Anna took monastic vows, following the example of other members of her family and many other aristocratic men and women of her time. She made the decision on the day she knew that she would die, but her family tried to dissuade her: it would be too great a commitment for someone as wealthy as she was to adhere to the oath of poverty, which as a nun she would have to take, what if she recovered and lived for a longer time? What would happen to her extensive property? But Anna, sure in her diagnosis that she was dying, cut them short: 'So what if God gave me my health back? Should we not give back a gift to the giver?' The Byzantine love of rhetorical devices such as *polyptoton* – using various grammatical forms of the same word - apparently did not leave Anna even at her deathbed.

She then began to say her goodbyes. She asked her sister to stay strong and remember that she would soon find a safe haven for all her troubles in the afterlife; she comforted her daughter and assigned the whole household to her care, particularly the women who would need assistance and protection, and discussed with her the affairs of her brothers and Anna's own sons, commending them to God and begging Him to grant them peace and harmony. She wished her nephew the emperor all the best, then joyfully she gave up her soul to the hands of her dear mother and the angels, leaving her mortal body behind. In death, she looked as if she had fallen asleep.

We do not know the actual date of Anna's death. According to Jean Darrouzès, editor of Tornikes' funeral oration, Anna's death went completely unnoticed; no ceremonies or official speeches that we know of marked the event, which he places sometime in 1153. The pronounced difference between Anna's entrance into life and her exit from it would have probably elicited some deeply philosophical comment from her, had she been able to make one after death; she would be the first to notice the complete reversal of circumstances. It is doubtful that she would have felt sad or bitter about it though: for the Byzantines, including emperors (or perhaps especially for emperors), it was important that the end of life should be Christian, painless, free of shame, peaceful, and that they would be well prepared to defend themselves in the judgment at Christ's 'terrible tribunal', as the standard petition of the Greek Orthodox liturgy repeats. By the time the Komnenoi came to power, the ideal death was one of monastic humility. Anna became a nun at the end of her life following the example of both her grandmothers and her mother. Her great-uncle Emperor Isaac I Komnenos had also died as a monk at the monastery of Stoudios, where he had happily held the humble post of porter. Her nephew Emperor Manuel would also take up the monastic habit shortly before his death about thirty years later.

Anna's obituary is a work of rhetoric, demonstrating all the traits of the genre: decorative language, praise for the departed and not a mention of any faults, propriety and decorum at every turn. One cannot expect to learn very much about the real person from an obituary; or rather, one has to read carefully and sometimes between the lines to find out anything of substance about them. Rhetorical platitudes are perennially present in obituaries. In theory at least the obituarist is supposed to be objective. But word choice can reveal the feelings of the author about the subject, and also subtly suggest and hint what is not appropriate to mention, as well as showing the worldviews, values and ideas of the obituarist.

What do we really learn about Anna from the obituary George Tornikes wrote for her? It appears that Tornikes was really fond of her and admired her exceedingly, but he was also uneasy, if not exactly out of his depth, and baffled, to say the least. His awareness that Anna was an extraordinary case, that there was no one like her, is clear, as is his difficulty to strike the right balance in doing justice to her uniqueness and simultaneously making sure not to make her look like a freak, a monstrous woman who behaved like a man. Anna herself has to deal with exactly the same difficulty in the *Alexiad*, as we have seen. Tornikes praises her 'virile virtues' and 'masculine intellect' effusively; in his world, a masculine woman was a woman who showed a praiseworthy desire to become better than her feeble and wicked sex. On the other hand, he takes great care to show that despite her 'masculine' intellect as demonstrated by her ability to be a writer of history – and other works – Anna performed, and excelled in, all the duties and obligations expected from a woman. He stresses Anna's devotion to her parents as much as Anna herself did, and he praises her for her love and support of her sister Maria in her affliction. Perhaps he insists so much on Anna's excellence in medicine because healing was traditionally the remit of women – at least until early modernity, when male doctors took over, marginalising midwives and women healers (and sometimes condemning them as witches for it). It was also proper of women to care for their families, and what is a stronger indication of hands-on care than nursing? For the same reason, Tornikes speaks in admiration about Anna's philanthropy, her charitable works that rendered her comparable to Dorcas the disciple of St Peter: alms to the poor, protection of the weak, the widows and the orphans.

And what a loving and devoted wife she was! Tornikes paints a romantic portrait of Anna with all the details about her love life such as he knew it; he assures us that she was a beautiful girl who did not turn to letters because of lack of physical charms like other women. He discusses her early engagement to a lovely boy who died young, then her marriage to her dashing, handsome, intellectual husband with whom she was truly in love and lived a blissfully harmonious life. He talks of her children and particularly her daughter Eirene Doukaina, who probably commissioned the obituary, with high praise. In insisting so much on Anna's appearance and her romantic and family life, Tornikes bears a striking resemblance to modern commentators who, in discussing extraordinary women, intellectuals or politicians, always place disproportionate emphasis on their marriage, their children, their appearance and clothes, compared to the men. At least Tornikes' excuse was that he lived and wrote in the twelfth century and that his culture, condemned by many modern historians of the eighteenth and nineteenth century as effeminate, paid attention to men's appearance too.

Chapter 9

The Afterlives of Anna Komnene

Oxford, England, 1929

On 5 December 1923, Mrs Georgina Buckler, age 53, received a letter from St Hugh's College, University of Oxford, informing her she had been accepted in the BLitt programme. She was to work on a thesis entitled: 'The Intellectual and Moral Standards of Anna Comnena'. Until that time, no scholar in the English-speaking world had dedicated a monograph to the twelfth-century Byzantine historian of whom Mr Gibbon had spoken so disparagingly. It took an upper-middle-class lady of a formidable pedigree in the Classics, whose path to education was not seamless, who had been married and was the mother of children, with considerable experience in public service (she served in the Red Cross during the First World War), and a commitment to 'good works' to take a serious interest in a fellow-scholar whose distant life in the twelfth-century bore certain similarities to her own.

Thirty-five years earlier, in 1888, young Miss Georgina Grenfell Walrond, as she was called back then, had entered Girton College, Cambridge to read Classics. She left without a degree. It was through no fault of her own; although she was a diligent, hard-working, prize-winning student, women were not granted qualifications at that time; being accepted to study was considered radical enough. And at any rate, Miss Walrond surely received the biggest prize that a woman could desire in meeting her future husband at Cambridge – was not this the point of this new-fangled business of women going to university after all? One cannot help being sarcastic; all the more so because after her marriage in May 1892, young Mrs Buckler's development as a scholar stalled; her husband's career took precedence over hers, and so did motherhood (a difficult experience for her, as she lost several babies in miscarriages or stillbirths; eventually she raised two daughters). But in the 1920s things had fortunately changed somewhat, and Georgina Buckler was awarded her B.A. and M.A. within the first year of her BLitt, which was soon turned into a DPhil.

Perhaps because Georgina Buckler's interest in Anna Komnene's work was not focused on the language and style of the *Alexiad* but on its 'moral and intellectual values', she could see the author and the text with fresh eyes. For a very long time, Byzantine texts had suffered from negative comparisons with classical literature. But judging the work on its own merit, and finding that it entitled its writer to be 'among the great historians, among those who make the dry bones of the past ages live,' Buckler could see the significance of the author and her world, and even possibly her relatability with Buckler herself and her own world. For at a time when women scholars worked hard to open their way through a hostile crowd of prejudices, an intellectual foremother was of paramount importance.

From Constantinople, Byzantium to Abbotsford House, the Scottish Borders

Buckler walked a lonely trail regarding her appreciation of Anna as a person and historian. The Anglophone audience knew the Byzantine princess mostly through Gibbon, whose attitude we have seen and need nor repeat. But there was another source, perhaps equally influential, if not strictly speaking a historical one, which Buckler had read: Anna was one of the characters in a novel by the extremely popular author and 'father of historical fiction' Sir Walter Scott. True, the novel, *Count Robert of Paris* (1832), Scott's penultimate work and only one with a Byzantine setting, was not among his most successful. Still it had its readership, wider than any scholar would ever dream of having (with the exception perhaps of Gibbon) and thus it contributed to the iconography of the pretentious and vain bluestocking who cuts a slightly ridiculous figure among the men, although she comes relatively better off than any other Byzantine character in the novel.

The story is about Hereward, a young Anglo-Saxon member of the Varangian guard at the service of Emperor Alexios, and his adventures in Constantinople when the crusaders arrive; Count Robert, whom we have seen earlier described by Anna as 'the crazy Latin', is initially Hereward's enemy and later his friend. The two become embroiled in (and fight against) the plots and schemes of the wily Greeks. Interestingly, Anna is not a conspirator in this story, simply because Scott dispenses with her brother and makes her an only child in the novel. Scott wants to drive home the idea that Byzantium is finished, since there is no true heir to the throne (Anna is married but childless in the novel, and poor Bryennios is a cowardly cad who conspires against his father-in-law, although he repents in the end). 'The way is now open for a Western ruler in Byzantium' is the moral of *Count Robert of Paris*; indeed, Count Robert's wife Brenhilda gives birth to their son in the Porphyra at the end of the novel.

But it is not all bleak in Scott's portrayal of Anna; as a fellow-writer, and despite Gibbon's pronouncements, Scott can recognise the power of her writing. In one memorable scene in which Anna is reading from her work in front of a fawning but basically unappreciative audience at court, young Hereward, the hero of the novel, is so captivated and moved by her narrative, that at the culmination of a battle scene in which his own brother dies, he drops his gigantic battle-axe and clasps his hands with an exclamation; her vivid depiction of men and arms, for which her very authorship was doubted by modern scholars, temporarily disarmed a young soldier. What author could hope for higher praise than this?

Formidable Edwardian Aunts in Interwar Britain

At about the time that Georgina Buckler was completing her doctoral dissertation, Scottish author Naomi Mitchison published a short biography of Anna Komnene. The book, entitled simply *Anna Comnena* (1928), came out as part of the series Representative Women. The timing was telling; in 1928, the Equal Franchise Act was signed in Britain, by which all women over the age of 21 were given the vote, taking one more step towards equality with men. It was also a remarkable year for Anna Komnene, with the publication of the first English translation of the *Alexiad* by Cambridge-educated scholar Elizabeth Dawes. Buckler's book was to follow soon, and Mitchison was aware of this; she states in a note in her bibliography that Buckler had kindly answered a number of her questions and hopes that the readers of her book will go on to read Buckler's, adding: 'If the information they want is anywhere,

I am sure it will be there, and I only hope they will not discover that anything I have written here is absolutely wrong!' For the newly emancipated, studying, working, voting women who wrote and bought these books, it was important to have historical precedents of strong women with an intellectual legacy. Anna the author and historian was far more interesting and relevant to these women than Anna the would-be empress.

Mitchison uses the infamous phrase by Gibbon ('the vanity of the female author') as epigraph to her book; it is not clear if this is an endorsement or a condemnation, and there are instances throughout the book where one might be excused to think either or both. She does appear to be somewhat uneasy about Anna's Byzantine context. Byzantium was still uncontestably viewed as a decadent dark age. As a socialist, Mitchison would be hostile to the perceived conservatism and religiosity of Byzantine society. It could not be helped; Anna belonged to a 'stupid', 'superstitious age', in a 'doomed civilisation' and her shortcomings were attributed to the age in which she had lived. On the other hand, Mitchison is one of the first writers who is interested in Anna the historian and not the power-hungry conspirator. Mitchison wants history to be 'as readable as a detective story!' and in her view 'this is one of Anna Comnena's strongest points'. It is Komnene's story-telling power that makes her a remarkable woman, worthy of being presented as an ancestor to woman writers of our age.

In her narrative account of Anna's slightly fictionalised story, Mitchison uses a plain and modern language and a storytelling mode that would make her book suitable for children. The didactic style of her writing fits well within the educational purposes of the series and would help the young girls and women who read it to familiarise themselves with the idea of a princess who was not just that, but also a formidable intellectual and a writer whose surviving work could be of interest to them. As a result, this medieval lady sounds rather Victorian or Edwardian, from spoilt child to young romantic princess in love with her prince to old Victorian aunt, formidable and rather out of sync with modern times, yet interesting and appealing:

> She would have been an alarming person for the younger generation to meet, old Aunt Anna whom one went dutifully to see from time to time at her nunnery, and who was so

Conclusion

Anna Komnene was undoubtedly an extraordinary woman; an important medieval historian and an author whose work is deemed interesting enough to be available in translation and in print in many languages almost a thousand years after it was written. Anna would have probably been happy and perhaps not surprised, had she known. She was misunderstood by her peers of later ages, owing largely to the widening chasm between her culture – the Greco-Roman world of Byzantium – and Western European culture. When Byzantium was mortally wounded by the Fourth Crusade and later destroyed by the Ottoman conquest, Anna became part of an extinct world, so to speak. Absorbed by the Ottoman Empire, with which it often seems to be conflated in the minds of modern day tourists, surviving partly in the Orthodox Church and its rites and through language (Greek – largely unknown and rather irrelevant to Western audiences), Byzantium is vaguely known today as a mysterious, exotic and rather sinister world. The very use of the adjective 'byzantine' to denote scheming intrigue and complexity suggests its negative presence – when it is not completely erased. That erasure or disparagement of Byzantium, due mainly to its political extinction and takeover by the Ottomans and their Islamic culture, to the centuries-long hostility between Greek and Latin Christianity, and to its condemnation as an obscurantist, backward civilization by the Enlightenment did not do Anna Komnene's posthumous life any favours.

The nineteenth and especially the twentieth century brought about changes in revolutionary fervour to revise and rewrite the world. History began to look beyond heroes, kings and wars; it discovered women and their achievements beyond the usual queens and consorts. Anna Komnene was rediscovered. Her work was re-read, and great French and German historians like Ferdinand Chalandon, Charles Diehl and Karl Krumbacher praised it and were impressed by the author herself as a character. Sadly, deeply ingrained misogynistic attitudes prevailed; Anna was interesting, an important 'authoress' but morally suspicious, perhaps even more so than her contemporaries would think. As we have seen, her work was misread; her rhetorical efforts to capture the good will of the reader were taken literally as complaints against 'the slings and arrows of outrageous fortune' who thwarted her ambition. Only in the twenty-first century did the persistent views of her as a power-hungry, ruthless woman who would sacrifice her own brother to her ambition finally begin to change. Why were people so eager to accept the version of evil Anna? For a number of reasons: because the desire for authorship is mistaken as a desire for authority, for executive power; because the power of received ideas is very great, especially when they suit misogynistic agendas; because the testimony of one male historian was enough to condemn a woman whose behaviour was outside the ordinary and therefore deemed suspicious.

Literature picked up on the performative role of Anna's lamentations long before academic research arrived at this conclusion. But as the novels exploring Anna's life and personality were written in 'minor' languages (Bulgarian and Greek) and their subject was obscure, they failed to make any waves and Anna remained unknown. Yet there is always hope. Anna's hunger for intellectual power, for knowledge, her love of poetry, the extraordinary family in which she was born and the turbulent times in which she lived make for a fascinating story; a story which she herself told better than anyone else ever could, but which can inspire future generations of writers to tell it again and again.

THE END

Appendix

A Note on Language

Readers may be surprised to see some words or names they know from other texts they have read on Byzantium with a different spelling than the one they are familiar with. Older literature tends to use the latinised forms of names (e.g. Alexius Comnenus, caesar instead of Alexios Komnenos, kaisar etc) but the more recent tendency in Byzantine Studies is to use the Greek forms. I follow the example of the latter in most cases, acknowledging that it is very difficult to apply a general rule where long usage and practical reasons make room for many exceptions. I hope this sufficiently explains the inconsistencies in this volume.

Glossary

Augusta: feminine form of Augustus. In Byzantium this was not a name but a title, accorded to the empress only. Empress Eirene, for instance, would be addressed as 'augusta' or Augusta Eirene, but only while her husband the emperor was on the throne.

Basileus, basilissa: king, queen, In Byzantine history and studies translated as emperor, empress. In Byzantine political theory and usage, these titles were reserved for the Byzantine rulers alone. The words that the Byzantines used for monarchs of European countries or any other were *rēx* and *rēgissa,* or the titles in the local languages transliterated into Greek (for example, *khanes* for khan, *zupanos* and *emirēs* for Slavic żupan and Arabic emir etc). In diplomatic correspondence with the Holy Roman Empire, the German emperor is always called *rēx*, not *basileus*. In twelfth-century texts, members of the royal family are also called *basileus / basilissa* as a courtesy, without implying crowned imperial status.

Boukoleon: a composite word from the Greek words *bous ke o leon* (ox and lion), this was the name of a palace on the shore on the southside of Constantinople. It took its name from a sculpture standing in front of it, which represented a lion attacking an ox.

Chrysobull: an imperial document written in scarlet-purple ink and sealed with the emperor's special golden (Gr. *chryse*) seal or bull.

Demes: associations or factions of organised supporters of the teams at the chariot races at the Hippodrome of Constantinople. There were four of those, named by the colour the racing teams wore: the Blues, the Greens, the Reds, and the Whites. By the fifth century the most powerful ones were the Blues and the Greens. Going beyond mere sports support, their role in politics was considerable: a case in point were the Nika riots, caused by an uprising of the *demes* which almost resulted in toppling the emperor Justinian. Later emperors tried to keep the *demes* happy with frequent games and by granting them a role in state ceremonial.

Despotes, Despoina: lord master, lady mistress. This title does not simply mean of noble birth but is accorded to persons who are in a position of authority over others. In the Komnenian court it was the title accorded to Anna Dalassene, for her executive powers. It is one of the standard names attributed to the Holy Mother of God, and as such it is a common given name among Greek women.

Domestikos ton scholon: Domestic of the Schools; commander of the army of the East.

Doukai, the: Greek plural for Doukas, the family name; collective noun for all the members of the family who bore that name; equivalent to House of Doukas (see also Komnenoi).

Doux: a title similar but not equivalent to duke (they come from the same Latin origin); in Byzantium it was not hereditary.

Dromon: a galley with two or three rows of oars and lateen sails.

Droungarios: admiral of the fleet.

Ekphrasis: literary description of a work of art – painting, object – or person abounding in ancient Greek and Byzantine rhetorical texts.

Ephoros: secular governor or guardian of a large institution.

TABLE 2. HOUSE OF DOUKAS

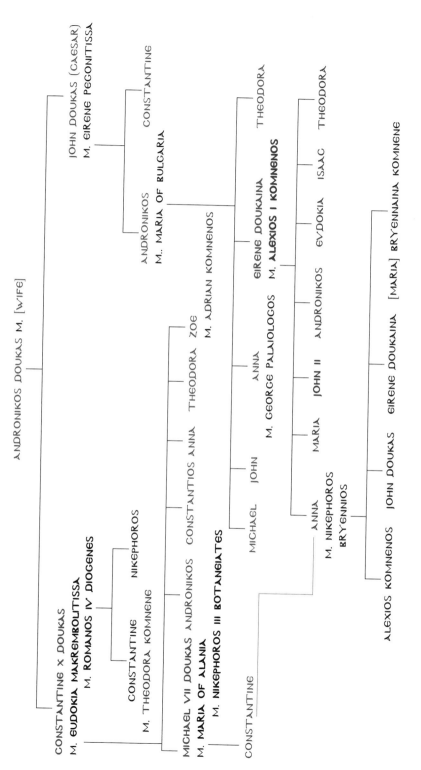

NB. Emperors and empresses are in bold characters

TABLE 3. HOUSE OF KOMNENOS

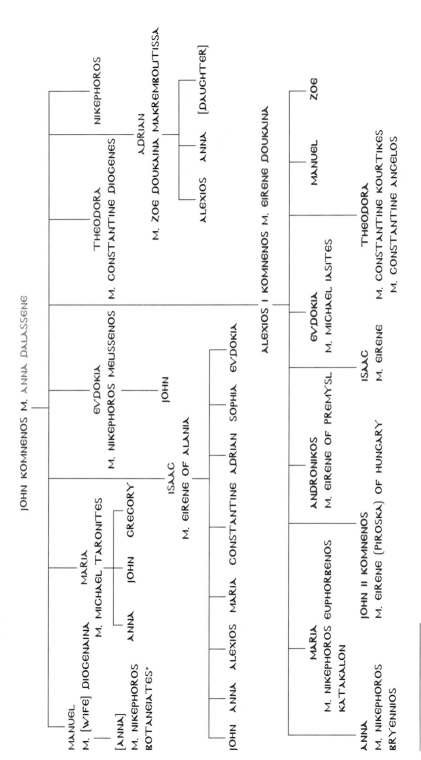

* Grandson of Emperor Nikephoros III Botaneiates from a previous marriage.

TABLE 4. THE PORPHYROGENITA GENERATION

CHILDREN AND GRANDCHILDREN OF ALEXIOS I KOMNENOS AND EIRENE DOUKAINA

1. ANNA KOMNENE
M. NIKEPHOROS BRYENNIOS
——

ALEXIOS KOMNENOS
JOHN DOUKAS
EIRENE DOUKAINA
[MARIA] BRYENNAINA KOMNENE

2. MARIA KOMNENE
M. NIKEPHOROS EUPHORBENOS KATAKALON

ALEXIOS KOMNENOS
ANDRONIKOS KOMNENOS
EIRENE DOUKAINA
[EVDOKIA KOMNENE]
[ANNA KOMNENE]

3. JOHN II KOMNENOS
M. EIRENE OF HUNGARY
——

ALEXIOS KOMNENOS
MARIA KOMNENE
ANDRONIKOS KOMNENOS
ANNA KOMNENE
ISAAC KOMNENOS
THEODORA KOMNENE
EVDOKIA KOMNENE
MANUEL I KOMNENOS

4. ANDRONIKOS KOMNENOS
M. EIRENE OF PRREMYSL
——

ALEXIOS

5. ISAAC KOMNENOS
M. EIRENE KAISARISSA
——

JOHN KOMNENOS
[MARIA] KOMNENE
ANNA KOMNENE
ANDRONIKOS I KOMNENOS
CONSTANTINE (COSTINTZES) [ADOPTED SON]

6. EVDOKIA KOMNENE
M. MICHAEL IASITES
——

[SON]
[DAUGHTER]

7. THEODORA KOMNENE
M. CONSTANTINE ANGELOS
——

JOHN DOUKAS
MARIA ANGELINA KOMNENE
ALEXIOS ANGELOS KOMNENOS
ANDRONIKOS DOUKAS
EVDOKIA ANGELINA KOMNENE
ZOE ANGELINA KOMNENE
ISAAC ANGELOS DOUKAS

8. MANUEL KOMNENOS
DIED AS AN INFANT

9. ZOE KOMNENE
DIED AS AN INFANT

Maps

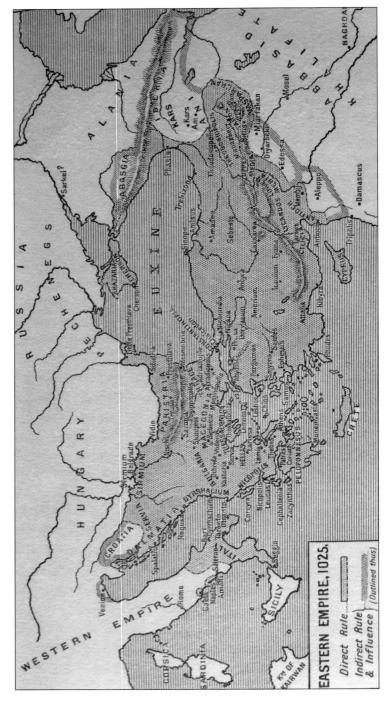

Map 1. The Byzantine Empire c. 1025, at the death of Emperor Basil II the Bulgar-Slayer. By permission UoG Sp Coll.

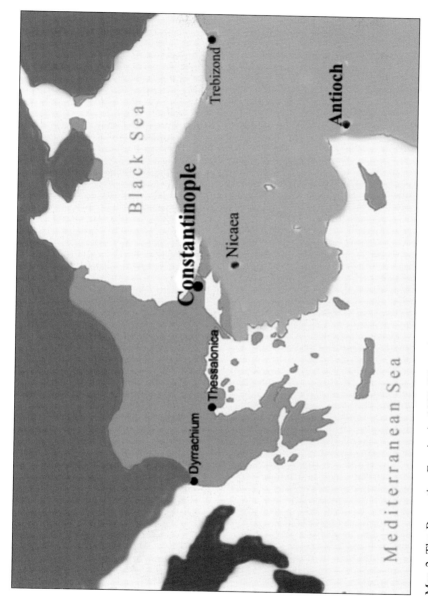

Map 2. The Byzantine Empire in 1081 CE, at the beginning of the reign of Anna Komnene's father, Emperor Alexios I Komnenos.

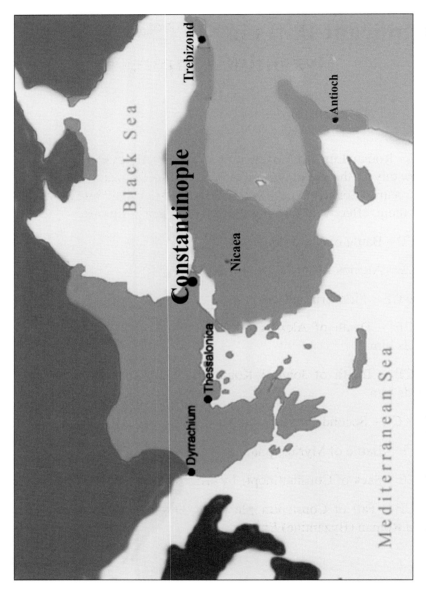

Map 3. The Byzantine Empire in 1148, as Anna Komnene began to write the *Alexiad*, during the reign of her nephew Manuel I Komnenos.

Significant Dates in the History of the Byzantine Empire

325 CE – Roman Emperor Constantine I ('the Great') lays the foundation of a new city on the site of ancient Greek colony of Byzantium, giving it his own name (Constantinou + Polis = Constantine's City) and moves his capital there, effectively forming the Eastern Roman Empire.

1074 CE – Battle of Mantzikert.

1081 CE – Alexios I Komnenos on the throne.

1096–9 CE – First Crusade.

1118 CE – Death of Alexios I Komnenos, son John II Komnenos succeeds him.

1143 CE – Death of John II Komnenos, son Manuel I Komnenos succeeds him.

1147–8 CE – Second Crusade.

1181 CE – Battle of Myriokephalon.

1204 CE – Sack of Constantinople by armies of the Fourth Crusade.

1453 CE – Fall of Constantinople to the Ottoman Turks. End of the Eastern Roman (Byzantine) Empire.

Timeline of Anna Komnene's Life[3]

1083, December 2 – Anna is born in the Porphyry Chamber (imperial birthing chamber) in Constantinople towards dawn. A manuscript found in a mosque that used to be the Church of Pammakaristos (All-Blessed) states: 'In the month of December, on the second, on the seventh day (Saturday), ninth hour (about three o'clock in the afternoon), seventh indiction (1083) was born the Porphyrogenita Lady Anna.'

1083, December – Anna, only a few days old, is engaged to Constantine Doukas Porphyrogenitos, 9-year-old son of former Emperor Michael VII Doukas and Empress Maria of Alania (or Abasgia), who has been her father Alexios Komnenos' co-emperor since 1081. Alexios places the imperial crown on Anna's head as co-empress of Constantine. Until her brother John's birth five years later (in September 1087), she is her father's heir, together with Constantine.

1085, September 19 – Friday, 5 o'clock in the afternoon. Maria Komnene, Anna's favourite sister, is born.

1087, September 13 – A long-awaited son and heir, John Komnenos, Anna's brother, is born. Anna describes the rejoicing of her parents and all their friends and well-wishers in the *Alexiad* and offers a description of the baby.

1090 (?) – Anna is raised in the household of her mother-in-law Maria of Alania, according to old custom. She will remain there until probably 1094. Anna is happy in that household; she is very fond both of Maria

---

3 This timeline is based on the information provided in the seminal genealogical study of the Komnenoi by Konstantinos Varzos, *Ē Genealogia tōn Komnēnōn [The Genealogy of the Komnenoi]*: Vol. I (Thessaloniki: Kentron Byzantinon Erevnon [Centre for Byzantine [Centre for Byzantine Research], 1984).

and Constantine and many years later she will praise and mourn them both in her book. Maria, who is very well educated herself, encourages the precocious young princess and nurtures her passion for education, particularly a Hellenic one, which was still frowned upon in some quarters as pagan.

1089/90 – Anna and Constantine are not acclaimed as co-emperors of Alexios any more, since there is now a male heir, John. In his *Material for History*, Nikephoros Bryennios mentions that Constantine was divested of the imperial titles owing to illness.

1091, September 19 – Andronikos Komnenos, Anna's second and favourite brother, is born in the Porphyry Chamber.

1092, September 1 (?) – John Komnenos Porphyrogenitos is crowned co-emperor of his father Alexios Komnenos in Hagia Sophia. This act seals the end of any hopes of the Doukai to return to the throne.

1093, January 16 – Sunday, 3.00 pm. Isaac Komnenos, Anna's third brother and fifth Komnenos sibling is born in the Porphyry Chamber. He was an intellectual like his big sister Anna, and apparently a prolific writer.

1094 – Maria of Alania, Anna's mother-in-law and guardian, is implicated in the conspiracy of Nikephoros Diogenes against Alexios. Diogenes was the son of Emperor Romanos IV Diogenes, and stepbrother of Maria's first husband, Emperor Michael. The conspiracy ends badly for Diogenes, who is apprehended in time and blinded. Maria is exiled to her estates in Serres, in the region of Central Macedonia in Greece. This was probably the end of Anna's and Constantine's engagement. Anna returns to live with her parents after having spent most of her childhood with Maria of Alania.

1094, January 14 – Evdokia, Anna's second sister and the sixth royal child is born in the Porphyry Chamber.

1095 – Constantine Doukas Porphyrogenitos, Anna Komnene's fiancé (or ex-fiancé) dies.

1096, January 15 – Tuesday, 3.00am. Theodora, the third sister of Anna and seventh royal child, is born in the Porphyry Chamber.

1097 – Anna, age 14, is married to Nikephoros Bryennios the Younger, age 16 (b. 1081).

1097–1118 – Anna is a wife and mother. Anna is also very close to her parents and especially her mother, Empress Eirene Doukaina, who by this time has increasingly become more indispensable to Alexios and accompanies him in his ceaseless military campaigns. Anna often accompanies her parents (and husband, since presumably he too participates in the military campaigns together with all the Komnenian military aristocratic men), as she clearly states in the *Alexiad*.

1102 – Birth of her first child, a son, Alexios Komnenos.

1103 – Birth of her second child, another son, John Doukas. It was not unusual in Byzantium to bypass the father's name and give the children names from the maternal family, if the latter was more illustrious and powerful.

1118, August 15 – Emperor Alexios I Komnenos dies and is succeeded by his son and heir, John II Komnenos. Some uncertainty as to the succession seems to have been at play, as more than one author mentions John's unusual behaviour at the time of his father's death, connecting it to a preference of Empress Eirene Doukaina, by that time all-powerful with Alexios, for her son-in-law. But only one author implicates Anna herself in this story, alleging that she conspired to become empress.

1118, November 28 – John II Komnenos is crowned Emperor of the Romans in Hagia Sophia. On the same day his fourth son Manuel, future Emperor Manuel I is born

1118–19 – Anna and Nikephoros allegedly conspire to assassinate John and seize the throne for themselves, but the conspiracy fails because of Nikephoros' unwillingness and 'sloth.'

1122 (?) – Anna's sons Alexios Komnenos and John Doukas marry on the same day. Their brides, princesses from Georgia, and their retinue had arrived at Constantinople on the day of Alexios' death. A long celebratory poem by court poet Theodore Prodromos suggests that the bridegrooms' proud parents Anna and Nikephoros were present, as well as their maternal grandmother Dowager Empress Eirene Doukaina and their uncle, Emperor John. The young men were led to the altar by the Emperor John II himself.

1123 (?), February 19 – Empress Eirene dies in the convent of Mother of God Full of Grace (*Theotokos Kecharitomēnē*). The year is uncertain, and some scholars give it as 1133, citing a mistake in the copying of the chronology in a manuscript.

1134–8 (?) – Nikephoros Bryennios dies in Constantinople after an illness contracted while during campaign with John II. His historical work *Material for History* which he had begun at the behest of his mother-in-law Empress Eirene Doukaina, remains unfinished.

1143, April 14 – Emperor John II Komnenos dies in a hunting accident near Antioch. His hand was scratched by his own poisoned arrow and he died of the complications caused probably by sepsis. His fourth son Manuel succeeds him on the throne.

1147 – Anna begins to write her magisterial work *Alexiad*, a history of her father's reign in fifteen books.

1153? – Anna dies in the convent of Mother of God Full of Grace.

Further Reading

This book, although informed by academic research, is addressed to the general public. For this reason I have opted for a less restricting format than an academic bibliography proper which would not mean very much to the non-specialist in Byzantine studies. My method in writing the book was simple: I read or re-read the original Greek texts, which I have used as the main source of my narrative throughout the book, as well as a large number of books (monographs, collective volumes and articles) on Anna Komnene, her work, her family, her world and her times. Sadly, much of that is not easily accessible to the non-academic reader as it would require the large-scale subscription to academic resources that only a university library can offer. On the plus side, we live in a fortunate age when many resources, previously inaccessible or difficult to access, even to specialists, are now available online. In writing this book, I have utilised the following databases, most of them freely accessible online:

Byzantine units of measurement:

http://www.anistor.gr/history/Byzantine_Units.pdf in http://www.anistor.gr/history/diophant.html

An excellent reconstruction of Constantinopolitan buildings and monuments: www.byzantium1200.com

Foundation of the Hellenic World: http://www.fhw.gr/choros/trapezounda/gr/webpages/ index.html

Thesaurus Linguae Graecae®: A Digital Library of Greek Literature: http://stephanus.tlg.uci.edu [Access via University of Glasgow Library]

Primary Sources – Greek

As stated in the Foreword, I used the original Greek texts available in the TLG (new version) and I have consulted the English, French, Spanish and Modern Greek translations where available. Unless stated otherwise, the translations of Greek text cited throughout the book are mine.

Anna Komnene
Athanasios Kambylis and Diether R. Reinsch (eds), Annae Comnenae, *Alexias*, Corpus Fontium Historiae Byzantinae, Series Berolinensis XL/1 (Berlin - New York: De Gruyter, 2001): 5-505

Eirene Doukaina
P. Gautier, 'Le typikon de la Théotokos Kécharitôménè', *REB*, vol. 43, vol. 4 (1985): 19-155

George Tornikes
J. Darrouzès, Georges and Dèmètrios Tornikès, *Lettres et Discours* (Paris: Centre National de le Recherche Scientifique, 1970)

John Zonaras
T. Büttner-Wobst, *Ioannis Zonarae epitomae historiarum libri*, xviii, vol. 3, *Corpus Scriptorum Historiae Byzantinae* (Bonn: Weber, 1897): 1-768

Kekaumenos
M.D. Spadaro, 'Raccomandazioni e consigli di un galantuomo', Hellenica 2 (1998): 44-242

Michael Italikos (for Anna Komnene's will)
P. Gautier (ed.), Michel Italikos, *Lettres et Discours*, Archives de l'Orient Chrétien 14 (Paris: Institut Français d'Études Byzantines, 1972), pp. 106-109

Michael Psellos
É. Renauld (ed.), Michel Psellos, *Chronographie ou histoire d'un siècle de Byzance (976–1077)*, 2 vols. (Paris: Les Belles Lettres, 1:1926; 2:1928 (repr. 1967): 1:1-154; 2:1-185

Nikephoros Bryennios
P. Gautier (ed.), Nicéphore Bryennios, *Histoire*, Corpus Fontium Historiae Byzantinae, Series Bruxellensis 9 (Brussels: Byzantion, 1975): 55-311

Niketas Choniates
J. Van Dieten, *Nicetae Choniatae Historia, pars prior*, Corpus Fontium Historiae Byzantinae, Series Berolinensis 11.1 (Berlin: De Gruyter, 1975): 1-635, 637-655

Theodore Prodromos

W. Hörandner (ed.), Theodoros Prodromos, *Historische Gedichte*, Wiener Byzantinistische Studien 11 (Vienna: Österreichische Akademie der Wissenschaften, 1974): 177-553

Theophylact of Ochrid

P. Gautier, *Theophylacte d'Achrida: Discours, Traités, Poésies*, Corpus Fontium Historiae Byzantinae, Series Thessalonicensis 16.1 (Thessalonica: Association for Byzantine Research, 1980): 179-211

Primary Sources in Translation (English, French, Modern Greek)

Anna Komnene, *Alexias*, tr. Aloë Sideri – in Modern Greek (Athens: Agra, 2005)

Anna Komnene, *The Alexiad*, tr. Elizabeth A.S. Dawes (1928) available online: https://sourcebooks.fordham.edu/basis/AnnaComnena-*Alexiad*.asp and https://en.wikisource.org/wiki/The_*Alexiad*

Anna Komnene, *The Alexiad*, tr. E.R.A. Sewter, rev. ed. Peter Frankopan (London: Penguin, 2009)

Anne Comnène, *Alexiade*, ed. and tr. Bernard Leib – in French (Paris: Société d'Édition Les Belles Lettres, 1967)

Babcock, Emily Atwater and A.C. Krey (eds.), *A History of Deeds Done Beyond the Sea by William, Archbishop of Tyre* (New York: Octagon Books, 1976)

Bryennios, Nikephoros, *Ylē Istorias* [*Material for History* – in Modern Greek], ed. Dimitris Tsougkarakis, tr. Despoina Tsouklidou (Athens: Kanaki Publishing, 1996). Unaccountably, this highly enjoyable text has not had an English translation until now; one will be available soon in the series Texts in Translation for Byzantinists by Liverpool University Press.

Constantine Porphyrogennetos, *The Book of Ceremonies*, tr. Ann Moffat and Maxeme Tall (Canberra: Australian Association for Byzantine Studies, 2012), vol. I & II

Edgington, Susan (ed.), Albert of Aachen, *Historia Ierosolimitana: History of the Journey to Jerusalem* (Oxford: Clarendon Press, 2007)

Eirene Doukaina, 'Kecharitomene: Typikon of Empress Irene Doukaina Komnene for the Convent of the Mother of God Kecharitomene in Constantinople', tr. Robert Jordan, in John Thomas and Angela Constantinides Hero, *Byzantine Monastic Foundation Documents: Volume 2* (Washington D.C: Dumbarton Oaks Research Library and Collection, 2000), pp. 649-724

Fulcher of Chartres, *A History of the Expedition to Jerusalem, 1095–1127*, tr. Frances Rita Ryan (New York: W.W. Norton, 1973)

George Tornikes, Hill, John Hugh and Laurita L. Hill, (eds.), *Historia Francorum qui ceperunt Iherusalem by Raymond d'Aguilers* (Philadelphia: American Philosophical Society, 1968)

Hill, Rosalind (ed.), *Gesta Francorum et aliorum Hierosolimitanorum: The Deeds of the Franks and the other Pilgrims to Jerusalem* (London: Nelson, 1962)

Isaac Komnenos, 'Kosmosoteira: Typikon of the Sebastokrator Isaac Komnenos for the Monastery of the Mother of God Kosmosoteira near Bera', tr. Nancy Pattercon Ševčenko, in John Thomas and Angela Constantinides Hero, *Byzantine Monastic Foundation Documents: Volume 2* (Washington D.C: Dumbarton Oaks Research Library and Collection, 2000), pp. 782-858.

John Komnenos, 'Pantokrator: Typikon of Emperor John II Komnenos for the Monastery of Christ Pantokrator in Constantinople', tr. Robert Jordan, in John Thomas and Angela Constantinides Hero, *Byzantine Monastic Foundation Documents: Volume 2* (Washington D.C: Dumbarton Oaks Research Library and Collection, 2000), pp. 725-281

Levine, Robert (ed.), *The Deeds of God through the Franks: A Translation of Guibert de Nogent's Gesta Dei per Francos* (Woodhouse: Boydell Press, 1997)

Psellus, Michael, *Fourteeen Byzantine Rulers: The Chronographia of Michael Psellus*, tr. E.R.A. Sewter (London: Penguin, 1966). Online translation also available: https://sourcebooks.fordham.edu/basis/psellus-chrono07.asp

William, Archbishop of Tyre, *A History of Deeds Done Beyond the Sea*, tr. and eds. Emily Atwater Babcock and A.C. Krey (New York: Octagon Books, 1976), vol.1

Prologue

The imaginary depiction of Anna Komnene writing the *Alexiad* in the convent of Mother of God Full of Grace is based on a number of primary and secondary sources. For the location and description of the convent on Kecharitomene see Eirene Doukaina, 'Typikon of Mother of God Full-of-Grace', in John Thomas and Angela Constantinides Hero, *Byzantine Monastic Foundation Documents: Volume 2* (Washington D.C: Dumbarton Oaks Research Library and Collection, 2000), pp. 649-724.

Anna's physical description is given by George Tornikes, 'Discourse on the Death of the Porphyrogenita Lady Anna Komnene (in French)', in J. Darrouzès, Georges and Dèmètrios Tornikès, *Lettres et Discours* (Paris: Centre National de le Recherche Scientifique, 1970).

Her writing at dusk is mentioned by herself in *The Alexiad*, tr. E.R.A. Sewter, rev. Peter Frankopan (London: Penguin, 2009).

Information on the First Crusade in based on Peter Frankopan, *The First Crusade: The Call from the East* (London: Vintage, 2012). For the Second Crusade see Jonathan Philips, *The Second Crusade: Extending the Frontiers of Christendom* (New Haven and London: Yale University Press, 2010) and Paul Stephenson, 'Anna Comnena's *Alexiad* as a Source for the Second Crusade', *Journal of Medieval History*, 29:1 (2003), 41-54.

Chapter 1: Power Games

The main primary sources for the generation of Anna's grandparents and the turbulent 1070s are Nikephoros Bryennios, Michael Psellos, John Zonaras (especially on the fate of Romanos IV Diogenes and the marriage of Nikephoros III Botaneiates and Maria of Alania). Anna Komnene gives a detailed account on the events surrounding Alexios' coup in the *Alexiad*, as well as information about all the main protagonists of those events. For more specific information on Maria of Alania, see Lynda Garland, Lynda and Stephen Rapp, 'Mary of "Alania": Woman and Empress Between Two Worlds', in Lynda Garland (ed.), *Byzantine Women: Varieties of Experience* (London & Burlington, VA: Ashgate, 2006), pp. 91-123.

For a detailed account of the battle of Manzikert, complete with maps and plans of the battlefield and including information on the main protagonists, see David Nicolle, *Mantzikert 1071: The Breaking of Byzantium*, illustrated by Christa Hook (Oxford: Osprey, 2013). John Julius Norwich in his *Short History of Byzantium* (London and New York: Viking, 1997) also offers a comprehensive view of the era.

The main sources throughout the book for Anna's maternal and paternal families come from two monumental works: Demetrios I. Polemis, *The Doukai: A Contribution to Byzantine Prosopography* (London: Athlone, 1968) and Konstantinos Varzos, *Ē Genealogia tōn Komnēnōn* [*The Genealogy of the Komnenoi* – in Greek]: Vol. I (Thessaloniki: Kentron Byzantinon Erevnon [Centre for Byzantine Research], 1984). Sadly only the former is available in English.

Chapter 2: The Chamber of the Porphyra

The *Alexiad* is the main primary source for its own author's birth, including the description of the Chamber of the Porphyra. On Anna's filial piety, see George Tornikes, John Zonaras and Anna Komnene's will in Michael Italikos. The ceremonies related to the birth, acclamations and baptism of imperial children are described in Constantine Porphyrogenitos, *The Book of Ceremonies*, tr. Ann Moffat and Maxeme Tall (Canberra: Australian Association for Byzantine Studies, 2012), vol. II, Chapter 42. Faidon Koukoules, *Vyzantinōn Vios kai Politismos* [*Life and Civilization of the Byzantines* – in Greek] (Athens: Papazisis, 1951), vol. IV gives a detailed description of many customs and traditions related to marriage, baptism, birth, and death in the Byzantine world. For the topography of Constantinople and its palaces, see Jonathan Harris, *Constantinople: Capital of Byzantium* (London: Bloomsbury, 2017 [2007]). A partial map of the area of the Great Palace and its surrounding buildings, including the little Palace of the Porphyra, is available in the illustrations of this book courtesy of the University of Glasgow Special Collections.

The tragic episode relating to Empress Evdoxia's childbirth is discussed in J. Lascaratos, D. Lazaris, and G. Kreatsas, 'A Tragic Case of Complicated Labour in Early Byzantium (404 AD)', *European Journal of Obstetrics and Gynecology*, 2002, 105:1, pp. 80-83; Alexander Kazhdan, 'Byzantine Hagiography and Sex in the Fifth to

Twelfth Centuries', *DOP*, 44 (1990), pp. 131-143, http://www.jstor.org/stable/1291623 [Accessed: 26/11/2013]

The connection between the Byzantine and English coronation rites is pointed out in Percy Ernst Schramm, *A History of the English Coronation*, tr. Leopold G. Wickham Legg (Oxford: Clarendon, 1937).

Varzos [*The Genealogy of the Komnenoi*, 1984] and Polemis (*The Doukai*, 1968) are again the go-to sources for all matters genealogical pertaining to the two great Houses.

Chapter 3: A Girl Grows Up in Byzantium

The main primary sources for Anna's family life and childhood are the *Alexiad* and George Tornikes' *Discourse on the Death of the Porphyrogenita Lady Anna the Kaisarissa* – the funeral oration or obituary written for her within two years after her death (Darrouzès, *Lettres et Discours*, 1970). In compliance with classical typology, a large part of this obituary describes in detail the life of the subject from birth to death; the content of such speeches can be formulaic and refer to an idealised childhood, but Anna's divergence from the norm suggests that at least the information regarding her education, or self-education, must be accurate to a degree. Being her personal friend (with all the caveats attached to the term in its specific social and cultural context), Tornikes would have heard the stories from Anna herself. Michael Psellos (d. *c.* 1074), from the generation of Anna's grandparents, has left a poignant description of the education of his young daughter Styliane, who sadly died age 9 or 10 – see Anthony Kaldellis (ed.), *Mothers and Sons, Fathers and Daughters: The Byzantine Family of Michael Psellos* (Notre Dame, Indiana: The University of Notre Dame Press, 2014); John Zonaras offers an assessment of Alexios I Komnenos' life and character in his *Epitome*. The infamous piece of advice that daughters should be locked inside the house comes from eleventh-century general landowner and archetypal grumpy old man Kekaumenos, author of the *Strategikon*, a book of advice for his son (M.D. Spadaro, 'Raccomandazioni e consigli di un galantuomo', *Hellenica* 2 (1998): 44-242). Theophylact of Ochrid (or Akhrid) addressed a speech to his young pupil Constantine Doukas, Anna's fiancé, and his mother Maria of Alania (P. Gautier, *Theophylacte d'Ach*rida, 1980).

For a fuller picture of life in eleventh and twelfth-century Byzantium, including cultural changes in private and public space, family relationships, women and children, eunuchs, science and learning, government and private life, the following works have been very helpful: Claire Nesbitt, 'Shaping the Sacred: Light and the Experience of Worship in Middle Byzantine Churches', *BMGS*, 36:2, 2012, pp. 139-160; Cecilia Hennessy, *Images of Children in Byzantium* (Farnham and Burlington: Ashgate, 2008); Koukoules, *Life and Civilization of the Byzantines,* 1951); Penelope Buckley, *The Alexiad of Anna Komnene: Artistic Strategies in the Making of a Myth* (Cambridge and New York: Cambridge University Press, 2014); Georgina Buckler, *Anna Comnena: A Study* (London: Oxford University Press, 1929); Garland and Rapp, 'Mary "of Alania"', 2006; A.-L. Caudano, 'Eustratios of Nicaea on Thunder and Lightning', *Byzantinische Zeitschrift* 105.2 (2012): 626-633; Dion C. Smythe, 'Middle Byzantine Family Values and Anna Komnene's *Alexiad*', in *Byzantine Women: Varieties of Experience 800–1200*, edited by Lynda Garland (Aldershot: Ashgate, 2006), pp. 125-139; Kathryn M. Ringrose, *The Perfect Servant: Eunuchs and the Social Construction of Gender in Byzantium* (Chicago and London: University of Chicago Press, 2003); Shaun F. Tougher, 'Byzantine Eunuchs: An Overview, with Special Reference to Their Creation and Origin', in *Women, Men and Eunuchs: Gender in Byzantium*, edited by Liz James (London and New York: Routledge, 1997); Louis Du Sommerard, *Deux Princesses d'Orient Au XIIe siècle: Anna Comnène Temoin Des Croissades*; *Agnès de France* (Paris: Librairie Académique Perrin et Cie, 1907); Larisa Orlov Vilimonović, *Structure and Features of Anna Komnene's Alexiad: Emergence of a Personal History* (Amsterdam: Amsterdam University Press, 2019); Paul Magdalino, 'Innovations in Government', in Margaret Mullet and Dion Smythe (eds.), *Alexios I Komnenos* (Belfast: Belfast Byzantine Enterprises, 1996), pp. 146-166.

Chapter 4: A Woman's Lot

In the *Alexiad*, Anna speaks of her husband Nikephros Bryennios often and always with high praise, love and regret; her turn of phrase and frequency of references to him convincingly demonstrate a real regard for him beyond rhetorical effusion. Both Zonaras and Choniates agree that Nikephoros was highly educated and had great influence in Alexios' administration, to the point that Empress Eirene preferred him as Alexios' successor over her own son John.

Most references to Anna's education and character come from Tornikes (Darrouzès, *Lettres et Discours*, 1970). Theodore Prodromos' orations on the marriage of the two sons of Kaisar Nikephoros Bryennios and Anna and on the funeral of Anna's daughter-in-law offer updates on family history (Hörandner, *Theodoros Prodromos*, 1974).

Anna's marriage, including the wedding ceremonial, married life and motherhood is based on information provided by the following works: Koukoules, *Life and Culture of the Byzantines*, vol. 4, 1951, pp. 70-147; Michael Jeffries, 'The Comnenian Prokypsis', *Parergon*, No. 5, 1987, pp. 38-53, https://doi.org/10.1353/pgn.1987.0009 [Access 8 June 2018]; Gary Vikan, 'Art and Marriage in Early Byzantium', *DOP*, Vol. 44 (1990), pp. 145-163, Stable URL: https://www.jstor.org/stable/1291624 [Accessed: 29-01-2019]; Ioli Kalavrezou 'Images of the Mother: When the Virgin Mary Became "Meter Theou"' *Dumbarton Oaks Papers*, Vol. 44 (1990), pp. 165-172, Stable URL: https://www.jstor.org/stable/1291625 [Accessed: 12-06-2019].

The intellectual milieu under Alexios I Komnenos' rule is discussed in Paul Magdalino, *Tradition and Transformation in Medieval Byzantium* (Aldershot and Brookfield: Variorum, 1984), especially in 'Byzantine Snobbery', pp. 58-78, and 'The Byzantine Aristocratic Oikos', pp.92-111; Robert Browning, 'Enlightenment and Repression in Byzantium in the Eleventh and Twelfth Centuries', in Robert Browning, *Studies on Byzantine History, Literature and Education* (London: Variorum Reprints, 1977), XV, 3-23; Ringrose, *The Perfect Servant,* 2003; Tougher, 'Byzantine Eunuchs', 1997; Joan B. Burton, 'Byzantine Readers', in *The Cambridge Companion to the Greek and Roman Novel*, edited by Tim Whitmarsh (Cambridge and New York: Cambridge University Press, 2008), pp. 272-281, esp. pp. 272-273; Kazhdan 'Byzantine Hagiography and Sex', 1990; Elizabeth Jeffreys, *Four Byzantine Novels: Theodore Prodromos, Rhodanthe and Dosikles; Eumathios Makremobolites,* Hysmine and Hysminias; *Constantine Manasses,* Aristandros and Kallithea;

Niketas Eugenianos, Drosilla and Charikles (Liverpool Liverpool University Press, 2014), especially Introduction pp. ix-xi, as well as the introductions to the individual novels.

Anna's education and intellectual attainment is described on the basis of the excellent works by Ruth Macrides, 'The Pen and the Sword: Who Wrote the *Alexiad*?' and Jakov Ljubarskij, 'Why is the *Alexiad* a Masterpiece of Byzantine Literature?' both essays in *Anna Komnene and Her Times*, edited by Thalia Gouma-Peterson (New York and London: Garland, 2000), pp. 63-81 and 169-185; Leonora Neville, *Anna Komnene: The Life and Work of a Medieval Historian* (New York: Oxford University Press, 2016); Leonora Neville, *Heroes and Romans in Twelfth-Century Byzantium: The Material for History of Nikephoros Bryennios* (Cambridge: Cambridge University Press, 2012).

The information on Anna's children is mainly derived from Varzos, *The Genealogy of the Komnenoi* (1984) and Polemis, *The Doukai* (1968).

General information in daily life in Byzantium is given in Marcus Rautman, *Daily Life in the Byzantine Empire* (Westport and London: Greenwood Press, 2006).

Chapter 5: The Power Factor

The primary sources for this chapter and specifically for the affairs relating to the succession of Alexios Komnenos and Anna's alleged conspiracy are the *Alexiad*, Books 6, 13, and 15 (the last one gives the affecting sequence of Alexios death); John Zonaras 747, 754-5, 759-64; Niketas Choniates John 2, 4-13 and George Tornikes 268-9. In Niketas' version there is a highly sexualised, immoral tone in the account of the alleged conspiracy, suggesting that the palace of the Komnenoi was a den of iniquity which fits in with his agenda of blaming that dynasty for the tragedy of 1204. Later in his account Niketas will include many more titillating horror stories about the immoral Komnenoi and their Jezebel-like women. Details about John Komnenos' hospital as well as other provisions made in the monastery which reveal interesting information about the Komnenoi and about John can be found in the Typikon (foundation charter) of the Monastery of Christ Pantokrator, in Thomas and Hero, *Byzantine Monastic Foundation Documents, Vol. 2,* pp. 725-781. In the same volume see also the typikon of Kosmosoteira, the monastic foundation of Isaac Komnenos, Anna and John's younger brother, pp. 782-858.

Important insights on imperial succession in general and the case of Alexios I and John II in particular are offered in the following texts: Peter Frankopan, 'Kinship and the Distribution of Power in Komnenian Byzantium', *The English Historical Review*, Vol. 122, No. 495 (Feb., 2007), pp. 1-34, Stable URL: http://www.jstor.org/stable/20108202 [Accessed: 24-03-2017]; Smythe, 'Middle Byzantine Family Values', 1996; Barbara Hill, 'Alexios I Komnenos and the Imperial Women', in *Alexios I Komnenos*, edited by Margaret Mullet and Dion Smythe (Beflast: Belfast Byzantine Texts and Translations, 1996), pp. 37-54.

The insights by Dr H.E. Counsell on Alexios' ailments in a private letter to Georgina Buckler are cited in her *Anna Komnene* (1929), p. 220.

Additional sources for this chapter: Neville, *Anna Komnene*, 2016; Darrouzès, *Lettres et Discours*, 1970, pp. 268-9, n.52 ; Neville, *Heroes and Romans*, 2012, esp. pp. 16-24; Edward Gibbon, *History of the Decline and Fall of the Roman Empire* (London, New York, and Toronto: Oxford University Press, 1907 [1781]), Vol. V., p. 263.

Chapter 6: The Contemplative Life: Writing the *Alexiad*

For the life of Anna in the convent of Full of Grace, the main primary source is the Typikon of Theotokos Kecharitomene [Mother of God Full of Grace] written by Empress Eirene Doukaina herself (Eirene Doukaina, 'Kecharitomene', trans. Robert Jordan (2000), pp. 649-724 – but I have used my own translations from the original text throughout. Part of the typikon signed by Empress Eirene's own hand is shown in Plate 5. The calculations of the values in coin and measurements are based on Despoina Nikolaidou, Neikolaos Giorkas, and Mary Fountouli, 'To nomisma sto Byzantino kosmo [*The Coin in the Byzantine World –* in Greek]', in *Ē Istoria tou Byzantinou Nomismatos* [*The History of the Byzantine Coin*], edited by Museum of Numismatics (Athens: Stavros Niarchos Foundation, 1998), pp. 74-75 and on the information provided in http://www.anistor.gr/history/Byzantine_Units.pdf.

The information on Anna's literary activity is from the *Alexiad* and from Tornikes' obituary (Darrouzès, *Lettres et Discours*, 1970).

Information about the Komnenian daughters and their marriages is also given by Zonaras, *Epitome*, 2.740.3.

The discussion on the intellectual activities of Eirene and Anna in the convent as well as the reception of Anna as an intellectual woman has been informed by my reading of the following texts: Browning, 'Enlightenment and Repression', 1977, pp. 3-23; Frankopan's comments in his translation of the *Alexiad*, 2009, p. 528 n.25; Judith Herrin, *Women in Purple: Rulers in Medieval Byzantium* (Princeton and Oxford: Princeton University Press, 2001); Barbara Hill, *Imperial Women in Byzantium 1025–1204: Power, Patronage and Ideology* (Harlow: Longman, 1999), pp. 165-198; Dion C. Smythe, 'Women as Outsiders', in *Women, Men and Eunuchs: Gender in Byzantium*, edited by Liz James (London: Routledge, 1997), pp. 149-167; Rae Dalven, *Anna Comnena* (New York: Twayne Publishers, 1972).

Vivid images of Anna the author have been depicted by Louis Du Sommerard, *Deux Princesses d'Orient,* 1907 and Naomi Mitchison, *Anna Comnena* (London: Gerald Howe, 1928). A very valuable discussion is offered by Neville in *Anna Komnene*, 2016, especially Chapter 8, 'A Room of One's Own', pp. 133-9.

Much great scholarship is available on the *Alexiad*, among which the following texts are prominent. The monograph by Penelope Buckley, *The Alexiad of Anna Komnene,* 2014 is the most thorough literary analysis of the text so far to my knowledge; additionally Jakov Ljubarskij, 'Why is the *Alexiad* a Masterpiece?', in Gouma-Peterson, *Anna Komnene,* 2000; Larisa Vilimonović, 'Gendering Politics: The Female Authorial Voice of Anna Komnene', Godišnjak za društvenu istoriju (Annual for Social History), 1, 2015, pp. 7-36, *TCEEOL*, https://www.ceeol.com/search/article-detail?id=304173 [Access 20 July 2018] and Vilimonović, *Structure and Features of Anna Komnene's Alexiad*, 2019.

The notorious view that Anna was not the author of the *Alexiad* was put forward by James Howard-Johnston, 'Anna Komnene and the *Alexiad*', in Mullet and Smythe, *Alexios I Komnenos*, 1996, pp. 260-302 and promptly and successfully refuted by Ruth Macrides in 'The Pen and the Sword', Gouma-Peterson, *Anna Komnene*, 2000, pp. 63-81.

Finally, the misogynistic bias in the assessment of women authors is accurately and perceptively discussed by Sophie Collins, *Who Is Mary Sue?* (London: Faber and Faber, 2018); Maroula Joannou,

'The Woman Writer in the 1930s: On Not being Mrs Giles of Durham City', in *Women Writers of the 1930s: Gender, Politics and History*, edited by M. Joannou, 1-15 (Edinburgh: Edinburgh University Press, 1999); Joanna Russ, *How to Suppress Women's Writing* (Austin: University of Texas Press: 1983).

Chapter 7: Anna and the First Crusade

The primary sources for the First Crusade are plentiful and mostly available in English. The *Alexiad*, as discussed, is the only Greek source for this world-changing event. Latin primary sources for the First Crusade which I have consulted for the writing of this chapter include: Fulcher of Chartres, *A History of the Expedition to Jerusalem*, 1973; Albert of Aachen, *Historia Ierosolimitana: History of the Journey to Jerusalem*, Edgington (ed.), 2007; Hill (ed.), *Gesta Francorum et aliorum Hierosolimitanorum*; Hill and Hill (eds), *Historia Francorum qui ceperunt Iherusalem by Raymond d'Aguilers*, 1968; Babcock and Krey (eds.), *A History of Deeds Done Beyond the Sea by William, Archbishop of Tyre*, 1976; Levine, (ed.), *The Deeds of God through the Franks: A Translation of Guibert de Nogent's Gesta Dei per Francos*, 1997.

There is a colossal amount of secondary literature on the First Crusade, out of which I consulted the following works, many of them accessible outside academic libraries and online: David Nicolle, *The First Crusade 1096–99: Conquest of the Holy Land* (Oxford: Osprey 2003); Thomas Asbridge, *The First Crusade: A New History* (London: Simon & Schuster, 2005); Peter Frankopan, *The First Crusade: The Call from the East* (Cambridge, Mass: The Bellknap Press of Harvard University Press, 2012); Jonathan Harris, *Byzantium and the Crusades* (London and New York: Bloomsbury, 2003); R.D. Thomas, 'Anna Comnena's Account of the First Crusade', *Byzantine and Modern Greek Studies* 15, 1991, pp. 269–312; Kyle Sinclair, 'Anna Komnene and Her Sources for Military Affairs in the *Alexiad*', *Estudios bizantinos* 2 (2014) 143-185; Eleni Sakellariou, 'Byzantine and Modern Greek Perceptions of the Crusades', in *The Crusades*, edited by Helen Nicholson (London: Palgrave, 2005), pp. 245-268; Penelope Buckley (in *The* Alexiad *of Anna Komnene*, 2014) reads the *Alexiad* as source for the First Crusade in new and ground-breaking ways.

My discussion of Alexios' archenemies, Bohemond and his father Robert, is based on Peter Frankopan, 'Turning Latin into Greek: Anna Komnene and the *Gesta Roberti Wiscardi*', *JMH*, 39:1 (2013), pp. 80-99; Emily Albu, 'Bohemond and the Rooster: Byzantines, Normans, and the Artful Ruse', in Gouma-Peterson, *Anna Komnene and Her Times*, 2000, 157-68; a very interesting study of the relationship between Alexios Komnenos and Bohemond to complement and/or contradict the *Alexiad* is Jonathan Shepard, 'When Greek Meets Greek: Alexius Comnenus and Bohemond in 1097–98', *BMGS* 12 (1988), pp. 185-277.

Aspects of the *Alexiad* as source of the First Crusade and of Anna's preoccupations as they emerge in it are based on essays by Paul Magdalino, 'Astrology', in *The Cambridge Intellectual History of Byzantium*, edited by Anthony Kaldellis and Niketas Siniossogloy (Cambridge: Cambridge University Press, 2017), pp. 198-214; John France, 'The Departure of Tatikios from the Crusader Army', *Bulletin of the Institute of Historical Research*, XLIV:110, November 1971; John France, *Victory in the East: A Military History of the First Crusade* (Cambridge: Cambridge University Press,1994), esp. p. 382; Peter Frankopan, 'Perception and Projection of Prejudice: Anna Comnena, the *Alexiad* and the First Crusade', in *Gendering the Crusades*, edited by Susan B. Edgington and Sarah Lambert (New York: Columbia University Press, 2002), pp. 59-76, and esp. p. 67.

Chapter 8: The Death of Anna Komnene

Anna Komnene's will has been edited by Stratis Papaioannou in *Byzantine Religious Culture: Studies in Honor of Alice-Mary Talbot*, edited by Denis Sullivan, Elizabeth Fisher and Stratis Papaioannou, (Leiden & Boston: Brill, 2012), pp. 99-121. Papaioannou's essay includes the full translation of the text, but again I use my own translation from the original Greek text (Gautier, *Michel Italikos*, 1972: 106-109). Information about her medical accomplishments and final days is from George Tornikes (Darrouzès, *Lettres et Discours*, 1970). My reading of Tornikes' funeral speech was informed by the following secondary texts: Stephen H. Moore, 'Disinterring Ideology from a Corpus of Obituaries: A Critical Post Mortem', *Discourse & Society,* Vol 13(4): 495–536,

2002; also by Darrouzès' comments and notes in his edition of Tornikes' text (Darrouzès, *Lettres et Discours* 1970); Buckler, *Anna Comnena* (1929) and Neville, *Anna Komnene* (2016).

Chapter 9: The Afterlives of Anna Komnene

The best and most comprehensive assessment of Anna Komnene's reception by later historians is offered in Neville, *Anna Komnene*, 2016, particularly Chapter 10, 'The "Fury of Medea"' (pp. 153-174).

For the fraught relationship between Classical and Byzantine studies, see Averil Cameron, *Byzantine Matters* (Princeton and Oxford: Princeton University Press, 2014), pp. 48-49. This short but succinct book is invaluable also for its insights into the place of Byzantium in popular perception today (especially pp. 10-11). For the disparagement of Byzantium, viewed as an irredeemable Dark Age, see also Judith Herrin, *Byzantium: The Surprising Life of a Medieval Empire* (London: Allen Lane 2007), esp. p. 321.

My account of Georgina Buckler, the first scholar to write a monograph of Anna Komnene in the twentieth century is based in the excellent essay by Buckler's granddaughter and eminent scholar Charlotte Roueché, 'Georgina Bukler: The Making of a British Byzantinist'. in *The Making of Byzantine History: Studies Dedicated to Donald M. Nicol*, edited by Roderick Beaton and Charlotte Roueché (Aldershot: Variorum, 1993), pp. 174-196. Buckler's book was a great source of inspiration for my own project. The background to Buckler's intellectual achievement is vividly depicted in Diana Wallace, '"History to the Defeated": Women Writers and the Historical Novel in the Thirties', *Critical Survey*, 15:2, 2003, p. 76-92.

The reception of Anna Komnene in modern literature is my particular field of expertise. The first and only English language canonical novel to portray Anna as a character is Sir Walter Scott's *Count Robert of Paris* (1832). This novel has an interesting history, as the published edition was not the novel as Scott had written it but a heavily edited version by his son-in-law J.G. Lockhart, who had considered Scott's original rather risqué! You can find out more about this intriguing case in my own essay 'Masculine Crusaders, Effeminate Greeks, and the Female Historian: Relations of Power in Sir Walter Scott's *Count Robert of Paris*', *JHF* 1:1, 2017, pp. 89-110. The new magisterial edition of all the Waverley novels by the Edinburgh University Press in the 2000s includes Scott's penultimate novel in its original, restored form: Walter Scott, *Count Robert of Paris*, edited by J.H. Alexander (Edinburgh: Edinburgh University Press, 2006).

My primary texts for this chapter are not Anna's works but works of fiction in which Anna is a major or minor character: Naomi Mitchison's *Anna Comnena* (1928); Susan Shwartz, *Cross and Crescent* (New York: Tor, 1997); Tracy Barrett, *Anna of Byzantium* (Laurel Leaf: Amazon, 2000); C.P. Cavafy, 'Anna Komnina [sic]', *Collected Poems*, tr. Edmund Keeley and Philip Sherrard, ed. George Savidis, Revised Edition (Princeton University Press, 1992); Vera Mutafčieva, *Egō, Ē Anna Komnēnē*, tr. Panos Stathoyannis, in Greek from Bulgarian original title:*Аз, Анна Комнина* [*I, Anna Komnene*, 1991] (Athens: Nea Synora Livanis, 1996); Maro Douka, *Come Forth, King*, tr. David Connolly (Kedros: Athens, 2003); Julia Kristeva, *Murder in Byzantium*, tr. C. Jon Delogu (New York, Columbia University Press, 2006 [2004]). For my discussion of some of these works I consulted the following secondary texts: Elizabeth Maslen, 'Naomi Mitchison's Historical Fiction', in *Women Writers of the 1930s*, edited by M. Joannou, 1999: 138-150); Maria Margaroni,'Byzantium: The Future Anterior of Europe?', in *Women: A Cultural Review*, 18:2, (2007) 223-225. I discuss Maro Douka and Vera Mutafchieva's portrayal of Anna Komnene in their respective novels in my chapter 'Reconfiguring the Template: Representations of Powerful Women in Historical Fiction: The Case of Anna Komnene', in *Gender and Authority*, edited by Adele Bardazzi and Alberica Bazzoni (forthcoming by Palgrave Macmillan).

Suggested General Reading

Cameron, Averil, *Byzantine Matters* (Princeton and Oxford: Princeton University Press, 2014)

Herrin, Judith, *Byzantium: The Surprising Life of a Medieval Empire* (London: Allen Lane 2007

Hughes, Bettany, *Istanbul: A Tale of Three Cities* (London: Widenfeld and Nicholson, 2017), esp. Part Five: City of War

Kaldellis, Anthony, *Streams of Gold, Rivers of Blood: The Rise and Fall of Byzantium, 955 A.D. to the First Crusade* (New York: Oxford University Press, 2017).

Kazhdan, Alexander (ed.), *The Oxford Dictionary of Byzantium* (New York and Oxford: Oxford University Press, 1991), 3 vols

Mango, Cyril, *Byzantium: The Empire of the New Rome* (London: Phoenix, 2005)

Norwich, John Julius, *A Short History of Byzantium* (London and New York: Viking, 1997)

Runciman, Steven, *A History of the Crusades: 1. The First Crusade* (London: Penguin, 1991 [1951]) (I am including this book more for the narrative style than for the scholarship, for which see literature Further Reading, Chapter 7.)

Venning, Timothy (ed.), *A Chronology of the Byzantine Empire* (Basingstoke and New York: Palgrave Macmillan, 2006)

Acknowledgements

I owe many thanks to a great number of people and organisations, whose help and support was vital in the writing of this book: the Dangerous Women Project, IASH, University of Edinburgh, for publishing 'Anna Komnene: A Dangerous Woman'; Danna Messer, my discerning editor, for salvaging it from the sea of forgetfulness that is the internet; The Society of Authors' Author's Fund, for their generous grant that supported me in more ways than just financially; the University of Glasgow Library Special Collections, for their wealth of material and generous permission to use some of it.

I am deeply grateful to all those scholars of Byzantium in general and of Anna Komnene in particular whose long and laborious research on the topic facilitated mine. We always stand on the shoulder of giants. First and foremost among them is the unforgettable Ruth Macrides, mentor and *basilissa*. I can never repay this debt. I would also like to thank Professor Leonora Neville for her kindness and encouragement, and for Dr Matthew Kinloch for the introductions. Thank you, Professor Panagiotis Agapitos, for your valuable guidance and suggestions. And thank you, Professor Peter Frankopan, for bringing Anna Komnene to a wider English-speaking audience and for always being her champion.

My heartfelt thanks to the team in Pen & Sword for their help and support throughout the writing and production of this book: commissioning editor and perceptive reader Dr Danna Messer, Claire Hopkins (thank you for your patience, Claire!) and Laura Hirst and all those who worked on the production and distribution of this book.

I am grateful to many friends and colleagues for their love, support and unstinting belief in me throughout: Helen Raftopoulos, Vassiliki Kolocotroni, Iro Filippaki, Marianne Gilchrist, Marie Meechan, Gillian Smith, Carolyn Donaldson, Victoria Robinson, and Duo Long.

Finally, I would like to thank my family, Nena Kolovou, Artemios Kolovos, Mary Kolovou and Andrew Mabin. Without you, neither this book nor I would be here.

Richard, the next one will be for you.

About the Author

Ioulia (Julia) Kolovou is a Greek-born writer and researcher based in Scotland. She studied History and Archaeology at the Aristotle University of Thessaloniki, Greece, Linguistics at the Universidad de Buenos Aires, Argentina, and Creative Writing in Scotland, achieving an MSc (Distinction) at the University of Edinburgh and a PhD at the University of Glasgow. She taught History and Classics (Greek and Latin language and literature) for over twenty years. She writes historical fiction and non-fiction and has published creative and academic work in various journals. *Anna Komnene* is her first full-length published book. She lives in Glasgow.

Index